The *Bhagavadgītā* in the *Mahābhārata*

Text and Translation

The University of Chicago Press, Chicago 60637
The University of Chicago Press, Ltd., London

Printed in the United States of America

85 84 83 82 81 1 2 3 4 5

Library of Congress Cataloging in Publication Data
Mahābhārata. Bhagavadgītā. English & Sanskrit.
The Bhagavadgītā in the Mahābhārata.
Includes bibliographical references.
I. Buitenen. Johannes Adrianus Bernardus van.
II. Title.
BL1130.A4B84 294.5'924 79-13021
ISBN 0-226-84660-1
ISBN 0-226-84662-8 pbk.

J. A. B. van Buitenen was George V. Bobrinskoy Distinguished Service Professor of Sanskrit and Indic Studies at the University of Chicago.

The *Bhagavadgītā* in the *Mahābhārata*

J. A. B. van Buitenen

The University of Chicago Press
Chicago and London

For Haven O'More, patron and friend

ná sá sákhā yó ná dádāti sákhye
sacābhúve sácamānāya pitváḥ /
ápāsmāt préyān ná tád óko asti
pṛṇántam anyám áraṇaṃ cid icchet //
sá íd bhojó yó gṛháve dádāty
ánnakāmāya cárate kṛśā́ya /
áram asmai bhavati yā́mahūtā
utāparī́ṣu kṛṇute sákhāyam //

Ṛgvedasaṃhitā 10.117.4; 3.

Contents

Foreword

There are many approaches to the *Bhagavadgītā* in the *Mahābhārata*. Most translators, commentators, and students treat the *Bhagavadgītā* as an entity or scripture isolated from its context, that very *Mahābhārata*, the Fifth Veda. But the *Mahābhārata* does not permit this attempted removal and interpretation, this tearing away from its great sacred body, for it refuses to render up and make clear its innermost treasures: as a brain does not function independent of the human or animal body in which it grew and has its roots, so with the *Bhagavadgītā* rooted in its body, the *Mahābhārata*.

Greater than any mountain, the *Mahābhārata* sits supreme, its top veiled in clouds, with powerful winds and bitter cold. Truly, it is said, the *Mahābhārata* gives birth, and also gives death. For it contains an account of the life and acts of the Supreme Ruler Himself, Creator and Destroyer of the universe, who binds human beings and all manifestations "on a chain, of which one end is life, the other death." What is not found within the *Mahābhārata* is not found anywhere. A great intellectual and spiritual mountain, it unveils itself only to the most passionate, intense, sincere, full of truth to themselves and others, athletic, death-defying, life-embracing, plunging-into-possibility climbers. Civilizations rise up and decay; the great mountain penetrates into the whole/holy possibility of Universal Manifestation—even, paradoxically, resting simultaneously in the Unmanifest Itself. Accordingly, as the *Ṛgveda* says,

> *all beings and manifestations are a fourth of Him, /*
> *three-fourths lies in the non-phenomenal His Unmanifestness.*

For the first time in English, or in any language outside of the Sanskrit, so far as we know, van Buitenen gives a translation of the *Bhagavadgītā* in the *Mahābhārata* based on the critical text. This means, first, as "straight" as a first-class Sanskritist can give it. It means down the throat. Raw. It means without bullshit, without mystification. It means clear, straight through. It means the real reader/student/passionate seeker/climber can start his work. He provides an accurate map of the site. Realize, that before van Buitenen's text and translation of the whole/holy *Mahābhārata* even the possibility of the site was a mystery; the mountain could not, really, be approached from any direction. Van Buitenen is/was a traditional scholar-translator: one who continues the Tradition (*vidyā*), one who carries-over, the builder over the stream/river, the passer-over, the Preserver.

Now we thank van Buitenen and praise him for his exertions over many years. This mystified one, this explorer and leader-into of the incredible and wondrous, this dear partner in the dance and music, this penetrant into strange and beautiful nonordinary states, this translator of the *Mahābhārata* (alas, unfinished by him) and its *Bhagavadgītā*.

And now van Buitenen is dead. We bless his name and memory. We mourn him. But we rejoice, also. We are inspired to continue his work on the principles he laid down. For now we have the means through his exertions to plunge into the great river running to the cosmic sea and find its mountain residing most centrally in that very Self (*ātmā*) we call our innermost Self (*ātmā*).

May all beings benefit and be blessed.

Haven O'More

Preface

In the course of translating the *Mahābhārata* I was bound to reach the point where, in that last moment of stillness before the battle, Arjuna shrinks away from its abomination, and Kṛṣṇa, his friend and charioteer, persuades him of its necessity. It was hardly the first time that I read the *Bhagavadgītā*, but it was the first time that I had to translate it, as part of the epic. I do not now recall whether it was my publisher or I who suggested that the *Gītā*, which is due to appear as part of volume IV of the *Mahābhārata* translation, might be usefully published separately as a paperback excerpt for those who would otherwise not have easy access to it.

In doing so I have attempted to preserve the epic context in which this celebrated episode occurs. The *Mahābhārata* itself provides it, and not just in the battlefield scene of the preamble to Kṛṣṇa's teaching. The entire episode of the *Gītā*, the *Bhagavadgītāparvan*, is appreciably longer—by about one half—than the eighteen chapters which both in India and the West have traditionally been taken as the complete body of the text. This *Book of the Bhagavadgītā* is the sixty-third of the Hundred Minor Books of the *Mahābhārata*, and forms the third episode of the *Bhīṣmaparvan, The Book of Bhīṣma*, the sixth of the Eighteen Major Books. While it is true that the eight initial chapters of the complete episode add nothing to the religious and philosophical significance of this Colloquy of Kṛṣṇa and Arjuna, still, from the point of view of the epic narrative, they are quite important. For, as they predict the death of Bhīṣma and the mourning it causes, they justify Arjuna's loathing of being a party to it. Thus these chapters provide the setting and the occasion of the *Gītā*. To round off the episode I have added in conclusion the chapter immediately following the *Gītā*, which brings us back to the battlefield.

It was decided to include the Sanskrit text in this edition to face the translation. The text reproduced is that presented by S. K. Belvalkar as part of the critical edition of the *Mahābhārata* prepared by the scholars of the Bhandarkar Oriental Institute at Poona.[1] For the *Gītā* itself this is virtually the Vulgate. I have added into it occasional variant readings, for which there is better authority, and have appended in my textual notes a further list of readings based on the early commentary of Bhāskara.

There are few among the scores of translations and commentaries of the *Bhagavadgītā* that I have not consulted over the last thirty years, but I want to single out a few which to me at least have been the most significant: the commentary of Rāmānuja, the notes of Etienne Lamotte, the French of Emile Senart, and the English of Franklin Edgerton.[2]

In the Introduction I have sought to avoid duplicating what has so capably been set forth by my predecessors and have instead drawn attention to specific issues that have been little dealt with or not at all. I hope that my brief remarks will contribute to the already vast body of scholarship on the *Gītā*.

The translation does not, of course, pretend to great novelty. I have tried to retain the friendly and at times intimate tone and the directness of language characteristic of this book, to clarify the significance of the technical terms, and to maintain the style of the continuing *Mahābhārata* translation. The last purpose allowed me to break with the traditional practice of enshrining each verse in its own paragraph, which thwarts easy reading and often blunts the thrust of the argument. In line with the rest of the translation, the *ślokas* have been rendered in prose, the other meters in verse.

My annotations likewise address themselves to the text itself, not to the comments of the multitudes of scholars from Śaṅkara and Bhāskara to R. G. Zaehner and Prabhupāda Bhaktivedānta. All these are available to the diligent student for edification and comparison.

It is today twenty-five years since I completed my first attempt at Sanskrit scholarship with a study of the *Bhagavadgītā* according to the philosopher Rāmānuja. Perhaps a sufficient interval has now elapsed for me to attempt the *Bhagavadgītā* according to the *Mahābhārata*.

Chicago, October 23, 1978 J. A. B. van B.

Publisher's Note: J. A. B. van Buitenen died on September 21, 1979, before this book was well into production. The University of Chicago Press wishes to acknowledge with thanks the considerable efforts of one of his students, James Fitzgerald of the University of Tennessee, in correcting proofs and in matching the translation to the text.

Introduction

The Bhagavadgītā in the Mahābhārata

The Book of the Bhagavadgītā (*Bhagavadgītāparvan*) begins with the blunt announcement by the bard Saṃjaya that Bhīṣma has fallen in battle. He reports this to his patron Dhṛtarāṣṭra, the father of Duryodhana, of whose army Bhīṣma was the supreme commander.

Dhṛtarāṣṭra, posthumous eldest son of the titular king of Kurukṣetra, Vicitravīrya, was born blind and therefore was excluded from the kingship which would otherwise have been his. Bhīṣma, whose death is reported, belonged to the generation immediately preceding Dhṛtarāṣṭra's. Bhīṣma, too, was the eldest son of a king of Kurukṣetra, Śaṃtanu, and, like Dhṛtarāṣṭra, would normally have succeeded to the throne; however, he had voluntarily given up all claims to the kingship. This peculiar affinity between the early lives of Bhīṣma and Dhṛtarāṣṭra, which antedates the central story of the *Mahābhārata*, and its consequences are the main causes of the war of which Saṃjaya reports the first victim, but which is yet to be faced in the *Gītā*. It is not just a successful narrative device that the death of Bhīṣma is first reported as an accomplished fact, then juxtaposed with the prior teaching of the *Gītā* which in the end seeks to justify the killing of him: each one is the condition of the other.

Bhīṣma renounced Śaṃtanu's throne when his father became infatuated with a lower-class girl, Satyavatī, whose own father insisted on the marital condition that the throne should descend in Satyavatī's

In text and notes, references to the *Mahābhārata* are given by Major Book (1–18), by chapter (1, etc.), and on occasion by verse (1, etc.). This reference is then followed by the number of the volume of my translation (I–III) and the number of the page on which the quoted passage occurs. Thus *MBh.* 5.149.47; III, 464, refers to the 47th verse in the 149th chapter of Book 5, which is to be found on page 464 of Volume III of my translation.

line, not Bhīṣma's. Bhīṣma's formal assent to this condition[1] introduces all the later complications of succession. His oath, undertaken to aid his father, becomes a curse on his father's posterity.

Satyavatī bears Śaṃtanu two sons, the elder of whom dies afflicted by possession.[2] The second, Vicitravīrya, marries two princesses fetched for him from the court of the Kāśis by Bhīṣma. He is a voluptuary[3] and dies heirless. The line of Satyavatī, for which Bhīṣma forswore the kingdom, seems extinct before it has begun. Satyavatī, however, invokes the law of levirate, and her premarital son Kṛṣṇa Dvaipāyana, elder half-brother of Vicitravīrya, begets for the latter the blind Dhṛtarāṣṭra by the elder princess, and by the younger the possibly leukodermic Pāṇḍu.[4] Since his blindness excludes Dhṛtarāṣṭra from the kingship,[5] his junior Pāṇḍu becomes king. To confuse matters further, Pāṇḍu soon leaves with his two wives for a hunter's life in the wilderness, where he has five sons, the eldest Yudhiṣṭhira, the middlemost Arjuna. Dhṛtarāṣṭra begets a hundred sons, the eldest of whom, Duryodhana, is born a year after Yudhiṣṭhira. At Pāṇḍu's death the five Pāṇḍavas return to Kurukṣetra to the court of Dhṛtarāṣṭra, who has been regent in Pāṇḍu's absence at Hāstinapura. While the Pāṇḍavas are recognized as legitimate, their title to succession is clouded; moreover, Duryodhana was already in place, though a minor. Duryodhana plots to send the Pāṇḍavas into exile.[6] They go underground and later marry Draupadī, the daughter of the king of Pāñcāla, who thereby becomes their powerful ally.[7] The Hāstinapura Kauravas make their peace with the Pāṇḍavas by partitioning the kingdom.[8] Yudhiṣṭhira settles in at Indraprastha and institutes a Vedic Consecration. As part of the ritual he engages in a game of dice with Duryodhana and loses all. The penalty for losing is thirteen years of exile.[9] After their exile the Pāṇḍavas demand their share of the kingdom back; Duryodhana refuses; both parties prepare for war.[10]

What has happened to Bhīṣma meanwhile? Very little. His function as regent of Kurukṣetra came to an end with Pāṇḍu's ascension, and he lives in retirement at the court of Hāstinapura, a grandfatherly presence, a counselor whose advice is ignored. The family teachers Droṇa and Kṛpa have similarly retired and stayed on. All subsist on Duryodhana's dole.[11] Their sympathies are with the Pāṇḍavas, but when war comes, they have no choice but to side with their patrons. Besides, Duryodhana has now elevated Bhīṣma to supreme commander of his troops and allies.[12] He is therefore the first target.

War is now at hand, and the abomination of it is unspeakable. In a royal joint-family the sons have first engaged in a partition of ancestral property, a procedure in itself of questionable morality, and are now about to wage war over the entire patrimony. While the

Pāṇḍavas were clearly wronged, the only way to right the wrong is by committing the greater wrong of destroying the entire family. Indeed, the first to fall is Bhīṣma, the most venerable guru of the family, the only survivor of the grandfather generation, hence "grandfather" par excellence, who, by his lifelong honoring of his oath of celibacy, is the paragon of rectitude and truthfulness, the benefactor and sage adviser of all. He is the first to be sacrificed in this war, and is it a wonder that Arjuna shrinks from sacrificing him, as well as Droṇa, Kṛpa, etc.? Arjuna's dilemma is both a real one and, despite Kṛṣṇa's sarcasm, an honorable one. In effect, on the level of *dharma* Arjuna will be proved to have been right; but in the *Gītā* Kṛṣṇa offers him the choice of another level of values, which will absolve him from guilt.

In the light of all this it cannot be reasonably argued that the setting of the *Gītā* is a random choice dictated by purely dramatic (read: melodramatic) considerations.[13] The preamble tells us that Bhīṣma is dead, that Arjuna's reluctance to fight in this war was therefore fully justified, and that consequently a need existed to override Arjuna's reluctance with a higher truth, so that in fact *that* will come about which we know is *already* the case. This is a very subtle narrative weaving that requires the preamble so often forgotten and that also masterfully contrasts the high dilemma of the *Gītā* with the chapter following immediately—the formal approval-seeking by Yudhiṣṭhira.

Indeed, if the compilers had felt so inclined, they could have found other places for the *Gītā* among the one hundred thousand couplets of the text. For instance there is *MBh.* 5.151, where not Arjuna but Yudhiṣṭhira himself voices the dilemma: "How can war be waged with men we may not kill? How can we win if we must kill our gurus and elders?" Here Arjuna provides the answer: "It is not right to retreat now without fighting," largely on his mother Kuntī's authority.[14] And Kṛṣṇa adds: "That is the way it is." End of discussion. Again, the *Gītā* might have been consigned to the *Mokṣadharma* section of the *Mahābhārata*, where so many philosophical colloquies and indeed some *gītās*[15] have been collected. For that matter anywhere else, as the self-styled *Anugītā*, "Sequel to the *Gītā*," shows: this text has been accommodated in *MBh.* 14, *The Book of the Horse Sacrifice*.[16]

The fact is that the *Gītā* occurs where it does for excellent reasons. Among the many ways of looking at the *Gītā* is as a creation of the *Mahābhārata* itself. At the time when all the materials that were to go into the final redactorial version of the great epic (which transformed the *Bhārata* into the *Mahābhārata*) were collected, materials that hailed from many milieus and many centuries, a change of sensitivity away from the war books had taken place, a change from the martial spirit toward a more reflective and in certain ways more quietistic mood. The war had ceased to be a glorious event for celebration and was to be regarded as a horrendous, blood-curdling finale to an eon. The discussions concerning war and peace in *MBh.* 5, *The Book of the Effort*, uncover in the future combatants a reluctance to embark on armed conflict that overshadows a hesitant acceptance of it as a fate predestined for warriors. The ambivalence that tilts toward the negative culminates in the *Gītā*, where it swings to the positive. The armies have now been drawn up and arrayed in battle formations. Warriors have been assigned their targets. The momentum can no longer be checked.

> There were berserk men there, clutching their weapons—twenty thousand standards commanded by champions. There were five thousand elephants, all the chariot trains, footmen and commanders, carrying bows and swords and clubs by the thousands in front and by the thousands in back. The other kings were largely stationed in this sea of troops where Yudhiṣṭhira himself was positioned, with thousands of elephants, tens of thousands of horses, thousands of chariots and foot soldiers, relying on which he marched to attack Duryodhana Dhārtarāṣṭra. Behind followed hundreds of thousands and myriads of men, marching and shouting in thousands of formations. And in their thousands and tens of thousands the happy warriors sounded their thousands of drums and tens of thousands of conches.[17]

At this point the composers allow us one more moment of stillness before the tempest, in which we see both the reluctance of an Arjuna downing his bow Gāṇḍīva, and his acceptance of *kṣatriya* duty and fate on the urging of Kṛṣṇa. There will be no more happy warriors, only resigned ones.

The architects of the literature of the *Mahābhārata* do not shy from showing their debts. The *Gītā* is the final climax of reluctance and acceptance often voiced before. It is also the beginning of the war and it draws on the chapters that follow it to describe its own mise-en-scène, as, e.g., in 6.47, where Duryodhana gives the heartening speech amplified in *Gītā* 1. Soon all the reluctant acceptance will, as these chapters show, be drowned in the oceanic tides of battle.

Who then is Kṛṣṇa who persuades Arjuna to accept the warrior's fate? He is a Vṛṣṇi prince, for the nonce acting as Arjuna's charioteer, a seemingly subordinate role to which he has agreed in order to be a noncombatant in the thick of battle. Loyal to both warring parties, he has conceded his troops to Duryodhana and his presence to Arjuna.[18] It is not atypical for the Kṛṣṇa of the *Mahābhārata* to be active on the sidelines, for, albeit important, he is not central to the main story. His first encounter with the Pāṇḍavas occurs when he recognizes them behind their disguise as young brahmins on the day they win Draupadī and, with her, the alliance with Pāñcāla.[19] Later he brings a lavish wedding gift to their marriage.[20] Together with Arjuna, but on two chariots moving as one, Arjuna and Kṛṣṇa lay fire to the Khāṇḍava Forest.[21] He encourages Arjuna to sue for his sister Subhadrā, lends him his chariot to abduct her, and appeases her irate relatives.[22] He is the guiding spirit in Yudhiṣṭhira's Consecration;[23] in the killing of Jarāsaṃdha;[24] at the Consecration itself, when he slays his challenger Śiśupāla.[25] There are more contacts, the most important his fruitless embassy to the enemy to ward off the war.[26] An old comrade of Arjuna, his relative by marriage and uncle to his son Abhimanyu, Kṛṣṇa comes well prepared as his friend's charioteer.

This role assumed by Kṛṣṇa, because of the conventional camaraderie between warrior and driver, provides the intimacy which makes his exhortations possible and appropriate. Traditionally the *sūta*, on the chariot of the warrior, is witness to the warrior's triumphs and occasional lapses; in danger he protects him. The triumphs of the warrior he celebrates in song, hence *sūta* also means "bard"; the lapses he condemns in private. The warrior Pradyumna berates his charioteer for withdrawing from battle; the other spiritedly replies that it is his duty to save his master.[27] Arjuna, acting as Prince Uttara's charioteer, scolds Uttara unmercifully when he tries to flee.[28] Kṛṣṇa does the same to Arjuna. There is an easy familiarity between Kṛṣṇa and Arjuna born from dangers braved together, heightened by the old ties of friendship and marriage. There is more: not only are Arjuna and Kṛṣṇa comrades in arms in this life; they are also the reincarnations or repersonifications of the ancient warrior pair Nara and Nārāyaṇa, who have long since retired to a hermitage at Badarī on the Ganges.[29] Historically they might even be successors to the divine and heroic pair of Indra and Viṣṇu. It does not matter; their association in the *Mahābhārata* suffices to place them together now.

As a person Kṛṣṇa oscillates between the heroic and the divine; in the *Mahābhārata* he has until now been treated more as a hero than as God. There have been passing theophanies before,[30] but the epic sees in him principally the hero, sometimes beleaguered,[31] but always triumphant. His divine nature will need to be explained, and he will do so himself.

To sum up: The *Bhagavadgītā* was conceived and created in the context of the *Mahābhārata*. It was not an independent text that somehow wandered into the epic. On the contrary, it was conceived and developed to bring to a climax and solution the dharmic dilemma of a war which was both just and pernicious. The dilemma was by no means new to the epic, nor is it ever satisfactorily resolved there, yet the *Gītā* provides a unique religious and philosophical context in which it can be faced, recognized, and dealt with. Whatever the further thrust of Kṛṣṇa's teaching and its elaborations, the *Gītā* addresses itself in the first place to a specific issue that the Bhārata war posed to a more reflective age, whose attitude toward violence was changing.

The Bhagavadgītā as Revelation

In the sacred literature of Hinduism the *Bhagavadgītā* occupies both an extremely important and a very peculiar place. Its importance as a religious text is demonstrated by its uniquely pan-Hindu influence. There are other texts that have found a somewhat comparable universal acceptance in Hinduism, for example the *Mahābhārata* and *Rāmāyaṇa*, and some of the *Dharmaśāstras* such as *Manu* and *Yājñavalkya*,[32] but because of their subject matter, scope, and objectives their religious importance has not been felt so profoundly as that of the *Gītā*. Although these works often bear on matters religious and ethical, their message is overshadowed by the *Gītā*'s. In later literatures expressing a religious inspiration the fundamental texts belong either to specific schools, like the great Mīmāṃsā and Vedānta commentaries, or to specific sects, like many of the *Purāṇas*; neither of these sets of works has the suprascholastic or suprasectarian relevance of the *Gītā*. At the same time many of these texts, for instance in Vedānta, assert this relevance of the *Gītā*, as witness Śaṅkara's, Bhāskara's, and Rāmānuja's commentaries, to mention only a few. However variously such scholars may interpret the *Gītā*, its authority is not at issue. The devotional *Purāṇas* of course breathe with the life of the *Gītā*.

It is this universal acceptance of the revelatory relevance of the *Gītā* that makes it so unique. For even before it was composed or "revealed" (ca. 200 B.C. is a likely date), orthodox thought had defined the nature and scope of revelation in such terms as might well have excluded the *Gītā*, or firmly consigned it to a lower level of authority where it would have withered away or at best been retained as a sectarian work of limited appeal.

What was "revelation" for the orthodox brahmanist thinker in 200 B.C.? Primarily the *brahman*, a word that in one of its connotations designates the Veda. The more general terms used were *śruta*, "that which is heard," and *śruti*, "knowledge by hearing." As the words indicate, revelation was conceived as a body of knowledge orally transmitted by a teacher to his pupil, who thus heard it. Although almost any teaching could be so described, the terms had the specialized meaning of that teaching which a *śrotriya*, an expert in *śruti*, conveyed to a student who had passed through the second birth of initiation: that is to say, at best a student from the three twiceborn classes, but most commonly a brahmin. This teaching would ideally comprise the entire Vedic corpus from the oldest hymns to the *Upaniṣadic* texts, but practically limits were set upon it by the branch (*śākhā*) of a particular Veda (e.g., *Yajurveda*) to which teacher and student belonged.

Despite these limitations of class and hereditary affiliation, this was the *brahman* that was heard. It was without beginning, for it stretched backward through the uninterrupted succession of teachers and students to the beginning, when it was given along with creation and then discovered by the primordial seers. It was without an author, human or divine, since it was part of creation; moreover, were it authored it would of necessity be flawed by the author's imperfections, and its authority diminished. It thus validated itself insofar as it was the sole source of knowledge about matters lying beyond the senses.

None of these criteria for revelation seem to apply to the *Gītā*. It is not beginningless, for it was uttered at the start of the *Mahābhārata* war which ushered in the Kali Age. It is authored, for Kṛṣṇa speaks it. It is not self-validated, for God validates it. In fact, only a small part of official *śruti* itself escapes the severe limits that the early Exegetes of the Veda, the Mīmāṃsakas,[33] imposed on its authority. They divided the corpus into three broad categories: Injunction (*vidhi*), Recital (*mantra*), and Commentary (*arthavāda*). Recital encompasses all the lines of the four Vedas, which may have their place in a ritual for such purposes as invoking gods, but really illuminate us about nothing. Commentary (literally: discussions of meaning and purpose) comprises the bulk of the later texts of *Brāhmaṇas*, *Āraṇyakas*, and *Upaniṣads*, in which matters pertaining to the ritual are described, explained, praised, or condemned. This category has some derivative meaning, but stands in need of the authority of the principal class, the Injunction.

The basic text of the Exegetes, the *Karma-mīmāṃsā-sūtras* (*sūtras* for the Enquiry into the Act), ascribed to Jaimini and certainly pre-*Gītā*, defines its scope in the first two *sūtras*: "In consequence [of the earlier study of the Veda] there arises therefore the desire of knowing the *dharma*" (1.1.1), and "*Dharma* is the meaningful purpose defined by the urging [of the Veda]" (1.1.2). These assertions establish that *dharma* is a meaningful and beneficial action which Injunctions urge a qualified person to engage in for specified reasons. Jaimini's concern is principally with those acts of *dharma* that are prescribed, or can be construed as being prescribed, in the Vedic corpus. He is not concerned with actions whose consequences are predictable from experience, but with the ritual acts that are declared to have a reward totally unpredictable by any other means than Vedic statement. For example, there is the Injunction that "He who desires heaven should sacrifice with the *jyotiṣṭoma* rite." Now there is nothing in our experience or any further knowledge we may gather from sensory perception or deduction that can validly convey to us that through the performance of a specific variant of the Soma sacrifice a person will attain heaven (itself a suprasensory goal), if he so desires. It is therefore in such self-validating injunctions to a course of ritual action that revelation ultimately resides.

This characteristic of revelation puts stringent limitations on its authority and its scope: all validity lies in Injunction, which has Vedic ritual as its scope. Thus the Veda has no authoritative bearing on anything that is already an accomplished fact, only on acts yet to be accomplished. For example, butter is a matter of fact, and nothing that the Veda has to say about butter adds an iota to our knowledge of it, *except* about what can be done with butter ritually for a purpose escaping our perceptions and deductions.

This view and definition of revelation limit its human relevance to those who have the interest and the means to perform a sacrifice in order to satisfy a need. If one is rich and young, he may as yet have no desire for heaven; conversely, a poor, middle-aged farmer who wants a son and needs rain does not have the means to satisfy either desire.

The limited purpose of the Veda inevitably created a need for some sort of revealed authority to cover matters for which it did not provide. This secondary authority is vested in the large body of *smṛti*, a word that means "recollection" but is practically used to signify "tradition." Jaimini devotes a chapter[34] to this important corpus: he concedes a delegated authority to *smṛti* if it does not conflict with *śruti*. This is a broad concession, since *śruti* deals with so little. But the concept of *smṛti* has its own limitations: first of all *smṛti* must owe allegiance to the Veda (and this excludes all heterodox *smṛtis*), and it must deal with acts. Tradition, therefore, does not broadly comprise traditional knowledge. More precisely *smṛti* is the set of rules for acts of *dharma* that are not explicitly declared by *śruti*, but are implicitly derivable from it: when we find a *śruti*-observing brahmin *also* observing non-*śruti dharmas*, the presumption is that such acts are rooted in the Veda in that their actual practice is "recollected" in the behavior of that brahmin, whose knowledge of them was passed on to him by his teacher just as *śruti* was passed on to him.

The theory therefore is that orthodox behavior, i.e., the behavior of the orthodox, and the rules about it are validated implicitly by the Veda. Now this behavior covers a great deal of human action that is existentially relevant, e.g., life-cycle rites, law in the strict sense, the actions traditionally proper for class and life stage (*varṇāśramadharma*), etc. *Smṛti* is thus for all practical purposes far more important than *śruti*, yet dogmatically it has no authoritative standing without the latter. Like *śruti*, *smṛti* remains beginningless and authorless. When, as so often, the *Dharmaśāstra* is invoked with "Manu has said," this does not mean that the law originated in time with the person of Manu, any more than Mosaic Law is the Law of Moses. Manu simply recorded it.

Where does all this leave the *Gītā*? What is *its* basis of authority? From a *śruti* point of view it has not much of one. The only *dharma* it acceptably advocates is the *varṇāśramadharma* of Arjuna, who as a *kṣatriya* in the prime of his life should fight this war. What it says about the human soul, God, and their interrelations has some purpose only as a sort of *arthavāda* to the injunction *yudhyasva*, "Fight!" The *Gītā*'s notions about the avoidability of the consequences of acts is at least questionable. But by and large, as long as the text does not imply that the injunction originated with a person, Kṛṣṇa, at a specific time, that of the *Mahābhārata* war, but simply reaffirms Veda-based *smṛti*, it is not in contradiction with *śruti*.

So far the Mīmāṃsaka. But, trapped by the steely consistency of which only Indian *śāstra* seems capable, he has not realized that the *Gītā* has authority for all the wrong reasons: because it has a person as its author, because it was the product of time, and because it has no regard for *śruti*. Its author is Kṛṣṇa, who comes right out and reveals himself as God beyond the Veda; its time is a war that sorely tried the dictates of *dharma* in a way arousing sympathy; its rejection of a Mīmāṃsā type of orthodoxy is explicit and implicit. We have in the *Bhagavadgītā* a new sort of revelation: personal, historic, and original. These features are, to be sure, not entirely new to the *Gītā*. There are in the *Upaniṣads* whole passages in which individual persons presented as historic propound original views. But this fact has not struck the Vedānta students of the *Upaniṣads* either. For them these texts were part of *śruti* (beginningless, authorless). They were much more concerned with defining the *Upaniṣads* as valid and meaningful, if need be on Mīmāṃsā terms, than with pointing to their novelty. Nor has the *Gītā* struck them as novel, though their use of it goes a long way toward implying that it is so.

The Vedāntists would have had problems with the *Gītā* if they had attempted to define its authority outside *śruti* and *smṛti*. The great commentators ignore the issue, if in fact they saw it. Śaṅkara, who ultimately does not accept the notion of God, has no problem with him on the level of practicality.

The Blessed Lord [he begins his commentary] after creating this

> world and desiring to make it permanent, created in the beginning the Prajāpatis Marīci, etc., and taught them the *dharma* defined by activity, which is declared by the Veda. Thereafter he created others, Sanaka, Sanandana, etc., and taught them the *dharma* of withdrawal from activity, defined as knowledge and dispassion. For the *dharma* declared by the Veda is of these two kinds. . . . After a long time, when the *dharma* was overwhelmed by *adharma* as a result of the performers' judgment and knowledge having dwindled because of the rise of desire, and *adharma* was growing strong, the original creator Viṣṇu, named Nārāyaṇa, desirous of assuring the stability of the world, undertook, so they say, birth, using a particle of himself, from Devakī by Vasudeva, in order to protect the brahminhood of the brahmins on earth: for by the protection of brahminhood the Vedic *dharma* itself would be protected, since the variety of classes and stages of life depend on it. This Blessed Lord was perceived as born, as it were, as an embodied person, as it were, by virtue of his own power of illusion, doing, as it were, a favor to the world. For, though having no purpose of his own, but out of desire to show favor to the creatures, he taught the twofold Vedic *dharma* to Arjuna, who was drowning in the ocean of sorrow and confusion, with the thought that the *dharma* would again grow strong if it were accepted and performed by notably virtuous men. It is this *dharma* as taught by the Blessed Lord which the all-wise lord Vedavyāsa expressed in the 700 verses called the *Gītā*.[35]

In this passage Śaṅkara makes his own view quite clear: The *Gītā* is a composition (*upanibandha*) by Vyāsa, the author of the *Mahābhārata*, recounting the Lord's teachings to Arjuna about the duties of class and life stages; these duties depend on the brahmins for their adjudication, and the brahmins are protected by the Lord in order to safeguard the Vedic *dharma*. As the creator's word, the *Gītā* affirms *śruti* and *smṛti*.

The position of Bhāskara has in part to be reconstructed, for unfortunately the beginning of his introduction is lost. After some quotations from the *Mahābhārata* he concludes that

> the *śūdra*, etc. [viz., women and even lower classes], may only *listen* to the epic, and even then only listen to the *narrative* part of the epic, not to the passages that set forth the hidden significance of the Vedānta (i.e., the *Upaniṣads*), such as the *Sanatsujātīya*, the *Mokṣadharma*, the *Gītā*, for there is the *smṛti* which prohibits [the *śūdra*] from learning the Veda, listening to it, understanding its import, and acting upon it.[36]

Bhāskara therefore appears to treat the *Gītā* practically as an *Upaniṣad*, not just *smṛti* but near-*śruti*.

Rāmānuja concludes his preamble, which contains his basic theodicy, as follows:

> Nārāyaṇa . . . has descended, seemingly to rule the world but actually to alleviate the burdens of *saṃsāra* even of the likes of us, and so become visible to all mankind. . . . Slaking the thirst of all with the elixirs of his glances and words animated by boundless mercy, kindness, and tenderness, he has made Akrūra, Mālākāra, and others the most ardent Bhāgavatas by revealing the multitudes of his beauty, goodness, etc.; until, at last, while pretending to exhort Arjuna to fight, he has revealed the *bhaktiyoga*, promoted by *jñāna-* and *karmayoga*, which in the Vedānta [i.e., the *Upaniṣads*] is declared to be the means of attaining man's supreme end [viz., release], and of which he himself is the object.[37]

For Rāmānuja no Advaitic hedging with "as it were, as it were," but the physical presence of God converting Akrūra and the others into believers; still, he takes the view that the *Gītā* reaffirms the *bhakti* doctrine of the *Upaniṣads*. For all three Vedāntins, then, the *Gītā* is confirmation of what existed before in *śruti*, either the Vedic *dharma*, or the hidden meaning of the *Upaniṣads*, or their devotional message. They do not address themselves to the question of why God took the time to repeat what was already available, or why they themselves commented on it.

The answer to the latter question is of course that they could not ignore the *Gītā*. The prestige of the text in the Vedānta school of thought goes back to the *Vedāntasūtras*, themselves ascribed to Bādarāyaṇa. While the *Gītā* refers to "*Brahmasūtras*" (13.4), this is likely to have been some collection antedating Bādarāyaṇa, perhaps as an appendix to the *Karmamīmāṃsāsūtras*. For Bādarāyaṇa quotes the *Gītā* twice. As usual there is no hint in the *sūtras* themselves about this matter. However, the earliest commentators whose works survive, Śaṅkara, Bhāskara, and Rāmānuja, unanimously quote the *Gītā* as the source for *sūtras* 2.3.45 (*api smaryate*, "this is also declared by *smṛti*") and 4.1.10 (*smaranti ca*, "and they declare it in *smṛti*").

We must, in my opinion, accept the traditional assignment of sources to the *sūtras*, and also accept that this tradition goes back as far as Bādarāyaṇa himself. For these two assumptions are in accord with the facts of (1) the near unanimity of commentators who otherwise hold conflicting views on the interpretation of the *sūtras*, so that the source is not an issue, and (2) the sheer impossibility, *at any time*, of construing with any degree of likelihood a set of scriptural sources for the *sūtras* without the aid of an unassailable tradition. The context of the *Gītā* quotations in the *Vedāntasūtras* is here unimportant. The important thing is that the *Gītā is* quoted. Both of the citations are strictly speaking unnecessary, since in each case there is already a reference to *śruti*. Therefore, that a *Gītā* quotation was nevertheless deemed appropriate attests to the near-*śruti* prestige of our text at a very early date.

Yet the *Gītā* does not identify itself with *śruti*. In fact, as we shall see,[38] Kṛṣṇa can be quite outspoken in his criticism of *śruti*. The tradition with which the *Gītā* prefers to link itself is a *kṣatriya* one: "I have revealed this eternal [*karma*-] Yoga to Vivasvat, who transmitted it to [his son] Manu, who told it to [his son] Ikṣvāku" (4.1), who is the founder of the Solar Dynasty of kings. Again: "Through action alone did Janaka, etc., attain to perfection" (3.20), and Janaka was a king who shone in his debates with brahmins.

I do not wish to raise once more the specter of "*kṣatriya* philosophers," Pravāhana,[39] Buddha, Mahāvīra, and now apparently Kṛṣṇa, for I think it is without substance. What such a *kṣatriya* alignment means is not that there existed independently a strain of *kṣatriya* thought zealously and secretively concealed from bramins who were hermetically sealed off from it; but that new thought might identify itself as "new" by calling itself non-brahmin, i.e., not in line with those hidebound orthodox Vedic specialists who could think only old thoughts.

For, despite his perfunctory bows to received orthodoxy, Kṛṣṇa is quite aware that he has new things to say, disguised as old things, older than the oldest brahmin: "Thus has come down the tradition of Yoga (= *karmayoga*) which the royal seers knew. Over a long span of time this Yoga was lost. What I have propounded to you today is this same ancient Yoga . . . for this is the ultimate mystery" (4.2–3). Kṛṣṇa's "today" is revealing: he is speaking *in time* about matters so long forgotten that until today they have remained a complete mystery. Kṛṣṇa reveals himself: "I am opaque to all. . . . No one knows me" (7.25–26). Again: "I shall proclaim to you . . . this most mysterious insight, . . . the royal wisdom, the royal mystery" (9.1–2); "listen to my supreme word which I shall pronounce to you" (10.1). Arjuna is converted: "You yourself tell me so, Keśava; I know that all this is true. . . . You yourself know yourself. . . . How may I know you, yogin?" (10.13–15; 17). So Kṛṣṇa responds: *hanta te kathayiṣyāmi*: "Well, then, I shall tell you!" and God reveals himself: "Hari, the great sovereign of Yoga, revealed to Arjuna his supreme supernal form" (11.9), in the marvelous transfiguration of chapter 11. This is a personal and unprecedented self-revelation: "Out of grace for you, Arjuna, have I revealed myself, . . . my highest form which no one but you has ever beheld" (11.47).

If it is true that in so many respects the *Bhagavadgītā* deviates from the old acceptable *śruti*, how did it come to be accepted as a source text with an authority close to that of *śruti*? One may consider that it was just the deviation that commended it. Brahmanism was going through an upheaval in the late centuries B.C. There were new doctrines abroad that were being commonly accepted by the thoughtful. The doctrine of rebirth and particularly the dismal view taken of it were gaining wide currency and could not really be accommodated by the old system that saw in acts the cure of all afflictions. The cure *was* the affliction, for it was the acts themselves that were pointed to as the cause of endless reincarnation.

Movements, which even found royal favor,[40] emphasized the misery of life and the need for (and possibility of) escape from it. New values were being stressed: The renunciation displayed by the universal teacher whose life was austere beyond reproach but whose gravity did not mask his compassion for man in need of spiritual help. Around him an order of similarly renouncing disciples, all otherworldly and, being homeless, willing to live by the liberality of the faithful. A doctrine that could be understood on every level of society and that promised alleviation of the ills of existence. A refreshing proximity between the saintly and the common people. A shared distaste of the taking of life and a disgust for those who lived by this means, professionally or sacerdotally. A growing distance from a social class that proclaimed its ancient authority with less and less to show for it except quick quacksalver palliatives for temporary relief. Elsewhere the enthusiasm for savior gods found jubilant voice, gods who could be worshiped and beseeched for the grace that would liberate instantly; who could be imagined, praised, sung, and sculpted; about whom delightful stories could be told and retold and woven into myths; with whom one could identify the crude icons of the village and the abstract conceptions of the new schools of thought.

There was much in the new values and perceptions that a thoughtful brahmin, of however venerable and hallowed a Vedic clan, and a proud prince, of however distinguished and glorious an old dynasty, could live with and even embrace. But for one fatal flaw: the lack of a consistent supramundane view of an ordered world and society. Neither the religious enthusiasts nor the unsocialized ascetics could offer stability to an expanding society that was badly in need of it. And here Kṛṣṇa came to the fore, a hero from their own tradition, revered in the Aryan heartland as a mighty yet kindly God, who was made to reveal himself as the guarantor of social stability, and the upholder of the *dharma* of class and life stage, who yet had the answer to the doctrine of rebirth that the heterodox had appropriated, who put their wisdom, philosophies, and renunciations in their place and who revealed himself as the savior of all. Who would not with Saṃjaya reflect on his discourse and rejoice anew and anew, or with Arjuna recover his wits, shed his doubts, and do as Kṛṣṇa said?[41]

Act, Karman and Yoga

The attention and deliberation devoted by Indian, especially Hindu, thinkers to the nature of actions, their components, their conditions, and their consequences are to the non-Indian student staggering. This phenomenon began with the earliest of the Vedas and has continued to this day. During this time, which spans the entire life of Indian civilization, emphases obviously have changed. The changes are, however, no means of periodization, for at almost any one time, close irreconcilable views were being held.

Certain characteristics of the Indian "act" should be mentioned at the outset. It was never centrally regarded as an indifferent or spontaneous form of behavior; that acts of such types existed was recognized but not as relevant to serious discussion. Rather, the act was a performance with precise definition as to circumstance, subject, objective, and result. We may call the act, thus viewed, "ritual" in the sense that it was repeatable under the proper conditions and served a purpose that, while it could be desired by an individual person, was valid only insofar as it functioned within a set of values that transcended that person and to which he by his performance bore witness.

The first stage of such acting was in the sacrificial context of the older Veda. An act (*karman*) was a rite directed at a deity by a person, representing himself or a group, to insure the continued functioning of the power of that deity and hence the stability of the cosmos as far as it was governed by that deity, and the fulfillment of the person's desire as far as that was not at variance with cosmic stability. From the beginning one may recognize a dual purpose of the act: to maintain the cosmic status quo and to allow a person's expansion within it.

The second stage, which may be dated by the later literature of the *Brāhmaṇas* (ca. 800–700 B.C.) exhibits a breathtaking extension of this dual purpose and hence of the act. The act of sacrifice is magnified: the sacrifice itself is viewed as the necessary condition of the maintenance of the cosmos as a whole, without the mediation of partial divine powers, and all its appurtenances are subordinated to the fact of sacrifice. The deities themselves become such appurtenances, losing practically all importance except for their existence as recipients of *mantras* and sacrificial substances. The act itself is paramount as the generator of that power which keeps the universal wheel rolling: it ceaselessly renews, even recreates, the cosmos; its power source is the *brahman*, the creative potency of the ritual utterance and performance. The sacrificing person, unlike the deity, does *not* become a mere appurtenance, for the act is his; on the contrary, his role and options develop commensurately. While the act grows richer and more expensive, so that only the great of the land can afford it, the labor, patronage, and outlay of the sacrificing person are immensely rewarded with personal fruits: there is not a rite unavailable to accommodate his every desire. A mighty host of priestly specialists, growing with the act, divide the ever-increasing functions among themselves. They are the brahmins that have specialized in and henceforth belong to one of the four Vedas and receive the rich fees that complete the act. They have access to power as immense in its display as it is mysterious in its source.

At the height of this development a reaction occurred that marks a third stage. While there probably always were lone figures who sought their own path outside the cosmos of the act, they are now given voices of their own. In the later Vedic texts of the *Upaniṣads* (from 600 B.C. on) a new emphasis is placed on deliberation, not about the proper ways of performing an act and the significance of its constituent rites, but about the universal power or principle underlying it all, which in the act mediates between microcosm and macrocosm and unites the two. Mediation implies two levels and raises questions of priority and hierarchy. Is this primordial creativeness continuous in creation, or is creation of a lower level of effective reality? If the act mediates, what is the required bond between the "soul" of the universe and the "soul" of the performer?[42] Is creativeness that of a consciousness paralleling human consciousness or of a substance transforming itself? With these variously presented and answered questions, thinking remains within the domain of the act; the reaction to "mere" acting is that of a thoughtful address to the metaphysics of the act.

There was also a revolution brewing. It is ironical that the very magnitude, the very irresistibility of the act helped foster a newly articulated concept that in certain circles would destroy the act. It was becoming dubious, at least, whether all this accumulated power of so many acts could be spent in a lifetime. Everything in nature constantly renews itself through death and rebirth by virtue of the inherent creativeness of growth. Likewise the mysterious power of man's acts might well wash over the temporary boundary of his death into a new birth and life, into reincarnation.

Such a notion could be viewed positively, as suggesting a possible infinity of the good life; but by and large it was not. There is little in the powerful optimism of the *Brāhmaṇas* and, to a high degree, of the early *Upaniṣads* that prepare us for the disgust with which disaffected spirits view sacrifice and rebirth. The Lord Buddha, at the request of a group of wealthy old brahmins of Kosala, holds forth on the modern brahmins. After describing their original purity ("Refined, tall, of fine color and high fame were those brahmins because of their practice of their own Laws, intent upon both task and avoidance of misdeeds"), he goes on:

> Then came their ruin. Seeing bit by bit their king expand, with his finely decked women, his well-wrought chariots yoked with thoroughbreds, his colorful stitchings, his palaces and well-laid-out chambers, thriving with herds of cows, waited on by bevies of comely women, those brahmins began to covet that vast human luxury. They composed *mantras* then and there, approached Okkaka and said, "Your riches are abundant. Sacrifice, you have much wealth. Sacrifice, you have much money!" Prompted by the brahmins, that king, a bull among warriors, sacrificed up horses, humans, and animals and offered the Vājapeya in unbridled fashion; and he gave riches to the brahmins: cows, beds, clothes, finely decked women, etc.

The brahmins keep prompting, until "cows, sweet as lambs, filling pails with milk, never hurting anyone with foot or horn—the king had them seized by the horns and slaughtered by the sword," so that "the *kṣatriyas*, self-styled brahmins, and others protected by rank destroyed the repute of their caste and fell prey to desires."[43] By this time the Buddha has proclaimed the Four Noble Truths and the Eightfold Path, which imparted a liberating insight into the cause of the misery that is life and rebirth, and the method of transcending it, without benefit of "acts" and the services of priests.

In Hinduism too, though there the evils of rites and rebirth were muted, there was a movement toward *saṃnyāsa*, renunciation, and the turning away from acts, at the same time that old-style brahminism kept maintaining the need for action as the only guarantee against chaos.

It is against this complex background, of the diminished but continuing prestige of the Veda (now almost wholly subservient to ritualism) and the demand for the orthodoxy of *dharma*, of *saṃsāra* of rebirth now assumed to result from acts, of the mystical philosophies among the orthodox that were held superior to the practical philosophy of the act, with the correlated tendencies toward *saṃnyāsa*, and of the total rejection of the Veda and brahmin authority by the heterodox who advocated the asocial pursuit of personal salvation—it is against this background that Kṛṣṇa's doctrine of the act needs to be viewed.

Kṛṣṇa's argument for action is two-pronged: he defends the right kind of action against, on the one hand, the overzealous advocates of Vedic ritualism and, on the other, the propounders of the doctrine that all acts should be given up. His argument is at once simple and complex: simple, because he finds cause to propose that action is both necessary and unproductive of rebirth; complex, because he attempts to hold on to the orthodoxy of social action while revolutionizing it from within, and at the same time to demolish the heterodoxy of renunciation-at-any-price without discarding the value of renunciation per se. These were the issues of the time, and Kṛṣṇa addresses them before going on to the consolations of personal religion.

In the narrative of the *Gītā*, Kṛṣṇa, faced with Arjuna's renunciation, at the outset stipulates two assumptions: (1) that the soul survives the body (2.16–30) and (2) that one must observe one's own *dharma*. On these two assumptions most of his further argument is predicated. The first assumption he does not spend time arguing but takes for granted. The second one is argued at length.

By shirking his *dharma*, Kṛṣṇa submits, Arjuna rightly brings on his head the scorn of his peers (2.33–36). As it happens, if Arjuna does observe his *dharma* he cannot lose: surviving he has the earth, dying he has heaven (2.37).

This argument, of course, displays fine old *kṣatriya* conviction. But now, in 2.38, Kṛṣṇa introduces a new proposition: "Holding alike happiness and unhappiness, gain and loss, victory and defeat, yoke yourself to the battle, and so do not incur evil." According to this injunction, one should observe one's own *dharma* (in Arjuna's case: fighting) with disregard of personal consequences. It is this disinterestedness, and this alone, which is the spirit about which he will set forth the *yoga*: yoked with this spirit (*buddhi*) Arjuna will cut away the bondage of the act (2.39).

Any translator will have difficulty in giving a satisfactory rendering of the word *yoga*. First of all, let the reader not mistake the *yoga* of the *Bhagavadgītā* for the Yoga of Patañjali or, worse, Haṭha-Yoga or even Kuṇḍalinī Yoga. The word *yoga* and cognates of it occur close to 150 times in the *Gītā*, and it needs attention. The root is *yuj-*, which means "to yoke," as one yokes horses to a chariot. This literal meaning occurs in the *Mahābhārata*: when battle is at hand, the warriors call for the Yoke,[44] i.e., the yoking of the horses to the war cars, wagons, and other war equipment. The word *yoga* always refers to a strenuous effort to which a person has committed himself. It can be applied reflexively to the warrior himself: *yuddhāya yujyasva* (2.38), "Yoke yourself to the battle!"

This reflexive usage is usual in the *Bhagavadgītā*: *yoga* is a self-yoking to a particular effort to win a goal. In doing so a person may have tools with which he, so to say, girds himself: hence he is *buddhiyukta*, "yoked with the spirit" as his instrument (*buddhyā yuktaḥ*, instrumental case, 2.39). One girds oneself *for* a course of action, e.g., fighting (*yuddhāya*, dative case), which then is the goal. But also *in* a course of action (*karmaṇi*, locative case) or *through* a course of action (*karmaṇā*, instrumental case), which *then* will lead to a further goal.

Thus the word *yoga* denotes a broader concept than "discipline

(= method)" which Edgerton chose *par faute de mieux*. It is not the case that *yoga* has so many different "meanings," but that the central meaning is a complex one that in English is not exhausted by one equivalent. *Yoga* is always of somebody, in something, with something, for some purpose; *yoga* in an absolute sense hardly occurs in the *Gītā* at all. (Divine *yoga* is a special case to which we shall return.) When *yoga* occurs by itself it is oftentimes an abbreviation for *karma-* or *bhakti-yoga*. *Yoga*, then, implies (1) the process of a difficult effort; (2) a person committed to it; (3) the instrument he uses; (4) the course of action chosen; and (5) the prospect of a goal.

Thus, in 2.39, "Now hear how this spirit applies in practice (*yoga*)," the word *yoga* covers the entire spectrum, with the instrument, viz., the spirit, specially mentioned. Henceforth *buddhi* should be primarily understood as that instrument in *yoga*. The ultimate goal of the *yoga* is mentioned at once (2.39): the doing away with the "bondage of the act." The word *buddhi*, too, defies attempts at single renderings. The old definition "the *buddhi* consists in resoluteness" is helpful: the *buddhi* is a high cognitive faculty that is always geared to purposeful action. "Spirit" covers some of this; "mental attitude" is too passive. Despite their apparent multiplicity of meanings in somewhat technical contexts, words like *yoga*, *karman*, and *buddhi* are not arcane technical terms, but words in common usage. If their contextual implications are at times obscure to us, they were immediately understood by Kṛṣṇa's audience.

Having put forward his proposition that acting is necessary and not binding when done disinterestedly, Kṛṣṇa immediately confronts those who have made themselves the arbiters of *dharma*, the ritualists. He calls them unenlightened, fond of debating the Veda, holding that their notion of Veda is all there is, and he points out that the acts they propagate lead to rebirth: their pleas are to the benighted who act for pleasure and power and who have not the singleness of purpose of the true spirit (2.41–44). These charges strike the Mīmāṃsakas where they are vulnerable. Exegetes and advocates of the act, they stress the personal reward for the sacrificer from his act. We must keep in mind that the ritualists did not constitute a church with the power to enforce the performance of ritual acts. They might be "priests," but not the priests of a church: they were the ritual specialists whose livelihood was the execution of rites that others ordered. Necessarily they played on the potential patron's self-interest. Any rite, Jaimini maintains, is done for personal interest (*puruṣārtha*).[45] Even where he concedes that there are minor rites which subserve a major one (*kratvartha*), that major rite is *puruṣārtha*. A person's interests can be legion (*ananta*, 2.41). For the simplest of Vedic rites, the twice-daily fire offering (*agnihotra*), no less than ten varieties are listed that produce specific rewards.[46] And all these self-interest rites, so Kṛṣṇa holds, "bring on rebirth as a result of the acts" (2.43). The ritualist doctrine therefore needs total reformation.

The thesis of this reformation is expressed in one sentence: "Your entitlement is only to the rite, not ever at all to its fruits." Here, in "entitlement," *adhikāra*, we have a real technical term from Mīmāṃsā. It covers the sum total of those properties such as birth, initiation, and stage of life, as well as specific purpose—that qualify and thereby entitle a person to perform a certain act and reap the reward of his performance. Kṛṣṇa proposes to strike "specific purpose" from the *adhikāra* and maintains that doing so will automatically strike the reward of the rite.

But striking the purpose of acts is equivalent to striking a majority of acts. It leaves only the category of the "set act" (*niyataṃ karma*, 3.8), and the only "set act" that Kṛṣṇa is interested in here is *varṇāśramadharma*.

What is a set act? Mīmāṃsā in general divides acts into three classes: regularly recurring (*nitya*), e.g., the daily *agnihotra*, the fortnightly New and Full Moon offerings; occasional (*naimittika*), e.g., expiation and life-cycle rites; and desiderative (*kāmya*), i.e., rites undertaken to satisfy a certain desire. It is these *kāmya* rites that produce, according to Kṛṣṇa, the consequences that tie the performer to the chain of rebirth; and the other classes of rites have the same effect if they are undertaken with a certain desire in mind. The performer's desire is ritually stated in his *saṃkalpa*, "intention," at the beginning of the act. For Kṛṣṇa the entire structure of reward-seeking acts is a fabric of delusion. Such acts are far inferior to the *yoga* of acting with singlemindedness (2.49). If relinquishing such acts means giving up a goodly part of the Veda, so be it. That kind of Veda belongs to the workaday world of polarities, which needs to be transcended (2.45). "When you have the desire to cross over this quagmire of delusion, then you will become disenchanted with what is supposed to be revealed, and the revealed itself" (2.52). This "disenchantment" is *nirveda*, quite possibly a pun, for it may also mean "Veda-lessness." "When your spirit of purposiveness stands unshaken, at cross-purposes with the revealed truth and immobile in concentration, then you will have achieved *yoga*" (2.53), i.e., the application of that spirit to a selfless course of action. This spirit is *śrutivipratipannā*: in opposition to *śruti*.

Kṛṣṇa does not necessarily think that *kāmya* acts are all there is to the Veda: they are the inventions of the florid-spoken nitwits who delight in debating the Veda and hold that *nānyad asti*, "there is nothing else" (2.42). The truly knowing brahmin has as much, or as little, use for the Veda as for a well when the water overflows everywhere (2.46). Kṛṣṇa has no quarrel with Vedic ritual pursued in the right spirit: after all, it is through the ritual of sacrifice, coeval with creation, that men enhance the being of the gods and the gods that of men (3.10 ff.) And such ritual action will not be binding if it is taken selflessly; the world is in bondage to karmic consequences only when sacrifice is offered for another reason than for the sake of sacrifice: *yajñārthāt*, in which we may recognize the Mīmāṃsaka's *kratvartham*. Such action is the true *brahman* of the Veda; it has to be "kept rolling along" (3.15 ff.), but for unselfish purposes, "to hold the world together" (3.17 ff.)

Indeed, God himself is a *karmayogin*, for "if I were not to move in action, untiringly, at all times, Arjuna, people all around would follow my lead. These people would collapse if I did not act; I would be the author of miscegenation; I would assassinate these creatures" (3.23 f.). God's wisdom here is in striking contrast with the confusion of Arjuna, who thought that *he* would destroy his family and bring about miscegenation (1.39 ff.). On the surface, Kṛṣṇa observes, the acting of the sage and of the ignorant man look the same—so be it, do not confuse them: "The wise man should take kindly to all acts, but himself do them 'yoked,' in a disciplined fashion" (3.26), that is, yoked with *buddhi* to disinterested acting.

Some of this sounds confusing to Arjuna (3.1–2). If it is true when Kṛṣṇa says that insight (the spirit, *buddhi*) is superior to the act (e.g., 2.49), why should Arjuna not stick to insight and forget about this horrible act of war? And his response sets off Kṛṣṇa's attack on "inaction." Some of Kṛṣṇa's discourse may sound confusing to us, but it should not, as long as we keep his categories in mind.

Kṛṣṇa was not the only one within the brahmin tradition who connected the *karman* of death and rebirth with the lust for reward from acts. In *Mahābhārata* 5, *The Book of the Effort*, there occurs a semiphilosophical teaching attributed to the sage Sanatsujāta under somewhat similar circumstances: dreading that the next day's news about the Pāṇḍavas' reaction will mean war, Dhṛtarāṣṭra asks for consolation from Sanatsujāta, having heard that the sage maintains there is no death. The sage responds that there is no re-death, if one conquers the distractions of folly by the study-practice of *brahman* absorbed in the *ātman*. This process is contrasted with the normal practice of ritual by those who "covet the fruits of their acts" and who in consequence "follow after the *karman* that results, and so do not cross over death," i.e., the realm of rebirth and death, toward non-death, or release from rebirth. But he who "thinks and destroys those fruits as they try to arise"—i.e., in Kṛṣṇa's terms, he who by having the right spirit (*buddhi*) destroys the fruits of his acts, viz., his *karman*, before it has a chance of coming into being and still has not a *buddhi* that is "antagonistic" to acting per se out of "disrespect" for acting—he "eats like death the fruits of the acts as they arise. Therefore wise is the one who forsakes his desires."[47] It does not matter whether Sanatsujāta anticipates Kṛṣṇa or vice versa. What matters is that both saw the way of having the act and eating its *karman*.

Action, Nonaction, and the Place of Knowledge

Kṛṣṇa completes his one-verse manifesto that the Mīmāṃsaka's *adhikāra* bears only on the performance of acts, not the reaping of their rewards, with the admonition: "Be not motivated by the fruits of acts, but also do not purposely seek to avoid acting" (2.47). To convey the idea of "purposely seeking," Kṛṣṇa uses the word *saṅga*, "attachment, self-interest," exactly the same covetous attitude that he condemns in those who act for the sake of rewards. He therefore clearly states his view that the avoiders of acts may be similarly guided by self-seeking desire. He quickly associates the upholders of this "deliberate inaction," or, if you will, "creative nonaction," with followers of illumination philosophies.

He answers Arjuna's question, "Why act at all?" (3.1) with the statement that he himself has of old expounded that there are two positions one can take: a *yoga* of knowledge, and the *yoga* of action which he has just defended. While this might seem to authenticate the path of knowledge, Kṛṣṇa immediately attacks what must have been a highly visible aspect of it: "A person does *not* avoid incurring *karman* (*naiṣkarmyam aśnute*) just by not performing acts, nor does he achieve success by giving up acts (*saṃnyasanād eva*)" (3.4). After all, acting comes naturally: no one ever does *not* act even for an instant (3.5). Besides, the piety of the renouncer is by no means assured: behind his serene façade he may well indulge in daydreams of sensual delights (3.6). The superior man performs the *yoga* of action while renouncing (*asaktaḥ*, viz., the fruits) (3.7). So perform the set acts that are given with creation (3.8–15): he who does not do so lives in vain (3.16), whereas the man satisfied with his immortal soul has no action-for-reward to perform (*tasya kāryaṃ na vidyate*) (3.17). As we have seen, a wholly unmotivated God does himself perform acts, for the well-being of the world.

At this point Kṛṣṇa in passing borrows a notion from Sāṃkhya: ultimately it is material nature that acts on itself, while the soul stays aloof (3.27). Also in passing he etymologizes *saṃnyāsa*, which literally means "throwing it all down." But on what? Throw it on me, says Kṛṣṇa (now as God granting that this material nature is part of his being) and go on to fight (3.30).

Thus Kṛṣṇa by juxtaposition has associated the ancient "*yoga* of knowledge" with the practice of rejection of action, which he then condemns as ineffective (3.4), self-deceptive (3.5), hypocritical (3.6), antisocial (3.16; 20 ff.), uninformed (3.27), and unfeasible (3.33). We have not heard a good word about *jñānayoga* yet.

Kṛṣṇa returns to his theme in 4.18: "He is possessed of the right spirit (*buddhi*), when he can discern that there are no karmic consequences in acting (*karmaṇy akarma*) but that there are such in nonacting (*akarmaṇi karma*). Thus, yoked (*yukta*, i.e., with the right *buddhi* to action) he can perform any act" (4.18). Why? Because he does acts without the ritual intention (*saṃkalpa*) for any desired result (*kāma*) (4.19), so that, although fully engaged in an act (*karmaṇy abhipravṛtto 'pi*), he does not at all make any (sc., *karman: naiva kiṃcit karoti saḥ*) (4.20).

Moreover, the practices of sacrificers of substances (butter, soma, etc.), of ascetics practicing study and knowledge (4.28), of "yogic" controllers of the breath (4.29), of fasters (4.30) all have the same structure and spring from action (4.32). Those whose practices include knowledge (and this category certainly includes the *karmayogin*) rate above the traditional sacrificers of substances. In this way all action culminates, finds its fulfillment (*parisamāpyate*), in the knowledge that accompanies the action (4.33). In other words, from this vantage point a *yoga* of knowledge is really part and parcel of a *yoga* of acting.

Arjuna gives Kṛṣṇa an opportunity to make his views even clearer. To his question which of the two Kṛṣṇa prefers, the renouncing of acts or the *yoga* of actions, the answer is predictable: *karmayoga* (5.1–2). Once more Kṛṣṇa sees no real difference between the two: both lead to the highest goal, and by practicing the one a person also finds the fruit of the other (5.4). Kṛṣṇa does manage to discern one difference, which evaporates: "Renunciation is hard to accomplish without the *yoga* (sc., of action): yoked with the *yoga* the sage soon obtains *brahman*" (5.6), "for though acting, he is not tainted (by the *karman*)" (5.7). "He knows, 'I do not at all make any (*karman*)' " (5.8) is a repeat of 4.20, and as in 3.30 he casts all *karman* off, now on *brahman* (5.10), which, as so often in the *Gītā*, is the material-nature phase of God. This nature is again the realm of all action in 5.14.

At this point one might well wish for greater clarity on Kṛṣṇa's part about the issue: Who really is the agent in all this acting? The received Mīmāṃsā doctrine is that the agent is simply and justly the person, in fact the self: he does the acting and so the consequences rightly accrue to him. But the newer Sāṃkhya doctrine sees greater complexity here—and this doctrine is rather congenial to Kṛṣṇa, who is a transcendentalist. Sāṃkhya posits two categorically different orders of being: *puruṣa*, and *prakṛti* (*natura naturans et naturata*). It is in this *prakṛti* that all activity goes on, necessarily, for in his pure state the *puruṣa* is eternally unchanging. But, when the *puruṣa* gets (somewhat mysteriously) involved with *prakṛti*, or, in more practical terms, when the soul finds itself in its *prakṛti*-produced body, it identifies itself, by its faculty of subjectification (*ahaṃkāra*), with that body—wrongly and fatefully so, for this identification keeps it in bondage. So the soul thinks, "I am the agent" (3.27). Once a person recognizes that in action only material factors act on one another, he escapes the lien on his acts and their fruits (*na sajjate*) (3.28).

This assumption also provides a rationale for a person's acting-yet-not-acting ("my body acts, not I, the soul"), but it is a different rationale than is generally understood in *karmayoga*: "It is I who act but I act without a desire for the fruits by virtue of my spirit, and so I have no *karman*." Kṛṣṇa, however, apparently has little interest in the distinction, for his overriding concern is that a person can act without *karman*, however one might philosophically confront this issue. His Vedānta successors recognize the distinction and hold, with Mīmāṃsā, that the self/soul/person is both the agent of his acts and the experient of their fruits (*kartṛ* as well as *bhoktṛ*) and reject the Sāṃkhya view that only *prakṛti* acts, and that the *puruṣa* is solely the experient (*bhoktṛ*).

Kṛṣṇa continues to insist on the identity of renunciation and activity: "He is both a renouncer and a (*karma-*) *yogin* who performs the task set for him without interest in its fruits" (6.1) and "what they call 'renunciation' is precisely this *yoga*" (6.2). And now, having made his point abundantly clear, it is almost with relief that he can adopt the positive side of *saṃnyāsa*, the serenity that contemplation and meditation give to a person and the vision of higher goals that they open to him: the contentment of the pure self, the beatitude of *brahman*, and finally the faith in and love for God, who then deems him the most accomplished man of *yoga*. At this point Kṛṣṇa can move on to the *yoga* of *bhakti*.

God and Bhakti

Etienne Lamotte has remarked that "bhakti . . . is the specifically Hindu form of the religious sentiment, which can be and will be found over and over again in every cult and every sect, whichever it may be."[48] He is undoubtedly right if one with him takes "religious" to mean a practiced faith to which the acceptance of a personal God is central. But the statement can be misleading if it is understood to mean a self-evident, spontaneously recurring, ingrained monotheism. The *Gītā* itself may easily reinforce such an understanding, for, some fleeting references to minor deities aside, the text places central an articulate monotheistic concern. If unwarned, one might well come away with the idea that India confessed the monotheism of a God whose name was Kṛṣṇa. Fortunately, the word *bhakti* itself gives warning.

The word is an action noun derived from the root *bhaj-*. As is well attested from the earliest texts onward, the meaning of "sharing" is central to this root. The vast concept of sharing allowed of specialization, and meanings developed in two directions: offering someone else a share in something; and accepting or adopting something as one's allotted share. The latter usage evolved further into "declaring for, choosing for." It is the last of these meanings that governs later uses of the word *bhakti*.

The word *bhakti* is not confined to religious usage; it also occurs in contexts that are not religious in intent, in the *Mahābhārata*, and as late as Viśākhadatta's play *Mudrārākṣasa*. The basic connotation is that of loyalty (the opposite is "disaffection"): a subject may be loyal to his king, a servant to his master, and so on. But it is not always a sentiment directed toward one's superiors; the same root is also used for a man and a woman choosing each other carnally. But the notion of a loyal choice persists; and, as all loyalty, *bhakti* presupposes the possibility of other choices.

In religion, choices were legion. Although we are sparsely informed, we have little reason to assume that the age of the *Gītā* did not know the variety of sects and cults that later times so abundantly present. On a folk level the Vedic god Indra continued to be worshiped and prayed to for rain. There is evidence of a Sun cult. Fire worship of a kind persisted in the Vedic sacrifices. That there was a flourishing Śiva cult cannot be doubted. Very little is known about Goddess religions, but they are likely to have existed in several forms. The veneration of ancestors was more a domestic than a social worship, but it added to the richness of religious forms. Cults of chthonic powers like snakes and Yakṣas are evident. Also, a completely new god, Skanda Kārttikeya, appears in the northern pantheon, and surely not without sectarian pressure. In Buddhism and Jainism homage was paid to the great teachers—homage that a Hindu would consider *bhakti*. And then as now there undoubtedly existed *grāmadevatās* and *kuladevatās*, village and family deities. In this abounding polytheism a person needed *bhakti* to find for himself his *iṣṭadevatā*, "the god of his choice," to whom he could demonstrate his loyalty.

Sometimes such *bhaktas*, persons who have declared themselves for a particular god, are referred to as *ekāntins*, people who have withdrawn from the crowd to be with their god in solitude and privacy (*ekānte*), taking him as it were aside and addressing him privately, as in the theatre (*ekānte* is also a stage term) one character may take aside another and whisper to him what the others should not hear.

Bhakti, then, appears as a form of religiosity specifically Hindu in that it allows a religious man to create out of a social polytheism a personal monotheism. While he becomes ever more firmly a monotheist, the surrounding polytheism will continue to provide the believer, by the old process of henotheism, with metaphors for the supremacy of his god. Other gods become God's servants, or components imaginable in God's manifestations, or forms God assumed in his periodic incarnations. Whole pantheons now exist for God's glorification, so that the believer may stride through his world and discern that those who worship other gods are in fact engaged in the worship of an embodiment of *his* God, and therefore need not be disturbed in their simple faith.

Who then is the God of *bhakti*, what is he, and why? To the believer the identity of his God in a civilization that left many choices was a matter of passionate concern. On *what* God is he might lovingly dwell forever. *Why* he is is for the believer a question of unfathomable absurdity. To the outsider, however, the question has some relevance.

If we go by the literary sources, the literature preceding the *Gītā*, we find very little to make us expect to see soon the full glory of a transcendent personal God, who can be approached and known only with love. The later Veda had reduced the gods of the hymns to perfunctory invisible presences that were invoked to partake of offerings, in the context of a ritual event whose importance far surpassed their own. "Religious" speculation centered on the homologizing of sacrifice and cosmos and the finding of identities that would render intelligible the fact that the sacrifice kept generating the universe.

The generative power itself went by several names, one of which was *brahman*. When eventually the person of the sacrificer—an everyman, the one responsible for the unleashing and controlling of this generative power—began to be drawn into the speculations and homologies were perceived between the universe and its motive force, and the human person and his vital force, the emphasis shifted. A person's vital force too went by several names, one of which was *ātman*. Soon the homologies between macrocosm and microcosm were built up into perceptions of identity: *ahaṃ brahmāsmi*, "I am *brahman*"; *tat tvam asi*, "you are that." The "divine," the cosmic force, which was also spirit, was immanent in the human person.

Refinements were made in the perception of *brahman*. There was a higher, disembodied unmanifest *brahman*, and a lower *brahman* that was embodied and manifest. Hierarchy is causality. The Unmanifest, the unuttered and unevolved, is the source of the

Manifest. It is the ultimate and irreducible cause which is continuous in the manifest, the uncreated creator of a creation which is his self-creation. It is the transcendent that yet is immanent.

Once on this track some thinkers pushed on to the original autonomy of this transcendent being, which was spirit, an order separate from creation at the same time that creation was inseparable from it. But was it inseparable? Were the two *brahmans* perhaps separate orders of being, each with its own autonomy? Some assumed a creativeness abstracted from the spirit, a female womb to this male principle, a *prakṛti* to his *puruṣa*, which was the underlying cause of the manifest world, which was the body to his soul. And is this "soul" a single entity, immanent in the many individual souls, as the one fire is in the sparks that fly off it? Yes, said some: individual souls are but reflections, or components, of the one soul. No, said others, there are countless numbers of individual soul monads that together constitute the order of *puruṣa*; and they, so to say, have microcosmified the macrocosm which now consists in innumerable bodies and souls. Both of these concepts are valid, said still others: there is the supersoul never involved with *prakṛti*, which transcends the individual souls that are embodied; and they added yet a third ontological order to those of *puruṣa* and *prakṛti*.

All these speculations, however irreconcilable the final positions, remained in a continuum of thought that took off from the two forms of the one *brahman*. But there were persons, like Gautama Siddhārtha, who broke the continuum. As a healer he refused to care about soul in order to go on with the task of alleviating sorrow, and declined to address all the confusing issues of soul, supersoul, and body. If one attempts to identify the variety of views with the later labels of schools, one comes up with at least three views that were nontheistic: Mīmāṃsā, Sāṃkhya, and Buddhism; one that was semitheistic, Yoga; and one that was potentially both nontheistic and theistic: Vedānta. All these labors of thought hardly prepared the soil for a hardy, thriving theism.

Nevertheless, it is possible to say that pre-*Gītā* thought had fashioned a niche for a supreme God before there was one. And that when God decided to enter the scene he found his role waiting to be stepped into. The role was that of a transcendent supreme being who was to a certain extent immanent in, but not identical with, individual souls, and to a lesser extent immanent in the physical creation.

His role was to stand immovable on a pedestal. He was not a lawgiver, for *dharma* was already given. Hence he was also not a God of Justice—or, for that matter, necessarily even a just God—for divine justice was already taken care of by the *dharma* which through *karman* ruled on the rewards of the good and the punishment of the wicked. As a father he was otiose, since a separate mother took care of parturition. He was eternal and self-sufficient, and in his self-sufficiency knew the bliss of wanting nothing.

This was the best that philosophy could deliver. But with this potential image it also delivered a number of descriptions of God that the *Gītā* could rightfully adopt—not because it wished to legitimize Kṛṣṇa in the terms of orthodoxy but because it continued the thoughts of *Upaniṣads* and proto-Sāṃkhyan texts. As the supreme being Kṛṣṇa is indeed the higher *brahman*; the eternal, unborn, undying one; the highest abode; the final stride; the resting place of the universe; the unmanifest beyond the unmanifest; the light beyond darkness; the source and dissolution of the entire universe; the supreme *puruṣa*; the highest of *puruṣas*; the seed of all creatures; a being beyond knowledge and inconceivable, more minute than the minute, sun-hued; the supersoul; the Placer; the *Akṣara*; and so forth and so on. But what these descriptions stress above all is the Supreme's transcendence, his paramountcy, his inaccessibility, in short his supremacy.

But then there were gods who existed without benefit of philosophers, who were sought out by the multitudes that had wants these gods might fill. In a god of gods, in God, they needed, if not justice, at least love; if not a father, at least an uncle; if not law, at least the loophole of grace; if not creation, at least the illusion of it; if not revelation, at least advice. Urgently sought was for God to give a sign of his presence, for him to appear among men in whatever form he might care to assume, for him to descend from his supremacy and use his boundless power to right wrongs and restore order.

Kṛṣṇa provides for all these needs. Although as God he has all the lofty qualities that had already been ascribed to the supreme being, qualities that would have cut him off from all consoling contact with the world, he has descended in the person of Kṛṣṇa, a familiar hero in the *Mahābhārata*, aloof from involvement in the war but nevertheless partisan, who has found a friend in Arjuna. In the narrative of the epic this friendship antedates the revelation of Kṛṣṇa's divine nature and his transfiguration, and this sequence is characteristic of *bhakti*. In *bhakti* there must be an extremely close, one-to-one relationship between God and each loyal follower, so that God can disclose his divinity gradually and to one at a time. One already hears the loving laments of later *bhaktas* who long for a glimpse, however fleeting, of the God they adore and who pine away like deserted lovers in the desolation of his absence. One also foresees the role that is to be played by the indirect yet visible manifestation of a God in an icon, and perhaps, as in the case of Kṛṣṇa, his mythological transformation into the most captive objects of love, the child and the young lover. There is nothing of such a transformation yet in the *Mahābhārata*, or for that matter in the *Gītā*, but the seeds are present in the very conception of a God who descends and takes on human form.

The God who chooses to descend remains nameless. As God, Kṛṣṇa does not refer to himself by name, except once (7.19). Characteristically, in the long list of divine Ubiquities, he makes only casual mention of his present human identity: "Among the Vṛṣṇis I am Vāsudeva, among the Pāṇḍavas Arjuna; of the hermits I am Vyāsa, of sages Kavi Uśanas" (10.37). Equally casual is his mention of Viṣṇu: "Of the [Vedic group of the] Ādityas I am Viṣṇu, of celestial lights the shining sun, of [the storm gods] the Maruts I am Marīci, to the constellations I am the moon" (10.21), just as of the Rudras he is Śiva and of the Yakṣas Kubera (10.23). If God's name is Viṣṇu, Kṛṣṇa is not aware of it. Arjuna addresses him twice with *Viṣṇo*, "O Viṣṇu!" (11.24; 30), but he also identifies him with Vāyu, Yama, Agni, Varuṇa, the moon, Prajāpati, and Brahmā (11.39), and there is nothing in the *Gītā* elsewhere to hint that Kṛṣṇa was an *avatāra* of a specific God, Viṣṇu. The *Gītā* is suprasectarian.

Still, extremely important as the human dimension of God is for his *bhakta*, he remains a God that philosophers could recognize. He defines his relation to individual souls and material nature in the terms of an early quasi-theistic Sāṃkhya: "My material nature (*prakṛti*) is eightfold, comprising [the order of] earth, water, fire, wind, ether, mind (*manas*), spirit (*buddhi*), and ego (*ahaṃkāra*). This is my lower nature (*aparā*), but know that I have another higher nature (*prakṛtiṃ parām*), which comprises the order of souls (*jīvabhūtām*): it is by the latter that this [world: *idam*] is sustained" (7.4–5). The doctrine of the eight-*prakṛti* evolution, i.e., the five elements and three cognitive faculties, appears in sections of the *Mokṣadharma* of the *Mahābhārata* as an early stage[49] of the more complex evolutionary scheme of classical Sāṃkhya. In that doctrine the "soul" is still the creative, or at least initiative, force in an evolution seen on a cosmic scale, and is therefore single. But, when gradually the speculations on evolution shifted from the macrocosmic to the microcosmic, from the constitution of nature at large to that of the person, the separatist tendency of Sāṃkhyan thinking demanded, so to say, a soul per body. Nevertheless the more ancient, in fact *Upaniṣadic*, idea of a single "soul" persisted on a macrocosmic level. (In classical Yoga there are vestiges of this concept.[50]) Into the old polarity "soul: *prakṛti*," a new order of plural individual souls inserted itself. This led into two directions; the polarity of "soul: *prakṛti*" was restated as "souls: *prakṛti*," or the two polarities were combined in "Soul: souls: *prakṛti*." There, as in the statement of the *Gītā*, the dual scheme was extended: the Soul relates to the souls as the souls relate to *prakṛti*. Hence the universal Soul, i.e., the transcendent single spirit, has a higher *prakṛti* composed of the order of the individual souls. That such a transcendent *puruṣa* could be, and was, deified is not surprising.

But, to return to the *Gītā*'s own concerns, which were hardly theoretical or even theological, how does God, when he is called upon to manifest himself in his real, supreme divinity, reveal himself? As the bearer of all the transcendental properties that earlier thought had already named, as the creator who impregnates the *brahman* womb, which then sets in motion the actual creation, and as a spirit partially immanent in the domain of *prakṛti*, on which all action and fruit may be cast off. More concretely he reveals himself in his royal aspect, in the metaphors of his Ubiquities, where he is master or exemplar of any group that comes to mind. And most concretely, and overwhelmingly so, does he stand revealed by his transfiguration in chapter eleven.

Neither has the *Gītā* forgotten its theme nor Kṛṣṇa his mission: Arjuna's moral preparation for this war. And Arjuna's vision of God turns from the awed contemplation of God in his majesty (11.15–24) to the horrifying sight of God as war, devouring the warriors who like moths fly into his flaming mouths (11.25–31). God identifies himself as Time, which is death. And he gives Arjuna the final, absolving admonition: "Slay Droṇa, Bhīṣma, Jayadratha, Karṇa, and the other heroic warriors: I have already killed them. Do not tarry! Be merely my tool, Left-handed Archer!" (11.34). For, as God declares in the final verse of the chapter (11.55): "Only he comes to me, Arjuna, who acts for me, who holds me as the highest, who is devoted to me without self-interest and without any animosity against any creature."

How, finally, is Kṛṣṇa's teaching of *bhakti* related to his teachings of action and knowledge? I do not believe that he wishes to present them as equally valid options, or he would have done so. He has given new meaning to, and with it new hope for, the ordered life of action according to class and life stage; on the surface he has advocated the stoicism of acting for its own sake. He has rather ignored the benefits of knowledge and sharply warned against the dangers of blanket renunciation for the sake of release. Now he supplants the stoicism with the enthusiasm of the believer acting in God's name and for his glorification, and replaces the salvation-seeking knowledge with that knowledge of God that only *bhakti* can bring (11.47; 54).

Tradition sees the summation of his teaching in his *caramaśloka*, the "last" verse:

sarvadharmān parityajya mām ekaṃ śaraṇaṃ vraja /
ahaṃ tvā sarvapāpebhyo mokṣayiṣyāmi mā śucaḥ //

Abandon all the Laws and instead seek shelter with me alone.
Be unconcerned, I shall set you free from all that is evil.

6(63) *The Book of the Bhagavadgītā*

6.14–40 (B. 13–42; C. 495–1532)
14 (13; 495). Saṃjaya returns from the battlefield and reports to Dhṛtarāṣṭra that Bhīṣma has been killed by Śikhaṇḍin (1–10).
15 (14; 508). Dhṛtarāṣṭra asks about the circumstances of the killing, which he also imputes to Arjuna: Was Bhīṣma not invincible? (1–15). Was Bhīṣma deserted? Who guarded him? (15–30). Praise of Bhīṣma's prowess (35–40) and his battle with Rāma (40–45). The Kauravas' predicament at Bhīṣma's death (45–60). How did the battle proceed? (60–75).
16 (15–16; 588). Saṃjaya's reply. His gifts as witness (1–10). Duryodhana orders his brother Duḥśāsana to protect Bhīṣma and his chariot (10–20). In the morning both armies march out splendidly (20–35). The glorious aspect of Bhīṣma (40–45).
17 (17; 636). Both armies mass (1–5). Bhīṣma exhorts his troops (5–10). The splendors and banners of the Kaurava allies (10–35).
18 (18; 676). The tumult at the onset of battle (1–5). The numbers of the Kaurava army (5–15).
19 (19; 695). Yudhiṣṭhira consults Arjuna about their battle formation; the Thunderbolt array is decided on (1–15). Disposition of the Pāṇḍavas and their troops (15–35). Portents appear (35–40).

20 (20; 741). Description in triṣṭubhs *of the Kaurava forces (1–15).*
21 (21; 760). Upon that sight Yudhiṣṭhira despairs but is encouraged by Arjuna: Kṛṣṇa is on their side (1–15).
22 (22–24; 777). Description in triṣṭubhs *of the Pāṇḍava forces (1–15). Both armies are exultant (15–20).*

23–40. The Bhagavadgītā proper

23 [1] (25; 830). At Dhṛtarāṣṭra's bidding Saṃjaya recounts the preparations for imminent battle. Duryodhana exhorts Droṇa and his troops: they are superior (1–10). Bhīṣma sounds his battle cry, the Pāṇḍavas respond with their conches (10–15). Arjuna orders his driver Kṛṣṇa to bring the chariot between the armies (20–25). On seeing all his family opposing him, Arjuna is overcome with compassion and relinquishes his desire for a war that will destroy the Law (25–40). He sits down, refusing to fight (45).
24 [2] (26; 879). Kṛṣṇa accuses Arjuna of cowardice (1). Arjuna asks his advice in this dilemma (5–10). Kṛṣṇa replies that his pity for his enemies is misplaced. Souls are eternal; death and rebirth are just phases of existence. One should practice equanimity (10–15). Existence is unending; only the body ends: the soul survives all killing and sheds bodies like clothes. There is no cause for pity (15–25). Even if one does not believe in the soul's eternity, birth and death are matters of fact. Still, the soul is eternal (25–30). What really counts is observing your Law, and this war is heaven-sent. Refusing to fight means disgrace. Fight, for if you lose you gain heaven, if you win you gain earth (30–35). Action with singleness of purpose transcends Vedic Law, with its scattering of purposes and its inspiration by desires for pleasures and power: that sort of action brings on rebirth. But the ritual entitlement does not *require a desire for fruits: relinquish them and act without motive (35–50). Arjuna asks for a characterization of man without motive. He is equable, disinterested, serene, and disengaged from sense objects (50–65), while the self-seeking man is a plaything of circumstances. This serenity is* brahmanirvāṇa *(65–70).*
25 [3] (27; 951). Arjuna is confused about insight and

action. Kṛṣṇa explains that there are two positions: a discipline of knowledge and one of action. The latter course is the natural one, but should be taken disinterestedly (1–5). Acts, except those purely for sacrifice, bind one to rebirth. Sacrifice is given with creation and through it gods and men prosper one another; ultimately brahman *itself is based on sacrifice. So, one has to keep the wheel turning, but without self-interest (5–20). So does God, in order to set an example for those unable to rise above mere binding action (20–25). The domain of action is the lower nature, but the soul is confused and identifies with it. Arjuna should leave the domain of action to God, and fight unselfishly, otherwise confusion will rule the ignorant. One's own* dharma, *though deficient, is better than doing another's perfectly (25–35). Desire and anger compel a man to evil: therefore control your senses (35–40).*

26 [4] (28; 994). Kṛṣṇa has proclaimed this yoga *immemorially. How is Arjuna to understand this? Kṛṣṇa too has known many births, i.e., incarnations, to set right the Law. This knowledge produces* bhakti *(1–10). Kṛṣṇa's actions do not produce personal* karman. *People are confused whether to act or not to act (10–15). Action does* not *produce* karman *if done disinterestedly (15–20). There are all sorts of action leading to* brahman, *for all action culminates in insight, which purifies totally even the worst sinner. Such action does not bind (20–40).*

27 [5] (29; 1036). While renunciation and action both redeem, action is superior. Both lead to the same goal, but the former needs the latter, viz., action that renounces fruits (1–5). Leave action to brahman, *its domain, and you will not be bound (5–10). It is nature that acts, and this fact confuses people; the wise see no differences between creatures: all is* brahman *(15).* Brahman *is the beatitude attained to by the serene who have mastered the senses (20–25).*

28 [6] (30; 1065). Renunciation is disinterested action, which leads to serenity and equanimity (1–5). The yogin *should sit apart, concentrate, and disengage himself: thus he attains* nirvāṇa *in God (5–15). The conditions and consequences of* yoga *(15–25). The* yogin *sees himself and God in all creatures (25–30). The fleeting mind can be held in check, but with difficulty. When, however, the* yogin *strays, his labor is not lost but is rewarded with a*

better new life (30–40). The successful yogin *attains release; the best one attains* bhakti *for God (45).*
29 [7] (31; 1112). Kṛṣṇa propounds the knowledge of himself. He has two prakṛtis, *one material, the other made up of individual souls; God himself transcends both (1–5). He is the defining property of all creatures, which rest in him, while he transcends them. However, the creatures' modes of being, influenced by the three* guṇas, *produce an illusion that can be overcome with great difficulty (5–15). Among four kinds of* bhaktas *the uniquely loyal adept stands out and is especially beloved of God (15). People ignorantly worshiping other deities indirectly worship God, though he remains opaque to them (15–25). The ignorant can come to know God when their evil* karman *is burnt away (25–30).*
30 [8] (32; 1142). Description of brahman, *individual soul,* sarga, adhibhūta, adhidaivata, *and* adhiyajña *(1). He who thinks of God in his last hour reaches him. Therefore Arjuna should fight (1–5). Description of God (5–10). The manner of concentrating on God (10–15). On emergence and dissolution: only the Unmanifest remains, which is God (15–20). The two paths of the dead: to release and to rebirth (20–25).*
31 [9] (33; 1170). The Royal Mystery of release. God creates universes by his natural pulsation, but he is not bound (1–10). The deluded ignore God, the wise venerate him, with bhakti *and sacrifice, of which he is all the circumstances; but sacrifice alone leads to rebirth (10–20). God is the recipient of all rites, even the humblest. Every act should be done as an offering to him, and release is assured even if one is a criminal or of low birth (20–30).*
32 [10] (34; 1205). No one knows God's origin, but he is the origin of all creatures and their virtues. This insight inspires bhakti, *and in response God dispels one's ignorance (1–10). Arjuna asks about God's divine* yoga *and ubiquities (10–15). Kṛṣṇa describes himself as the first of any group (15–35). He supports the universe with a particle of his being (40).*
33 [11] (35; 1247). Arjuna prays for a vision of God as himself. Kṛṣṇa vouchsafes him divine sight and displays his supernal being. Arjuna tremblingly describes him as sovereign and as fearful—the God also of death (1–30). Kṛṣṇa describes himself as Time and exhorts Arjuna to wage war (30). Arjuna praises Kṛṣṇa (35–45). Kṛṣṇa

declares only Arjuna can see him so, then resumes his familiar appearance (45–50). Kṛṣṇa declares that only bhakti *enables one to perceive him (50–55).*
34 [12] (36; 1302). Description of the most adept bhaktiyogin, *his dedication, relinquishment, serenity, and virtues, and his paying heed to God's Law just set forth (1–20).*
35 [13] (37; 1323). On kṣetra *and* kṣetrajña *(1–5). The virtues of the knower (5–10). On* brahman *(10–15). On* prakṛti *and* puruṣa *(15–20). The ways of discerning the soul (20–25). The omnipresence of God (25–30). The transcendence of the individual self (30).*
36 [14] (38; 1356). The Large Brahman *as the womb of nature (1). Description of the* guṇas sattva, rajas, *and* tamas *and their effects (5–20). Description of the one who has transcended the* guṇas *(20–25).*
37 [15] (39; 1383). The parable of the Aśvattha tree (1). Glorification of the Supreme Person (1–15). The two Persons, and God, the third (15–20).
38 [16] (40; 1403). The divine and demonic properties (1–5). The assumptions of the demonic and their follies (5–15), and their infernal end (15–20).
39 [17] (41; 1427). The consequences of a person's guṇa *on faith (1–5), food (5–10), sacrifice (10), asceticism (10–15), donations (20). The uses of* OṂ, tad *and* sat *(20–25).*
40 [18] (42; 1455). The natures of saṃnyāsa *and* tyāga*: what never is to be renounced: sacrifice, asceticism, and donation (1–5). Influence of* guṇas *on renunciation (5–10). Sāṃkhyan notions of act and body (10–15). The* guṇas' *bearing on knowledge (15–20), action (20–25), agent (25), intelligence (25–30), fortitude (30–35), happiness (35). The ubiquity of the* guṇas *(40). The tasks of the* varṇas *(40): the need to perform one's natural task disinterestedly (45). Becoming* brahman *leads to* bhakti, *which inspires God's grace and brings release (50–60). Kṛṣṇa's final word (60–65). The teaching of the* Gītā *to a* bhakta *inspires God's love, and the listener will be released (65–70). Saṃjaya's praise of the Colloquy of Kṛṣṇa and Arjuna (70–75).*

6(64). The Book of the Slaying of Bhīṣma

41 (43; 1533). When Arjuna takes up his bow again,

the Pāṇḍava troops cheerfully make war music. Gods and demigods appear, to watch the battle (1–5). Then Yudhiṣṭhira lays down his weapons and starts to walk toward Bhīṣma on the opposite side. His brothers, who raise anxious questions, and Kṛṣṇa follow him (5–20). The Dhārtarāṣṭras assume cowardice on Yudhiṣṭhira's part but are not certain (25–30). Yudhiṣṭhira seeks Bhīṣma's formal permission to fight him; this is granted (30–40). The scene is repeated with Droṇa (45–60), Kṛpa (60–70), and Śalya, whom Yudhiṣṭhira reminds of an earlier promise of help. Yudhiṣṭhira withdraws (70–80). Kṛṣṇa tries to persuade Karṇa to side with Yudhiṣṭhira's cause until Bhīṣma's death; he declines (80–90). Yudhiṣṭhira issues an invitation to any Kaurava to join him; Dhṛtarāṣṭra's bastard son Yuyutsu does so (90–95). The Pāṇḍavas rearm themselves while their troops praise them for their generous treatment of the enemies. War conches are sounded (95–100).

6(63) The Book of the Bhagavadgītā

Vaiśaṃpāyana uvāca /
14.1 *atha Gāvalgaṇir dhīmān samarād etya Saṃjayaḥ /*
pratyakṣadarśī sarvasya bhūtabhavyabhaviṣyavit //
dhyāyate Dhṛtarāṣṭrāya sahasopetya duḥkhitaḥ /
ācaṣṭa nihataṃ Bhīṣmaṃ Bharatānām amadhyamam //
Saṃjaya uvāca /
Saṃjayo 'haṃ mahārāja namas te Bharatarṣabha /
hato Bhīṣmaḥ Śāṃtanavo Bharatānāṃ pitāmahaḥ //
kakudaṃ sarvayodhānāṃ dhāma sarvadhanuṣmatām /
śaratalpagataḥ so 'dya śete Kurupitāmahaḥ //
5 *yasya vīryaṃ samāśritya dyūtaṃ putras tavākarot /*
sa śete nihato rājan saṃkhye Bhīṣmaḥ Śikhaṇḍinā //
yaḥ sarvān pṛthivīpālān samavetān mahāmṛdhe /
jigāyaikarathenaiva Kāśipuryāṃ mahārathaḥ //
Jāmadagnyaṃ raṇe Rāmam āyodhya Vasusaṃbhavaḥ /
na hato Jāmadagnyena sa hato 'dya Śikhaṇḍinā //
Mahendrasadṛśaḥ śaurye sthairye ca Himavān iva /
samudra iva gāmbhīrye sahiṣṇutve dharāsamaḥ //
śaradaṃṣṭro dhanurvaktraḥ khaḍgajihvo durāsadaḥ /
narasiṃhaḥ pitā te 'dya Pāñcālyena nipātitaḥ //
10 *Pāṇḍavānāṃ mahat sainyaṃ yaṃ dṛṣṭvodyantam āhave /*
pravepata bhayodvignaṃ siṃhaṃ dṛṣṭveva gogaṇaḥ //
parirakṣya sa senāṃ te daśarātram anīkahā /
jagāmāstam ivādityaḥ kṛtvā karma suduṣkaram //
yaḥ sa Śakra ivākṣobhyo varṣan bāṇān sahasraśaḥ /
jaghāna yudhi yodhānām arbudaṃ daśabhir dinaiḥ //
sa śete niṣṭanan bhūmau vātarugṇa iva drumaḥ /
tava durmantrite rājan yathā nārhaḥ sa Bhārata //

Dhṛtarāṣṭra uvāca /
15.1 *kathaṃ Kurūṇām ṛṣabho hato Bhīṣmaḥ Śikhaṇḍinā /*
kathaṃ rathāt sa nyapatat pitā me Vāsavopamaḥ //
katham āsaṃś ca me putrā hīnā Bhīṣmeṇa Saṃjaya /
balinā devakalpena gurvarthe brahmacāriṇā //
tasmin hate mahāsattve maheśvāse mahābale /
mahārathe naravyāghre kim u āsīn manas tadā //
ārtiḥ parā māviśati yataḥ śaṃsasi me hatam /
Kurūṇām ṛṣabhaṃ vīram akampyaṃ puruṣarṣabham //
5 *ke taṃ yāntam anupreyuḥ ke cāsyāsan purogamāḥ /*
ke 'tiṣṭhan ke nyavartanta ke 'bhyavartanta Saṃjaya //
ke śūrā rathaśārdūlam acyutaṃ kṣatriyarṣabham /
rathānīkaṃ gāhamānaṃ sahasā pṛṣṭhato 'nvayuḥ //
yas tamo 'rka ivāpohan parasainyam amitrahā /
sahasraraśmipratimaḥ pareṣāṃ bhayam ādadhat /
akarod duṣkaraṃ karma raṇe Kauravaśāsanāt //

Vaiśaṃpāyana said:
14.1 Then Gavalgaṇa's sagacious son Saṃjaya, who had an immediate
insight into all things past, present and future, returned from the
battlefield.[1] Grief-stricken, he hastened to the brooding Dhṛtarāṣṭra
and told him that Bhīṣma, peerless among the Bharatas, lay dead.
Saṃjaya said:
I am Saṃjaya,[2] great king. My homage, bull of the Bharatas!
Bhīṣma, son of Śaṃtanu, grandfather of the Bharatas, is dead! The
chief of all warriors, the summit of all archers, the grandfather of the
5 Kurus lies now on a bed of arrows. He on whose might your son
relied when he played the dice,[3] he, Bhīṣma, lies on the battlefield,
king, killed by Śikhaṇḍin. He who on a single chariot triumphed over
all the assembled kings on earth in a great battle at the city of the
Kāśis,[4] the great warrior, issue of the Vasus,[5] who fought Rāma
Jāmadagnya and was not killed by him, now lies killed by Śikhaṇḍin.
The equal of great Indra in heroic feats, a Himālaya in steadfastness,
an ocean in depth, the earth in forbearance, invincible lion of a man,
with arrows for teeth, a bow for his mouth, a sword for his tongue,
10 your father now lies felled by the Pāñcālya. He before whom the
mighty host of the Pāṇḍavas trembled in panic when they saw him
rise over the battlefield, as a herd of cows trembles before a lion, that
killer of armies, now, after saving your army for ten days, has gone
to his setting like the sun, his rare feat achieved. He who, unshakable
like Śakra, rained arrows by the thousands and in ten days slew a
million warriors in battle, lies, breathing his last, on earth like a tree
snapped by a gale, undeserving of his death in your misbegotten plan,
Bhārata!

Dhṛtarāṣṭra said:
15.1 How was Bhīṣma, the bull of the Kurus, killed by Śikhaṇḍin? How
did my father, who was an Indra, fall from his chariot? And what
became of my sons, Saṃjaya, when they had lost the mighty, Godlike
Bhīṣma, who had remained a celibate because of his father? When
that courageous archer, that powerful warrior, that tiger of a man
fell, what was their feeling? Profound grief chokes me when you tell
me that he is dead, that bull of the Kurus, unshakable hero, bull
among men.
5 Who were following him, as he pushed forward, who were ahead of
him, who stood by him, who turned away, who pressed on, Saṃjaya?
Who were the champions who brought up the rear when that
tigerlike warrior, that undefeated bull of the barons, dived into the
ranks of the enemy? Shredding the troops of the enemy as the
thousand-rayed sun shreds the darkness, that killer of his foes threw
fear into the hearts of the others and accomplished a rare feat on the
battlefield at the behest of the Kaurava!

grasamānam anīkāni ya enaṃ paryavārayan /
kṛtinaṃ taṃ durādharṣaṃ samyag yāsyantam antike /
kathaṃ Śāṃtanavaṃ yuddhe Pāṇḍavāḥ pratyavārayan //
nikṛntantam anīkāni śaradaṃṣṭraṃ tarasvinam /
cāpavyāttānanaṃ ghoram asijihvaṃ durāsadam //
10 *aty anyān puruṣavyāghrān hrīmantam aparājitam /*
pātayāmāsa Kaunteyaḥ kathaṃ tam ajitaṃ yudhi //
ugradhanvānam ugreṣuṃ vartamānaṃ rathottame /
pareṣām uttamāṅgāni pracinvantaṃ śiteṣubhiḥ //
Pāṇḍavānāṃ mahat sainyaṃ yaṃ dṛṣṭvodyantam āhave /
kālāgnim iva durdharṣaṃ samaveṣṭata nityaśaḥ //
parikṛṣya sa senāṃ me daśarātram anīkahā /
jagāmāstam ivādityaḥ kṛtvā karma suduṣkaram //
yaḥ sa Śakra ivākṣayyaṃ varṣaṃ śaramayaṃ sṛjan /
jaghāna yudhi yodhānām arbudaṃ daśabhir dinaiḥ //
15 *sa śete niṣṭanan bhūmau vātarugṇa iva drumaḥ /*
mama durmantritenāsau yathā nārhaḥ sa Bhārataḥ //
kathaṃ Śāṃtanavaṃ dṛṣṭvā Pāṇḍavānām anīkinī /
prahartum aśakat tatra Bhīṣmaṃ bhīmaparākramam //
kathaṃ Bhīṣmeṇa saṃgrāmam akurvan Pāṇḍunandanāḥ /
kathaṃ ca nājayad Bhīṣmo Droṇe jīvati Saṃjaya //
Kṛpe saṃnihite tatra Bharadvājātmaje tathā /
Bhīṣmaḥ praharatāṃ śreṣṭhaḥ kathaṃ sa nidhanaṃ gataḥ //
kathaṃ cātirathas tena Pāñcālyena Śikhaṇḍinā /
Bhīṣmo vinihato yuddhe devair api durutsahaḥ //
20 *yaḥ spardhate raṇe nityaṃ Jāmadagnyaṃ mahābalam /*
ajitaṃ Jāmadagnyena Śakratulyaparākramam //
taṃ hataṃ samare Bhīṣmaṃ mahārathabalocitam /
Saṃjayācakṣva me vīraṃ yena śarma na vidmahe //
māmakāḥ ke maheṣvāsā nājahuḥ Saṃjayācyutam /
Duryodhanasamādiṣṭāḥ ke vīrāḥ paryavārayan //
yac Chikhaṇḍimukhāḥ sarve Pāṇḍavā Bhīṣmam abhyayuḥ /
kaccin na Kuravo bhītās tatyajuḥ Saṃjayācyutam //
maurvīghoṣastanayitnuḥ pṛṣatkapṛṣato mahān /
dhanurhrādamahāśabdo mahāmegha ivonnataḥ //
25 *yad abhyavarṣat Kaunteyān sa-Pāñcālān sa-Sṛñjayān /*
nighnan pararathān vīro Dānavān iva Vajrabhṛt //
iṣvastrasāgaraṃ ghoraṃ bāṇagrāhaṃ durāsadam /
kārmukormiṇam akṣayyam advīpaṃ samare 'plavam /
gadāsimakarāvartaṃ hayagrāhaṃ gajākulam //
hayān gajān padātāṃś ca rathāṃś ca tarasā bahūn /
nimajjayantaṃ samare paravīrāpahāriṇam //
vidahyamānaṃ kopena tejasā ca paraṃtapam /
veleva makarāvāsaṃ ke vīrāḥ paryavārayan //

How could the Pāṇḍavas stand up to Śāṃtanava in battle and
fence off that unassailable victor when he devoured their ranks and
was about to attack them conclusively at close quarters? With arrows
for his teeth, a bow for his gaping mouth, a sword for his tongue, that
10 dreaded, violent, unapproachable man was mowing down their troops,
an undefeated conqueror beyond any other tigerlike men for all his
modesty–yet how did the Kaunteya[1] fell the unbeaten warrior in
battle? An awesome marksman with awesome arrows, he roved on
his superb chariot, plucking off the heads of his enemies with his
sharp barbs, and his mere appearance on the battlefield struck terror
in the mighty host of the Pāṇḍavas, which always shrank away as
before the irresistible fire of Doomsday–yet, after rallying my troops
for ten days, that shatterer of armies went to his setting like the sun,
his rare feat accomplished. An Indra, he pelted the enemy with a
relentless rain of arrows and in ten days smote a million warriors in
15 battle–now he lies undeservedly breathing his last on the ground like
a tree snapped by a gale, the Bhārata, because of my evil design.

How upon sighting Śaṃtanu's son had the small Pāṇḍava army the
power to strike out at Bhīṣma with his terrifying prowess? How did
the sons of Pāṇḍu join battle with Bhīṣma, how could Bhīṣma fail to
win, Saṃjaya, while Droṇa[2] was alive? How could Bhīṣma, the
greatest of fighters, find his death when Kṛpa[3] was near and the son
of Bharadvāja? How could a Śikhaṇḍin of Pāñcāla bring down the
paladin Bhīṣma, before whom even the Gods lost heart in battle?

20 He always rivaled the mighty Jāmadagnya in battle, and, in
prowess Śakra's equal, he remained undefeated by Rāma–and now
Bhīṣma, accustomed to opposing the strength of great warriors, lies
dead on the battlefield! Tell me how he died, Saṃjaya, for without
him we find no shelter. Who of my archers refused to desert that
unbeaten man, Saṃjaya; which heroes did Duryodhana order to his
protection? When, led by Śikhaṇḍin, all the Pāṇḍavas attacked
Bhīṣma, did the Kurus perchance desert the invincible man in fear?
He was a mighty, lofty cloud, roaring with the twang of his bowstring,
raining with the drops of his shafts, thundering with the clap of his
25 bow when he pelted Kaunteyas, Pāñcālas, and Sṛñjayas, smiting
enemy warriors, the hero, as the Thunderbolt-Wielder smote the
Dānavas[4]–a dreadful ocean of arrows, unapproachable domain of the
crocodiles of his shafts, rippling with bows, unendurable, bereft of the
haven of islands, impossible to swim in battle, eddying with the
whirlpools of clubs and swords, infested with sharklike horses, muddied
with elephants, drowning steeds, elephants, footmen, chariots in mass
with vehemence, washing away enemy heroes, burning with wrath
and splendor, scourge of his foe–what brave men put a halt to him as
the floodline halts the ocean?

Bhīṣmo yad akarot karma samare Saṃjayārihā /
Duryodhanahitārthāya ke tadāsya puro 'bhavan //
30 *ke 'rakṣan dakṣiṇaṃ cakraṃ Bhīṣmasyāmitatejasaḥ /*
pṛṣṭhataḥ ke parān vīrā upāsedhan yatavratāḥ //
ke purastād avartanta rakṣanto Bhīṣmam antike /
ke 'rakṣann uttaraṃ cakraṃ vīrā vīrasya yudhyataḥ //
vāme cakre vartamānāḥ ke 'ghnan Saṃjaya Sṛñjayān /
sametāgram anīkeṣu ke 'bhyarakṣan durāsadam //
pārśvataḥ ke 'bhyavartanta gacchanto durgamāṃ gatim /
samūhe ke parān vīrān pratyayudhyanta Saṃjaya //
rakṣyamāṇaḥ kathaṃ vīrair gopyamānāś ca tena te /
durjayānām anīkāni nājayaṃs tarasā yudhi //
35 *sarvalokeśvarasyeva Parameṣṭhi-Prajāpateḥ /*
kathaṃ prahartum api te śekuḥ Saṃjaya Pāṇḍavāḥ //
yasmin dvīpe samāśritya yudhyanti Kuravaḥ paraiḥ /
taṃ nimagnaṃ naravyāghraṃ Bhīṣmaṃ śaṃsasi Saṃjaya //
yasya vīrye samāśvasya mama putro bṛhadbalaḥ /
na Pāṇḍavān agaṇayat kathaṃ sa nihataḥ paraiḥ //
yaḥ purā vibudhaiḥ sendraiḥ sāhāyye yuddhadurmadaḥ /
kāṅkṣito Dānavān ghnadbhiḥ pitā mama mahāvrataḥ //
yasmiñ jāte mahāvīrye Śaṃtanur lokaśaṃkare /
śokaṃ duḥkhaṃ ca dainyaṃ ca prājahāt putralakṣmaṇi //
40 *prajñāparāyaṇaṃ tajjñaṃ saddharmaniratam śucim /*
vedavedāṅgatattvajñaṃ kathaṃ śaṃsasi me hatam //
sarvāstravinayopetaṃ dāntaṃ śāntaṃ manasvinam /
hataṃ Śāṃtanavaṃ śrutvā manye śeṣaṃ balaṃ hatam //
dharmād adharmo balavān saṃprāpta iti me matiḥ /
yatra vṛddhaṃ guruṃ hatvā rājyam icchanti Pāṇḍavāḥ //
Jāmadagnyaḥ purā Rāmaḥ sarvāstravid anuttamaḥ /
Ambārtham udyataḥ saṃkhye Bhīṣmeṇa yudhi nirjitaḥ //
tam Indrasamakarmāṇaṃ kakudaṃ sarvadhanvināṃ /
hataṃ śaṃsasi Bhīṣmaṃ me kiṃ nu duḥkham ataḥ param //
45 *asakṛt kṣatriyavrātāḥ saṃkhye yena vinirjitāḥ /*
Jāmadagnyas tathā Rāmaḥ paravīranighātinā //
tasmān nūnaṃ mahāvīryād Bhārgavād yuddhadurmadāt /
tejovīryabalair bhūyāñ Śikhaṇḍī Drupadātmajaḥ //
yaḥ śūraṃ kṛtinaṃ yuddhe sarvaśastraviśāradam /
paramāstravidaṃ vīraṃ jaghāna Bharatarṣabham //
ke vīrās tam amitraghnam anvayuḥ śatrusaṃsadi /
śaṃsa me tad yathā vṛttaṃ yuddhaṃ Bhīṣmasya Pāṇḍavaiḥ //
yoṣeva hatavīrā me senā putrasya Saṃjaya /
agopam iva codbhrāntaṃ gokulaṃ tad balaṃ mama //

When enemy-killer Bhīṣma did his work in the war for the benefit
30 of Duryodhana, O Saṃjaya, who were in front of him, who guarded
the right wheel of boundlessly august Bhīṣma, who vigorously blocked
the enemy's warriors in his rear, who stayed immediately ahead of
Bhīṣma to protect him, which heroes guarded the front wheel of the
battling hero? Who were the men who stood at his left wheel and
killed the Sṛñjayas, Saṃjaya? Who at his side pressed forward and
opened a difficult path ahead? Who were the ones who
counterattacked the heroes of the enemy in the mêlée, Saṃjaya? How
is it possible that when he was protected by heroes, and they by him,
they were unable to defeat quickly the troops of the barely defeatable
foes?

35 He was like the sovereign of all the worlds, Prajāpati Parameṣṭhin
himself–then how proved the Pāṇḍavas able to strike at him,
Saṃjaya? He was a haven for the Kurus in their battle with the
others, yet you tell me that Bhīṣma, tiger among men, himself has
drowned! It was because he could sigh with relief in the shelter of
Bhīṣma's might that my powerful son could dismiss the Pāṇḍavas–
how then did the enemy kill him? In old times my battle-crazy father
of the great vow was besought for his aid by Indra and the Gods when
they were embattled with the Dānavas; at the birth of this hero,
healer of the world, Śaṃtanu shed his grief, sorrow, and worry
40 because of the good fortune of a son–how can you tell me he is
killed, a man unsurpassed in the wisdom he held high, intent on his
strict Law, pure and steeped in the truths of the Vedas and their
branches! When I hear that Śāṃtanava has been slain, he who knew
the use of any weapon, a man of self-control, serenity, and spirit, I
know the rest of my army is lost. Lawlessness, I now know, has
prevailed over Law, if the Pāṇḍavas still want the kingdom after killing
their ancient guru!

One time Rāma Jāmadagnya himself, unequaled expert with all
weapons, rose to battle Bhīṣma over Ambā, and he was defeated.
What could be more grievous a blow than the word you bring of the
death of Bhīṣma, who equaled Indra in his feats, the greatest of all
45 bowmen? Surely greater yet than that slayer of enemy heroes Rāma
Jāmadagnya who many times defeated the hosts of the barons, greater
than the puissant Bhārgava, a berserker in war, must be Drupada's
son Śikhaṇḍin in splendor, heroism, and strength, if he slew that
triumphant champion, master of all arms, expert of the ultimate
weapon, the heroic bull of the Bharatas!

Which heroes followed the enemy-killer into the assembly of his
foes? Tell me, Saṃjaya, how Bhīṣma's battle with the Pāṇḍavas went.
The army of my son is now like a woman whose hero has been killed;
my troops are like a herd of cattle panicking because their herdsman

50 pauruṣaṃ sarvalokasya paraṃ yasya mahāhave /
parāsikte ca vas tasmin katham āsīn manas tadā //
jīvite 'py adya sāmarthyaṃ kim ivāsmāsu Saṃjaya /
ghātayitvā mahāvīryaṃ pitaraṃ lokadhārmikam //
agādhe salile magnāṃ nāvaṃ dṛṣṭveva pāragāḥ /
Bhīṣme hate bhṛśaṃ duḥkhān manye śocanti putrakāḥ //
adrisāramayaṃ nūnaṃ sudṛḍhaṃ hṛdayaṃ mama /
yac chrutvā puruṣavyāghraṃ hataṃ Bhīṣmaṃ na dīryate //
yasminn astraṃ ca medhā ca nītiś ca Bharatarṣabhe /
aprameyāṇi durdharṣe kathaṃ sa nihato yudhi //
55 na cāstreṇa na śauryeṇa tapasā medhayā na ca /
na dhṛtyā na punas tyāgān mṛtyoḥ kaścid vimucyate //
kālo nūnaṃ mahāvīryaḥ sarvalokaduratyayaḥ /
yatra Śāṃtanavaṃ Bhīṣmaṃ hataṃ śaṃsasi Saṃjaya //
putraśokābhisaṃtapto mahad duḥkham acintayan /
āśaṃse 'haṃ purā trāṇaṃ Bhīṣmāc Chaṃtanunandanāt //
yadādityam ivāpaśyat patitaṃ bhuvi Saṃjaya /
Duryodhanaḥ Śāṃtanavaṃ kiṃ tadā pratyapadyata //
nāhaṃ sveṣāṃ pareṣāṃ vā buddhyā Saṃjaya cintayan /
śeṣaṃ kiṃcit prapaśyāmi pratyanīke mahīkṣitām //
60 dāruṇaḥ kṣatradharmo 'yam ṛṣibhiḥ saṃpradarśitaḥ /
yatra Śāṃtanavaṃ hatvā rājyam icchanti Pāṇḍavāḥ //
vayaṃ vā rājyam icchāmo ghātayitvā pitāmaham /
kṣatradharme sthitāḥ Pārthā nāparādhyanti putrakāḥ //
etad āryeṇa kartavyaṃ kṛcchrāsv āpatsu Saṃjaya /
parākramaḥ paraṃ śaktyā tac ca tasmin pratiṣṭhitam //
anīkāni vinighnantaṃ hrīmantam aparājitam /
kathaṃ Śāṃtanavaṃ tāta Pāṇḍuputrā nyapātayan //
kathaṃ yuktāny anīkāni kathaṃ yuddhaṃ mahātmabhiḥ /
kathaṃ vā nihato Bhīṣmaḥ pitā Saṃjaya me paraiḥ //
65 Duryodhanaś ca Karṇaś ca Śakuniś cāpi Saubalaḥ /
Duḥśāsanaś ca kitavo hate Bhīṣme kim abruvan //
yac charīrair upastīrṇāṃ naravāranavājinām /
śaraśaktigadākhaḍgatomarākṣāṃ bhayāvahām //
prāviśan kitavā mandāḥ sabhāṃ yudhi durāsadām /
prāṇadyūte pratibhaye ke 'dīvyanta nararṣabhāḥ //
ke 'jayan ke jitās tatra hṛtalakṣā nipātitāḥ /
anye Bhīṣmāc Chāṃtanavāt tan mamācakṣva Saṃjaya //
na hi me śāntir astīha yudhi Devavrataṃ hatam /
pitaraṃ bhīmakarmāṇaṃ śrutvā me duḥkham āviśat //
70 ārtiṃ me hṛdaye rūḍhāṃ mahatīṃ putrakāritām /
tvaṃ siñcan sarpiṣevāgnim uddīpayasi Saṃjaya //
mahāntaṃ bhāram udyamya viśrutaṃ sārvalaukikam /
dṛṣṭvā vinihataṃ Bhīṣmaṃ manye śocanti putrakāḥ //
śroṣyāmi tāni duḥkhāni Duryodhanakṛtāny aham /

50 is gone. Now that he has been cast aside, he in whom dwelled the
greatest manly prowess in all the world, what are your thoughts?
What capacity for life have we left, Saṃjaya, now that we have
caused the death of our puissant father, who was the paragon of Law
in the world?

Now that Bhīṣma is dead, my poor sons must feel the despair of
travelers who see their ferry sink in fathomless water. My heart must
be as hard as iron if it does not burst upon the news of tigerlike
Bhīṣma's killing. How can this invincible man have been killed in
battle, that bull of the Bharatas in whom dwelled weapon sense,
55 sagacity, good planning, and immeasurable accomplishments? No
man can escape death, whether with weapons, heroics, austerities,
wisdom, fortitude, or renunciation. Time is surely the conqueror whom
no one escapes, if you tell me that Bhīṣma Śāṃtanava lies dead,
Saṃjaya. In my sorrow over my sons, without thinking of the misery
at hand, I had hoped of rescue from Śaṃtanu's son Bhīṣma. Where did
Duryodhana turn when he saw Bhīṣma fallen on earth like the sun,
Saṃjaya? Even upon deep reflection I do not see who will now survive
60 of my kings and theirs, who are lined up against each other. Harsh
is the Law of the baronage which the seers have set out before us,
if the Pāṇḍavas want kingship after killing Śāṃtanava, or if we want
kingship after causing our grandfather's killing. Yet, neither the
Pārthas nor my sons are at fault as long as they stand by the baronial
Law. This is the Āryan's task, even in grave emergencies: to be brave
to the best of his ability; and this task is based on Law.

How, my friend, did the sons of Pāṇḍu bring down Śāṃtanava
while he, undefeated for all his modesty, was killing off their troops?
How were the ranks yoked? How did the great-spirited men fight?
65 How did the enemy kill Bhīṣma, my father, Saṃjaya? What did
Duryodhana, Karṇa, and Śakuni Saubala have to say when Bhīṣma
was killed, or the crooked Duḥśāsana? That dangerous and
inhospitable gambling den on the battlefield, where the carpet for the
dicing had been spread out with the bodies of men, elephants, and
horses, and the dice rolled with the arrows, spears, clubs, swords, and
javelins–what slow-witted warrior gamblers entered that den to
gamble for the fearful stakes of their lives? Who won? Who lost?
Who carried off the prize? Who were knocked down other than
Bhīṣma Śāṃtanava? Tell me, Saṃjaya, for I have no more peace here:
now that I have heard that Devavrata, my father of fearsome might,
70 has been killed, I know only grief. And you, Saṃjaya, as though
feeding a fire with butter, are adding more flame to the great worry
over my sons that has grown in my heart.

Yes, I am sure my sons are in mourning now that they have seen
world-famous Bhīṣma cut down, after he had lifted and carried his
great burden. I am sure to hear of the miseries that Duryodhana has

tasmān me sarvam ācakṣva yad vṛttaṃ tatra Saṃjaya //
saṃgrāme pṛthivīśānāṃ mandasyābuddhisaṃbhavam /
apanītaṃ sunītaṃ vā tan mamācakṣva Saṃjaya //
yat kṛtaṃ tatra Bhīṣmeṇa saṃgrāme jayam icchatā /
tejoyuktaṃ kṛtāstreṇa śaṃsa tac cāpy aśeṣataḥ //
75 *yathā tad abhavad yuddhaṃ Kuru-Pāṇḍavasenayoḥ /*
krameṇa yena yasmiṃś ca kāle yac ca yathā ca tat //

Saṃjaya uvāca /
16.1 *tvadyukto 'yam anupraśno mahārāja yathārhasi /*
na tu Duryodhane doṣam imam āsaktum arhasi //
ya ātmano duścaritād aśubhaṃ prāpnuyān naraḥ /
enasā tena nānyaṃ sa upāśaṅkitum arhati //
mahārāja manuṣyeṣu nindyaṃ yaḥ sarvam ācaret /
sa vadhyaḥ sarvalokasya ninditāni samācaran //
nikāro 'nikṛtiprajñaiḥ Pāṇḍavais tvatpratīkṣayā /
anubhūtaḥ sahāmātyaiḥ kṣāntaṃ ca suciraṃ vane //
5 *hayānāṃ ca gajānāṃ ca śūrāṇāṃ cāmitaujasām /*
pratyakṣaṃ yan mayā dṛṣṭaṃ dṛṣṭaṃ yogabalena ca //
śṛṇu tat pṛthivīpāla mā ca śoke manaḥ kṛthāḥ /
diṣṭam etat purā nūnam evaṃbhāvi narādhipa //
namaskṛtvā pitus te 'haṃ Pārāśaryāya dhīmate /
yasya prasādād divyaṃ me prāptaṃ jñānam anuttamam //
dṛṣṭiś cātīndriyā rājan dūrāc chravaṇam eva ca /
paracittasya vijñānam atītānāgatasya ca //
vyutthitotpattivijñānam ākāśe ca gatiḥ sadā /
śastrair asaṅgo yuddheṣu varadānān mahātmanaḥ //
10 *śṛṇu me vistareṇedaṃ vicitraṃ paramādbhutam /*
Bhāratānāṃ mahad yuddhaṃ yathābhūl lomaharṣaṇam //
teṣv anīkeṣu yatteṣu vyūḍheṣu ca vidhānataḥ /
Duryodhano mahārāja Duḥśāsanam athābravīt //
Duḥśāsana rathās tūrṇaṃ yujyantāṃ Bhīṣmarakṣiṇaḥ /
anīkāni ca sarvāṇi śīghraṃ tvam anucodaya //
ayaṃ mā samanuprāpto varṣapūgābhicintitaḥ /
Pāṇḍavānāṃ sasainyānāṃ Kurūṇāṃ ca samāgamaḥ //
nātaḥ kāryatamaṃ manye raṇe Bhīṣmasya rakṣaṇāt /
hanyād gupto hy asau Pārthān Somakāṃś ca sa-Sṛñjayān //
15 *abravīc ca viśuddhātmā nāhaṃ hanyāṃ Śikhaṇḍinam /*
śrūyate strī hy asau pūrvaṃ tasmād varjyo raṇe mama //
tasmād Bhīṣmo rakṣitavyo viśeṣeṇeti me matiḥ /
Śikhaṇḍino vadhe yattāḥ sarve tiṣṭhantu māmakāḥ //
tathā prācyāḥ pratīcyāś ca dākṣiṇātyottarāpathāḥ /
sarvaśastrāstrakuśalās te rakṣantu pitāmaham //
arakṣyamāṇaṃ hi vṛko hanyāt siṃhaṃ mahābalam /
mā siṃhaṃ jambukeneva ghātayāmaḥ Śikhaṇḍinā //

brought on, so tell me all that happened there, Saṃjaya. Tell me all,
whether it was well-planned or misguided, that befell the kings of the
earth in battle as a result of that cretin's[5] witlessness. And tell me
entirely what Bhīṣma wrought in the battle, covetous of victory, all
75 the glorious exploits of that masterful warrior: how the battle unfolded
between the Kuru and Pāṇḍava armies, in what order and at what
time, how, and why.

Saṃjaya said:

16.1 The question becomes you, great king, and you deserve an answer.
But you must not place all the blame on Duryodhana. A man who is
faced with the bad consequences of his own misconduct has no cause
to blame another for his own wickedness. Great king, he who does
anything contemptible to people stands condemned to death by all the
world for perpetrating the forbidden. The Pāṇḍavas, themselves
innocent of deception, have with their councilors suffered deceit by
attending on you, but they have long since forgiven you in the forest.[1]
5 Listen then, protector of earth, to what I have seen—with my own
eyes or through the power of yoga—of the doings of horses, elephants,
and boundlessly splendid champions. Do not indulge your heart in
sorrow. Surely all this was destined long ago and is now coming to
pass, king.

After paying homage to your father,[2] the sagacious son of Parāśara,
by whose grace I have obtained final divine insight, I have vision
beyond the range of the senses and hearing from afar, king, and
knowledge of the thoughts of others, of past and present, and
awareness of portentous happenings, and power to move through the
sky. Also, by the gift of his boon I am inviolate to weapons in battle.
10 Listen then when I relate in full how that horrendous great war of the
Bhāratas unfolded, full of vicissitudes, and utterly confounding.

When the ranks had been marshaled and arrayed according to the
rules, great king, Duryodhana said to Duḥśāsana, "Duḥśāsana, yoke
at once the chariots that are to guard Bhīṣma, and immediately give
instructions to all troops. Now at last, after many years of careful
planning, I have reached the hour of the clash of Pāṇḍavas and Kurus
and their armies. I can think of no greater task than the protection in
battle of Bhīṣma, for if he is well protected, he will kill the Pārthas,
15 Somakas, and Sṛñjayas. The pure-spirited man has told me: 'I shall
not kill Śikhaṇḍin, for I have heard that he was once a woman.
Therefore I shall shun him in battle.' So I think that Bhīṣma should be
particularly protected against Śikhaṇḍin. Let all my troops concentrate
on destroying him. Let all the masters of arms, eastern and western,
from the south and north, guard grandfather, for a wolf may kill a
powerful lion, if left unguarded! Let us not allow Śikhaṇḍin like a

vāmaṃ cakraṃ Yudhāmanyur Uttamaujāś ca dakṣiṇam /
goptārau Phalgunasyaitau Phalguno 'pi Śikhaṇḍinaḥ //
20 *saṃrakṣyamāṇaḥ Pārthena Bhīṣmeṇa ca vivarjitaḥ /*
yathā na hanyād Gāṅgeyaṃ Duḥśāsana tathā kuru //
tato rajanyāṃ vyuṣṭāyāṃ śabdaḥ samabhavan mahān /
krośatāṃ bhūmipālānāṃ yujyatāṃ yujyatām iti //
śaṅkhadundubhinirghoṣaiḥ siṃhanādaiś ca Bhārata /
hayaheṣitaśabdaiś ca rathanemisvanais tathā //
gajānāṃ bṛṃhatāṃ caiva yodhānāṃ cābhigarjatām /
kṣveḍitāsphoṭitotkruṣṭais tumulaṃ sarvato 'bhavat //
udatiṣṭhan mahārāja sarvaṃ yuktam aśeṣataḥ /
sūryodaye mahat sainyaṃ Kuru-Pāṇḍavasenayoḥ /
tava rājendra putrāṇāṃ Pāṇḍavānāṃ tathaiva ca //
25 *tatra nāgā rathāś caiva jāmbūnadapariṣkṛtāḥ /*
vibhrājamānā dṛśyante meghā iva savidyutaḥ //
rathānīkāny adṛśyanta nagarāṇīva bhūriśaḥ /
atīva śuśubhe tatra pitā te pūrṇacandravat //
dhanurbhir ṛṣṭibhiḥ khaḍgair gadābhiḥ śaktitomaraiḥ /
yodhāḥ praharaṇaiḥ śubhraiḥ sveṣv anīkeṣv avasthitāḥ //
gajā rathāḥ padātāś ca turagāś ca viśāṃ pate /
vyatiṣṭhan vāgurākārāḥ śataśo 'tha sahasraśaḥ //
dhvajā bahuvidhākārā vyadṛśyanta samucchritāḥ /
sveṣāṃ caiva pareṣāṃ ca dyutimantaḥ sahasraśaḥ //
30 *kāñcanā maṇicitrāṅgā jvalanta iva pāvakāḥ /*
arciṣmanto vyarocanta dhvajā rājñāṃ sahasraśaḥ //
Mahendraketavaḥ śubhrā Mahendrasadaneṣv iva /
saṃnaddhās teṣu te vīrā dadṛśur yuddhakāṅkṣiṇaḥ //
udyatair āyudhaiś citrās talabaddhāḥ kalāpinaḥ /
ṛṣabhākṣā manuṣyendrāś camūmukhagatā babhuḥ //
Śakuniḥ Saubalaḥ Śalyaḥ Saindhavo 'tha Jayadrathaḥ /
Vinda-Anuvindāv Āvantyau Kāmbojaś ca Sudakṣiṇaḥ //
Śrutāyudhaś ca Kāliṅgo Jayatsenaś ca pārthivaḥ /
Bṛhadbalaś ca Kauśalyaḥ Kṛtavarmā ca Sātvataḥ //
35 *daśaite puruṣavyāghrāḥ śūrāḥ parighabāhavaḥ /*
akṣauhiṇīnāṃ patayo yajvāno bhūridakṣiṇāḥ //
ete cānye ca bahavo Duryodhanavaśānugāḥ /
rājāno rājaputrāś ca nītimanto mahābalāḥ //
saṃnaddhāḥ samadṛśyanta sveṣv anīkeṣv avasthitāḥ /
baddhakṛṣṇājināḥ sarve dhvajino muñjamālinaḥ //
sṛṣṭā Duryodhanasyārthe Brahmalokāya dīkṣitāḥ /
samṛddhā daśa vāhinyaḥ parigṛhya vyavasthitāḥ //
ekādaśī Dhārtarāṣṭrī Kauravāṇāṃ mahācamūḥ /
agrataḥ sarvasainyānāṃ yatra Śāṃtanavo 'graṇīḥ //
40 *śvetoṣṇīṣaṃ śvetahayaṃ śvetavarmāṇam acyutam /*
apaśyāma mahārāja Bhīṣmaṃ candram ivoditam //

jackal to kill the lion. Yudhāmanyu guards the left wheel, Uttamaujas the right, of Phalguna, while Phalguna himself protects Śikhaṇḍin. Duḥśāsana, take measures that Śikhaṇḍin, protected by the Pārtha and avoided by Bhīṣma, does not kill the son of the Ganges!"

When night had made way for dawn, there arose a great noise of kings shouting, "The yokes, lay on the yokes!" On all sides there was a terrifying din, with the calls of conch shell and drum, the battle cries, Bhārata, the whinnying of the horses, the rattle of the chariot wheels, the trumpeting of the large elephants, and the roars, the growling, and the arm-slapping[3] of the warriors. At sunrise the entire vast force of the Kuru and the Pāṇḍava armies stood yoked, great king. The golden-caparisoned elephants and the gold-decked chariots of your sons and the Pāṇḍavas dazzled like lightning-streaked clouds. The convoys of chariots looked like cities, and among them your father gleamed bright like the full moon. The warriors took their positions with bows, spears, swords, clubs, javelins, and other sparkling weapons in their assigned ranks. Elephants, chariots, foot soldiers, and horses were in place, O lord of your people, forming a catch net with their hundreds and thousands, and many-shaped tall standards were visible. There were thousands of standards of thousands of kings, on your side and the enemy's, brightly glittering with gold and colorful gems, aflame like blazing fires, like the rainbow banners of Indra flashing in Indra's palaces. Fully girt heroes eager for battle were watching with upraised weapons, sparkling, with hand guards tied on, their quivers full, and they appeared like bull-eyed Indras among men at the head of their troops. Śakuni Saubala, Śalya, Jayadratha of Sindhu, Vinda and Anuvinda of Avanti, Sudakṣiṇa of Kāmboja, Śrutāyudha of Kaliṅga, King Jayatsena, Bṛhadbala of Kośala, and Kṛtavarman the Sātvata were the ten tigerlike commanders of grand armies, bludgeon-like champions, past sacrificers of generous stipends; they and many other allies of Duryodhana, kings and sons of kings, shrewd and powerful, could be seen in their armor posted by their troops. Girt with black antelope hides, all bearing standards, hung with *muñja* threads, pouring out in Duryodhana's cause, consecrated to the World of Brahmā,[4] they stood in place, holding fast their ten opulent armies. The eleventh army of the Kauravas, that of the Dhārtarāṣṭra himself, was in front of all the others and headed by Śāṃtanava.

We saw undefeated Bhīṣma like the risen moon with his white turban, white horses, and white armor. Kurus and Pāṇḍavas gazed on

hematāladhvajaṃ Bhīṣmaṃ rājate syandane sthitam /
śvetābhra iva tīkṣṇāṃśuṃ dadṛśuḥ Kuru-Pāṇḍavāḥ //
dṛṣṭvā camūmukhe Bhīṣmaṃ samakampanta Pāṇḍavāḥ /
Sṛñjayāś ca maheṣvāsā Dhṛṣṭadyumnapurogamāḥ //
jṛmbhamāṇaṃ mahāsiṃhaṃ dṛṣṭvā kṣudramṛgā yathā /
Dhṛṣṭadyumnamukhāḥ sarve samudvivijire muhuḥ //
ekādaśaitāḥ śrījuṣṭā vāhinyas tava Bhārata /
Pāṇḍavānāṃ tathā sapta mahāpuruṣapālitāḥ //
45 unmattamakarāvartau mahāgrāhasamākulau /
yugānte samupetau dvau dṛśyete sāgarāv iva //
naiva nas tādṛśo rājan dṛṣṭapūrvo na ca śrutaḥ /
anīkānāṃ sametānāṃ samavāyas tathāvidhaḥ //

Saṃjaya uvāca /
17.1 yathā sa bhagavān Vyāsaḥ Kṛṣṇadvaipāyano 'bravīt /
tathaiva sahitāḥ sarve samājagmur mahīkṣitaḥ //
Maghāviṣayagaḥ somas tad dinaṃ pratyapadyata /
dīpyamānāś ca saṃpetur divi sapta mahāgrahāḥ //
dvidhābhūta ivāditya udaye pratyadṛśyata /
jvalantyā śikhayā bhūyo bhānumān udito divi //
vavāśire ca dīptāyāṃ diśi gomāyuvāyasāḥ /
lipsamānāḥ śarīrāṇi māṃsaśoṇitabhojanāḥ //
5 ahany ahani Pārthānāṃ vṛddhaḥ Kurupitāmahaḥ /
Bharadvājātmajaś caiva prātar utthāya saṃyatau //
jayo 'stu Pāṇḍuputrāṇām ity ūcatur ariṃdamau /
yuyudhāte tavārthāya yathā sa samayaḥ kṛtaḥ //
sarvadharmaviśeṣajñaḥ pitā Devavratas tava /
samānīya mahīpālān idaṃ vacanam abravīt //
idaṃ vaḥ kṣatriyā dvāraṃ svargāyāpāvṛtaṃ mahat /
gacchadhvaṃ tena Śakrasya Brahmaṇaś ca salokatām //
eṣa vaḥ śāśvataḥ panthāḥ pūrvaiḥ pūrvatarair gataḥ /
saṃbhāvayata cātmānam avyagramanaso yudhi //
10 Nābhāgo hi Yayātiś ca Māndhātā Nahuṣo Nṛgaḥ /
saṃsiddhāḥ paramaṃ sthānaṃ gatāḥ karmabhir īdṛśaiḥ //
adharmaḥ kṣatriyasyaiṣa yad vyādhimaraṇaṃ gṛhe /
yad ājau nidhanaṃ yāti so 'sya dharmaḥ sanātanaḥ //
evam uktā mahīpālā Bhīṣmeṇa Bharatarṣabha /
niryayuḥ svāny anīkāni śobhayanto rathottamaiḥ //
sa tu Vaikartanaḥ Karṇaḥ sāmātyaḥ saha bandhubhiḥ /
nyāsitaḥ samare śastraṃ Bhīṣmeṇa Bharatarṣabha //
apetakarṇāḥ putrās te rājānaś caiva tāvakāḥ /
niryayuḥ siṃhanādena nādayanto diśo daśa //
15 śvetaiś chatraiḥ patākābhir dhvajavāraṇavājibhiḥ /
tāny anīkāny aśobhanta rathair atha padātibhiḥ //
bherīpaṇavaśabdaiś ca paṭahānāṃ ca nisvanaiḥ /

Bhīṣma standing on his silver chariot and bearing the banner with the
golden palm tree, like the sharp-rayed sun against a white cloud. At
the sight of Bhīṣma at the head of his army, the Pāṇḍavas and the
great archers of the Sṛñjayas led by Dhṛṣṭadyumna shuddered. Like
small game facing a large yawning lion, all the troops of Dhṛṣṭadyumna
shivered with terror. There were eleven armies of yours, decked with
good fortune, Bhārata, and seven of the Pāṇḍavas protected by great
45 men. The two forces were like the two oceans clashing at the end of
the eon, whirling with crazed dolphins and tossed by large crocodiles.
Never before, sire, have we seen or heard of such a massing of armies!

Saṃjaya said:
17.1 All the kings of earth massed together, as it has been declared by
the blessed Lord Kṛṣṇa Dvaipāyana Vyāsa. The moon that day stood
in the sign of Maghā,[1] and in the heavens the seven great planets
converged in a blaze of light. When the sun rose, it seemed as though
it had split in two, and when it had fully risen in the sky it was
burning with a crest of flames. Jackals and crows made foreboding
noises on the burning horizons, hoping for corpses, in order to feast
5 on their flesh and blood. Every morning, day after day, the ancient
grandfather of Kurus and Pārthas, and the son of Bharadvāja,[2] both
tamers of their enemies, said upon rising in restrained voices, "Let
victory go to the sons of Pāṇḍu," but they campaigned for you, sire,
as they had pledged.

Your father Devavrata, who knew all the niceties of Law, convened
the kings and said to them, "This is the wide gate to heaven which is
now open to you, barons! Enter through it to share the worlds of
Śakra and Brahmā! This is the eternal road that has been trod by your
ancestors and theirs: honor yourselves by putting all your heart into
10 this war. For Nābhāga, Yayāti, Māndhātar, Nahuṣa, and Nṛga were
hallowed and reached the ultimate abode by feats like yours. It is a
breach of the Law for a baron to die of sickness at home, and his
everlasting Law is it to find death on the battlefield!" Thus
admonished by Bhīṣma, O bull of the Bharatas, the kings left and
returned to their troops, radiant on their superb chariots. Only Karṇa
Vaikartana, his advisers and relations, were compelled by Bhīṣma[3] to
lay down their weapons for the battle, bull of the Bharatas.

Lacking only Karṇa, your sons and the kings on your side rode out,
15 causing the horizons to resound with their lion roars. Their troops
sparkled with white umbrellas, with banners, with standards,
elephants, and horses, with chariots and footmen. With the sounds of
drums and cymbals and the beat of kettledrums, the earth shook

rathanemininādaiś ca babhūvākulitā mahī //
kāñcanāṅgadakeyūraiḥ kārmukaiś ca mahārathāḥ /
bhrājamānā vyadṛśyanta jaṅgamāḥ parvatā iva //
tālena mahatā Bhīṣmaḥ pañcatāreṇa ketunā /
vimalādityasaṃkāśas tasthau Kurucamūpatiḥ //
ye tvadīyā maheṣvāsā rājāno Bharatarṣabha /
avartanta yathādeśaṃ rājañ Śāṃtanavasya te //
20 sa tu Govāsanaḥ Śaibyaḥ sahitaḥ sarvarājabhiḥ /
yayau mātaṅgarājena rājārheṇa patākinā /
padmavarṇas tv anīkānāṃ sarveṣām agrataḥ sthitaḥ //
Aśvatthāmā yayau yattaḥ siṃhalāṅgūlaketanaḥ /
Śrutāyuś Citrasenaś ca Purumitro Viviṃśatiḥ //
Śalyo Bhūriśravāś caiva Vikarṇaś ca mahārathaḥ /
ete sapta maheṣvāsā Droṇaputrapurogamāḥ /
syandanair varavarṇābhair Bhīṣmasyāsan puraḥsarāḥ //
teṣām api mahotsedhāḥ śobhayanto rathottamān /
bhrājamānā vyadṛśyanta jāmbūnadamayā dhvajāḥ //
jāmbūnadamayī vediḥ kamaṇḍaluvibhūṣitā /
ketur ācāryamukhyasya Droṇasya dhanuṣā saha //
25 anekaśatasāhasram anīkam anukarṣataḥ /
mahān Duryodhanasyāsīn nāgo maṇimayo dhvajaḥ //
tasya Paurava-Kāliṅgau Kāmbojaś ca Sudakṣiṇaḥ /
Kṣemadhanvā Sumitraś ca tasthuḥ pramukhato rathāḥ //
syandanena mahārheṇa ketunā vṛṣabheṇa ca /
prakarṣann iva senāgraṃ Māgadhaś ca nṛpo yayau //
tad Aṅgapatinā guptaṃ Kṛpeṇa ca mahātmanā /
śāradābhracayaprakhyaṃ prācyānām abhavad balam //
anīkapramukhe tiṣṭhan varāheṇa mahāyaśāḥ /
śuśubhe ketumukhyena rājatena Jayadrathaḥ //
30 śataṃ rathasahasrāṇāṃ tasyāsan vaśavartinaḥ /
aṣṭau nāgasahasrāṇi sādināṃ ayutāni ṣaṭ //
tat Sindhupatinā rājan pālitaṃ dhvajinīmukham /
anantarathanāgāśvam aśobhata mahad balam //
ṣaṣṭyā rathasahasrais tu nāgānām ayutena ca /
patiḥ sarva-Kaliṅgānāṃ yayau Ketumatā saha //
tasya parvatasaṃkāśā vyarocanta mahāgajāḥ /
yantratomaratūṇīraiḥ patākābhiś ca śobhitāḥ //
śuśubhe ketumukhyena pādapena Kaliṅgapaḥ /
śvetacchatreṇa niṣkeṇa cāmaravyajanena ca //
35 Ketumān api mātaṅgaṃ vicitraparamāṅkuśam /
āsthitaḥ samare rājan meghastha iva bhānumān //
tejasā dīpyamānas tu vāraṇottamam āsthitaḥ /
Bhagadatto yayau rājā yathā Vajradharas tathā //
gajaskandhagatāv āstāṃ Bhagadattena saṃmitau /
Vinda-Anuvindāv Āvantyau Ketumantam anuvratau //

tumultuously, and the great warriors, shining with their gold upper-
arm and wrist bracelets and bows, appeared to the eye like walking
mountains. Bhīṣma, the marshal of the Kuru armies, stood there with
his great standard that bore a palm tree and five stars in the image
of a cloudless sun.

Your great royal archers, bull of the Bharatas, moved according to
20 Śāṃtanava's instructions. King Śaibya of Govāsana, followed by all
his princes, rode on a regal, bannered elephant worthy of kings.
Aśvatthāman, lotus-complexioned, marched out fully girt at the head
of all his troops, bearing his standard of the lion's tail. The seven
archers Śrutāyus, Citrasena, Purumitra, Viviṃśati, Śalya, Bhūriśravas,
and the great warrior Vikarṇa, followed Droṇa's son[4] on their
brightly colored chariots to form Bhīṣma's vanguard; and their fine
lofty chariots glowed and their gold-decked banners sparkled. The
standard of Droṇa, foremost of all teachers, was a golden altar
adorned with a pitcher, as well as a bow. The gem-studded standard
25 of Duryodhana, who led an army of many hundreds of thousands,
was a large elephant in precious stones. In front of him stood the
warriors Paurava, Kāliṅga, Sudakṣiṇa of Kāmboja, Kṣemadhanvan,
and Sumitra. On a precious chariot and bearing the emblem of the
bull the king of Magadha advanced, pulling on as it were the van of
his army. The force of the easterners, which looked like a mass of
autumn clouds, was in the charge of the Lord of Aṅga and great-
spirited Kṛpa. At the head of his column shone famed Jayadratha with
30 his beautiful standard, a silver boar; he commanded a hundred
thousand chariots, eight thousand elephants and sixty thousand
horsemen. That great force in the van of the armies, protected by the
Lord of Sindhu, glittered with its innumerable chariots, elephants, and
horses, O king. The lord of all the Kaliṅgas, and Ketumat marched
with sixty thousand chariots and ten thousand elephants. His grand,
mountainous elephants sparkled with their adornment of javelins,
catapults, quivers, and flags. The king of Kaliṅga, bearing a tree on
his fine standard, glistened with his white umbrella, golden breastplate,
35 and yaktail fan. Ketumat appeared on the battlefield riding an
elephant with a large colored goad like a sun riding a rain-cloud. King
Bhagadatta came like the Thunderbolt-Wielder on a beautiful elephant
in a blaze of splendor. Measuring up to Bhagadatta on the shoulders
of their elephants came Vinda and Anuvinda of Avanti, who were
beholden to Ketumat. The marching formation was like a fearsome

sa rathānīkavān vyūho hastyaṅgottamaśīrṣavān /
vājipakṣaḥ patann ugraḥ prāharat sarvatomukhaḥ //
Droṇena vihito rājan rājñā Śāṃtanavena ca /
tathaivācāryaputreṇa Bāhlīkena Kṛpeṇa ca //

Saṃjaya uvāca /
18.1 *tato muhūrtāt tumulaḥ śabdo hṛdayakampanaḥ /*
aśrūyata mahārāja yodhānāṃ prayuyutsatām //
śaṅkhadundubhinirghoṣair vāraṇānāṃ ca bṛṃhitaiḥ /
rathānāṃ nemighoṣaiś ca dīryatīva vasuṃdharā //
hayānāṃ heṣamāṇānāṃ yodhānāṃ tatra garjatām /
kṣaṇena khaṃ diśaś caiva śabdenāpūritaṃ tadā //
putrāṇāṃ tava durdharṣa Pāṇḍavānāṃ tathaiva ca /
samakampanta sainyāni parasparasamāgame //
5 *tatra nāgā rathāś caiva jāmbūnadavibhūṣitāḥ /*
bhrājamānā vyadṛśyanta meghā iva savidyutaḥ //
dhvajā bahuvidhākārās tāvakānāṃ narādhipa /
kāñcanāṅgadino rejur jvalitā iva pāvakāḥ //
sveṣāṃ caiva pareṣāṃ ca samadṛśyanta Bhārata /
Mahendraketavaḥ śubhrā Mahendrasadaneṣv iva //
kāñcanaiḥ kavacair vīrā jvalanārkasamaprabhaiḥ /
saṃnaddhāḥ pratyadṛśyanta grahāḥ prajvalitā iva //
udyatair āyudhaiś citrais talabaddhāḥ patākinaḥ /
ṛṣabhākṣā maheṣvāsāś camūmukhagatā babhuḥ //
10 *pṛṣṭhagopās tu Bhīṣmasya putrās tava narādhipa /*
Duḥśāsano Durviṣaho Durmukho Duḥsahas tathā //
Viviṃśatiś Citraseno Vikarṇaś ca mahārathaḥ /
Satyavrataḥ Purumitro Jayo Bhūriśravāḥ Śalaḥ //
rathā viṃśatisāhasrās tathaiṣām anuyāyinaḥ /
Abhīṣāhāḥ Śūrasenāḥ Śibayo 'tha Vasātayaḥ //
Śālvā Matsyās tathā-Ambaṣṭhās Trigartāḥ Kekayās tathā /
Sauvīrāḥ Kitavāḥ prācyāḥ pratīcyodīcya-Mālavāḥ //
dvādaśaite janapadāḥ sarve śūrās tanutyajaḥ /
mahatā rathavaṃśena te 'bhyarakṣan pitāmahaṃ //
15 *anīkaṃ daśasāhasraṃ kuñjarāṇāṃ tarasvinām /*
Māgadho yena nṛpatis tad rathānīkam anvayāt //
rathānāṃ cakrarakṣāś ca pādarakṣāś ca dantinām /
abhūvan vāhinīmadhye śatānām ayutāni ṣaṭ //
pādātāś cāgrato 'gacchan dhanuścarmāsipāṇayaḥ /
anekaśatasāhasrā nakharaprāsayodhinaḥ //
akṣauhiṇyo daśaikā ca tava putrasya Bhārata /
adṛśyanta mahārāja Gaṅgeva Yamunāntare //

Dhṛtarāṣṭra uvāca /
19.1 *akṣauhiṇyo daśaikāṃ ca vyūḍhāṃ dṛṣṭvā Yudhiṣṭhiraḥ /*

bird, with a trunk of chariots, a head of elephants, and wings of horses; and it attacked in all directions. It had been so arrayed, sire, by Droṇa and King Śāṃtanava, as well as the teacher's son,[5] Bāhlīka and Kṛpa.

Saṃjaya said:

18.1 Soon there was heard the heartrending, terrifying noise of warriors
ready to go to war, great king. The blare of conches, the roll of drums,
the trumpeting of elephants, the racket of chariot rims seemed to split
open the earth. The skies were instantly filled with the riot of
whinnying horses and roaring warriors, and the armies of your sons
and the irresistible Pāṇḍavas trembled in the clash. The gold-decked
5 elephants and chariots appeared, flashing like lightning-splashed rain
clouds. The many-shaped banners of your men, king of the people,
bearing royal insignia of gold, sparkled like fires. The shining rainbow
colors of your troops and the others' were bright as in Indra's
mansions, Bhārata. The warriors, armored in their golden cuirasses
that shone like fire and sun, seemed like flaming meteors. The bull-
eyed archers, with their upraised weapons, tied-on guards and
banners, glittered at the head of the armies.
10 Your sons, king, acted as Bhīṣma's rearguards. There were
Duḥśāsana, Durviṣaha, Durmukha, Duḥsaha, Viviṃśati, Citrasena, the
great warrior Vikarṇa, Satyavrata, Purumitra, Jaya, Bhūriśravas, and
Śala, and twenty thousand warriors followed them. Abhīṣāhas,
Śūrasenas, Śibis, Vasātis, Śālvas, Matsyas, Ambaṣṭhas, Trigartas,
Kekayas, Sauvīras, Kitavas, and the Eastern, Western and Northern
Mālavas, twelve peoples in all, with fighters ready to risk their lives,
15 protected grandfather in a mighty chariot column. There was an
army of ten thousand fierce elephants with which the king of
Magadha followed the chariot forces. There were sixty thousand times
a hundred men to guard the wheels of the chariots and legs of the
tuskers in the middle of the army. Many hundreds of thousands of
footmen, armed with bows, shields, swords, and clawed spears went
in the vanguard. Your son had eleven grand armies, Bhārata, and
they looked like the Ganges before its confluence with the river
Yamunā, mahārāja!

Dhṛtarāṣṭra said:

19.1 When Yudhiṣṭhira Pāṇḍava saw those eleven armies marshaled

katham alpena sainyena pratyavyūhata Pāṇḍavaḥ //
yo veda mānuṣaṃ vyūhaṃ daivaṃ gāndharvam āsuram /
kathaṃ Bhīṣmaṃ sa Kaunteyaḥ pratyavyūhata Pāṇḍavaḥ //
Saṃjaya uvāca /
Dhārtarāṣṭrāṇy anīkāni dṛṣṭvā vyūḍhāni Pāṇḍavaḥ /
abhyabhāṣata dharmātmā Dharmarājo Dhanaṃjayam //
maharṣer vacanāt tāta vedayanti Bṛhaspateḥ /
saṃhatān yodhayed alpān kāmaṃ vistārayed bahūn //
5 *sūcīmukham anīkaṃ syād alpānāṃ bahubhiḥ saha /*
asmākaṃ ca tathā sainyam alpīyaḥ sutarāṃ paraiḥ //
etad vacanam ājñāya maharṣer vyūha Pāṇḍava /
tac chrutvā Dharmarājasya pratyabhāṣata Phalgunaḥ //
eṣa vyūhāmi te rājan vyūhaṃ paramadurjayam /
acalaṃ nāma Vajrākhyaṃ vihitaṃ Vajrapāṇinā //
yaḥ sa vāta ivoddhūtaḥ samare duḥsahaḥ paraiḥ /
sa naḥ puro yotsyati vai Bhīmaḥ praharatāṃ varaḥ //
tejāṃsi ripusainyānāṃ mṛdnan puruṣasattamaḥ /
agre 'graṇīr yāsyati no yuddhopāyavicakṣaṇaḥ //
10 *yaṃ dṛṣṭvā pārthivāḥ sarve Duryodhanapurogamāḥ /*
nivartiṣyanti saṃbhrāntāḥ siṃhaṃ kṣudramṛgā iva //
taṃ sarve saṃśrayiṣyāmaḥ prākāram akutobhayam /
Bhīmaṃ praharatāṃ śreṣṭhaṃ Vajrapāṇim ivāmarāḥ //
na hi so 'sti pumāṃl loke yaḥ saṃkruddhaṃ Vṛkodaram /
draṣṭum atyugrakarmāṇaṃ viṣaheta nararṣabham //
Bhīmaseno gadāṃ bibhrad vajrasāramayīṃ dṛḍhām /
caran vegena mahatā samudram api śoṣayet //
Kekayā Dhṛṣṭaketuś ca Cekitānaś ca vīryavān /
ete tiṣṭhanti sāmātyāḥ prekṣakās te nareśvara /
Dhṛtarāṣṭrasya dāyādā iti Bībhatsur abravīt //
15 *bruvāṇaṃ tu tathā Pārthaṃ sarvasainyāni māriṣa /*
apūjayaṃs tadā vāgbhir anukūlābhir āhave //
evam uktvā mahābāhus tathā cakre Dhanaṃjayaḥ /
vyūhya tāni balāny āśu prayayau Phalgunas tadā //
saṃprayātān Kurūn dṛṣṭvā Pāṇḍavānāṃ mahācamūḥ /
Gaṅgeva pūrṇā stimitā syandamānā vyadṛśyata //
Bhīmaseno 'graṇīs teṣāṃ Dhṛṣṭadyumnaś ca Pārṣataḥ /
Nakulaḥ Sahadevaś ca Dhṛṣṭaketuś ca vīryavān //
samudyojya tataḥ paścād rājāpy akṣauhiṇīvṛtaḥ /
bhrātṛbhiḥ saha putraiś ca so 'bhyarakṣata pṛṣṭhataḥ //
20 *cakrarakṣau tu Bhīmasya Mādrīputrau mahādyutī /*
Draupadeyāḥ sa-Saubhadrāḥ pṛṣṭhagopās tarasvinaḥ //
Dhṛṣṭadyumnaś ca Pāñcālyas teṣāṃ goptā mahārathaḥ /
sahitaḥ pṛtanāśūrai rathamukhyaiḥ Prabhadrakaiḥ //
Śikhaṇḍī tu tataḥ paścād Arjunenābhirakṣitaḥ /
yatto Bhīṣmavināśāya prayayau Bharatarṣabha //

against him, how did he array his smaller forces in defense? How did the son of Pāṇḍu and Kuntī set up his defenses against Bhīṣma, who knew the battle formations of men, Gods, Gandharvas, and Asuras?

Saṃjaya said:

When the law-spirited King Dharma Pāṇḍava saw the armies of the Dhārtarāṣṭra, he said to Dhanaṃjaya, "Brother, we know from the instructions of the great seer Bṛhaspati that one should keep a smaller force tight, but spread out superior numbers at will. The formation of fewer troops against superior forces should be needlepointed—and our army is far outnumbered by the enemy. Form the defense according to the great seer's counsel, Pāṇḍava!"

At King Dharma's words Phalguna replied, "I shall set up the virtually invincible formation of the unshaken Thunderbolt, which was invented by the God who wields the thunderbolt, king. Bhīma, the greatest warrior of them all, who like a raging gale is impossible to withstand in battle by any enemy, shall fight at our head. That best of men, who is shrewd in the ways of war, shall be our front-line warrior and shatter the might of the enemy armies. When they see him, all the kings who follow Duryodhana will flee in confusion as small game before a lion. All of us will cling to Bhīma, greatest of warlords, as to a rampart where fear stops, as the Immortals cling to the Thunderbolt-Wielder. For there is no man on earth who can face up to the raging Wolf-Belly, that bull-like man of ferocious feats. Brandishing his diamond-hard club, Bhīmasena would lay dry the ocean itself if he attacked it with his tremendous speed. The Kekayas, Dhṛṣṭaketu, and the heroic Cekitāna stand here with their councilors looking to you, king of men, knowing we are the heirs of Dhṛtarāṣṭra!" So spoke the Terrifier, and at his words, friend, all the troops praised the Pārtha with apposite words on that field of battle.

When Dhanaṃjaya of the mighty arms had spoken, he, Phalguna, ordered the forces quickly and advanced. The vast army of the Pāṇḍavas, sighting the Kurus who were on the march, appeared like the dense stream of the rain-filled Ganges. Bhīmasena led the vanguard with Dhṛṣṭadyumna Pārṣata, Nakula, Sahadeva, and the valiant Dhṛṣṭaketu. Behind them the king himself had marshaled the grand army that surrounded him and with brothers and sons protected the rear. The two illustrious sons of Mādrī were Bhīma's wheel guards, while the fierce Saubhadra and Draupadeyas[1] guarded his back. The great warrior Dhṛṣṭadyumna Pāñcālya covered them in turn along with the champions of his army and excellent armsmen, the Prabhadrakas. Śikhaṇḍin was behind them, protected by Arjuna; and dedicated to the destruction of Bhīṣma, he advanced, bull of the

pṛṣṭhagopo 'rjunasyāpi Yuyudhāno mahārathaḥ /
cakrarakṣau tu Pāñcālyau Yudhāmanyūttamaujasau //
rājā tu madhyamānīke Kuntīputro Yudhiṣṭhiraḥ /
bṛhadbhiḥ kuñjarair mattaiś caladbhir acalair iva //
25 *akṣauhiṇyā ca Pāñcālyo Yajñaseno mahāmanāḥ /*
Virāṭam anvayāt paścāt Pāṇḍavārthe parākramī //
teṣām ādityacandrābhāḥ kanakottamabhūṣaṇāḥ /
nānācihnadharā rājan ratheṣv āsan mahādhvajāḥ //
samutsarpya tataḥ paścād Dhṛṣṭadyumno mahārathaḥ /
bhrātṛbhiḥ saha putraiś ca so 'bhyarakṣad Yudhiṣṭhiram //
tvadīyānāṃ pareṣāṃ ca ratheṣu vividhān dhvajān /
abhibhūya-Arjunasyaiko dhvajas tasthau mahākapiḥ //
pādātās tv agrato 'gacchann asiśaktyṛṣṭipāṇayaḥ /
anekaśatasāhasrā Bhīmasenasya rakṣiṇaḥ //
30 *vāraṇā daśasāhasrāḥ prabhinnakaraṭāmukhāḥ /*
śūrā hemamayair jālair dīpyamānā ivācalāḥ //
kṣaranta iva jīmūtā madārdrāḥ padmagandhinaḥ /
rājānam anvayuḥ paścāc calanta iva parvatāḥ //
Bhīmaseno gadāṃ bhīmāṃ prakarṣan parighopamām /
pracakarṣa mahat sainyaṃ durādharṣo mahāmanāḥ //
tam arkam iva duṣprekṣyaṃ tapantaṃ raśmimālinam /
na śekuḥ sarvato yodhāḥ prativīkṣitum antike //
Vajro nāmaiṣa tu vyūho durbhidaḥ sarvatomukhaḥ /
cāpavidyuddhvajo ghoro gupto Gāṇḍīvadhanvanā //
35 *yaṃ prativyūhya tiṣṭhanti Pāṇḍavās tava vāhinīm /*
ajeyo mānuṣe loke Pāṇḍavair abhirakṣitaḥ //
saṃdhyāṃ tiṣṭhatsu sainyeṣu sūryasyodayanaṃ prati /
prāvāt sapṛṣato vāyur anabhre stanayitnumān //
viṣvagvātāś ca vānty ugrā nīcaiḥ śarkarakarṣiṇaḥ /
rajaś coddhūyamānaṃ tu tamasācchādayaj jagat //
papāta mahatī colkā prāṅmukhī Bharatarṣabha /
udyantaṃ sūryam āhatya vyaśīryata mahāsvanā //
atha sajjīyamāneṣu sainyeṣu Bharatarṣabha /
niṣprabho 'bhyudiyāt sūryaḥ saghoṣo bhūś cacāla ha
vyaśīryata sanādā ca tadā Bharatasattama //
40 *nirghātā bahavo rājan dikṣu sarvāsu cābhavan /*
prādur āsīd rajas tīvraṃ na prājñāyata kiṃcana //
dhvajānāṃ dhūyamānānāṃ sahasā mātariśvanā /
kiṅkiṇījālanaddhānāṃ kāñcanasragvatāṃ ravaiḥ //
mahatāṃ sapatākānām ādityasamatejasām /
sarvaṃ jhaṇajhaṇībhūtam āsīt tālavaneṣv iva //
evaṃ te puruṣavyāghrāḥ Pāṇḍavā yuddhanandinaḥ /
vyavasthitāḥ prativyūhya tava putrasya vāhinīm //
sraṃsanta iva majjāno yodhānāṃ Bharatarṣabha /
dṛṣṭvāgrato Bhīmasenaṃ gadāpāṇim avasthitam //

Bharatas. The great warrior Yuyudhāna covered Arjuna's back, while
Yudhāmanyu and Uttamaujas of Pāñcāla guarded his wheels.

King Yudhiṣṭhira, son of Kuntī, was in the center of the army with
25 massive, crazed elephants like walking mountains. The great-minded
Yajñasena of Pāñcāla followed behind Virāṭa with his grand army,
ready to show his prowess in the cause of the Pāṇḍava. There were
tall standards on their chariots, king, luminous like sun and moon,
adorned with the finest gold and bearing many emblems. Behind them
came up the great warlord Dhṛṣṭadyumna with his brothers and sons
to protect Yudhiṣṭhira. Dwarfing the standards on the chariots of your
men and the enemy stood the single standard of Arjuna, his great ape.

Ahead of Bhīmasena as his vanguard marched many hundreds of
30 thousands of footmen armed with swords, spears, and javelins. Tens
of thousands of elephants with their temple glands running, brave,
mountainous beasts sparkling with golden caparisons like streaming
rain clouds, moist with rut, fragrant like lotuses, followed behind the
king like moving hills. Bhīmasena, shrewd and invincible, who dragged
behind him his terrible bludgeon-like club, pulled along a vast force.
The warriors who stood close by him were unable to look at him from
any side, for he was as hard on the eyes as the burning ray-garlanded
sun.

This was the Thunderbolt formation, lightning-flagged with bows,
unbreakable, terrifyingly pointing in every direction and watched over
35 by the Gāṇḍiva bowman,[2] which the Pāṇḍavas had marshaled against
your army, sire, a formation invincible in the world of men since it
was protected by the Pāṇḍavas themselves.

When at dawn the troops were waiting for the sun to rise, a moist
breeze began to blow and there was thunder in the clear sky. Fierce
whirling winds blew close to the ground carrying gravel, and the
stirred-up dust covered the world with darkness. A large fireball
streaked through the sky to the east, bull of the Bharatas, hit the
rising sun, and exploded with a huge noise. And while the troops
were being put on alert, bull of the Bharatas, a lusterless sun rose
noisily, and the earth trembled and cracked open with rumblings,
40 chief of the Bharatas. There were many portents in all directions, king,
and so thick was the dust that rose that nothing could be seen. The
banners, suddenly shaken by the wind and ringing with their streams
of bell-strings and golden wreaths, the lofty pennant-flying banners
that sparkled like the sun, made the sustained rustling noise one hears
in palmyra forests.

And so the tigerlike, war-loving Pāṇḍavas arrayed themselves in defensive formation against your son's army as though tapping the very marrow of your warriors with the spectacle of Bhīmasena standing up front with his club in his hand, bull of the Bharatas.

Dhṛtarāṣṭra uvāca /
20.1 *sūryodaye Saṃjaya ke nu pūrvaṃ*
yuyutsavo hṛṣyamāṇā ivāsan /
māmakā vā Bhīṣmanetrāḥ samīke
Pāṇḍavā vā Bhīmanetrās tadānīm //
keṣāṃ jaghanyau somasūryau savāyū
keṣāṃ senāṃ śvāpadā vyābhaṣanta /
keṣāṃ yūnāṃ mukhavarṇāḥ prasannāḥ
sarvaṃ hy etad brūhi tattvaṃ yathāvat //
Saṃjaya uvāca /
ubhe sene tulyam ivopayāte
ubhe vyūhe hṛṣṭarūpe narendra /
ubhe citre vanarājiprakāśe
tathaivobhe nāgarathāśvapūrṇe //
ubhe sene bṛhatī bhīmarūpe
tathaivobhe Bhārata durviṣahye /
tathaivobhe svargajayāya sṛṣṭe
tathā hy ubhe satpuruṣāryagupte //
5 *paścānmukhāḥ Kuravo Dhārtarāṣṭrāḥ*
sthitāḥ Pārthāḥ prāṅmukhā yotsyamānāḥ /
Daityendraseneva ca Kauravāṇāṃ
devendraseneva ca Pāṇḍavānām //
śukro vāyuḥ pṛṣṭhataḥ Pāṇḍavānāṃ
Dhārtarāṣṭrāñ śvāpadā vyābhaṣanta /
gajendrāṇāṃ madagandhāṃś ca tīvrān
na sehire tava putrasya nāgāḥ //
Duryodhano hastinaṃ padmavarṇaṃ
suvarṇakakṣyaṃ jātibalaṃ prabhinnam /
samāsthito madhyagataḥ Kurūṇāṃ
saṃstūyamāno bandibhir māgadhaiś ca //
candraprabhaṃ śvetam asyātapatraṃ
sauvarṇī srag bhrājate cottamāṅge /
taṃ sarvataḥ Śakuniḥ pārvatīyaiḥ
sārdhaṃ Gāndhāraiḥ pāti Gāndhārarājaḥ //
Bhīṣmo 'grataḥ sarvasainyasya vṛddhaḥ
śvetacchatraḥ śvetadhanuḥ saśaṅkhaḥ /
śvetoṣṇīṣaḥ pāṇḍureṇa dhvajena
śvetair aśvaiḥ śvetaśailaprakāśaḥ //
10 *tasya sainyaṃ Dhārtarāṣṭrāś ca sarve*
Bāhlīkānām ekadeśaḥ Śalaś ca /

Dhṛtarāṣṭra said:

20.1 When the sun had risen, who were the first
To exult in this battle, O Saṃjaya,
My troops who were led to the war by Bhīṣma,
Or the Pāṇḍavas who were then guarded by Bhīma?

Against whom rose the sun and the moon and the wind?
Against which of the troops did the predators roar?
Which youths showed faces serene of color?
Tell all of it, just as it really happened!

Saṃjaya said:

Both armies at march were much the same:
Both were in formation and were of good cheer,
Both looked in their colors like ridges of forest,
Both teemed with elephants, chariots, horses.

Both armies were vast and ferocious-looking,
Both, Bhārata, were irresistible,
They both poured out to conquer heaven,
Both were in the care of good, noble men.

5 The Kurus of Dhṛtarāṣṭra faced west,
The bellicose Pāṇḍavas looked to the east;
The Kauravas were like the army of Daityas,
The Pāṇḍavas' host was like that of the Gods.

The Pāṇḍavas had a good wind behind them,
Wild beasts roared against the Dhārtarāṣṭras,
And your son's elephants could not endure
The sharp pungent rut of the tuskers in front.

In the midst of his Kurus Duryodhana,
Who was glorified by his minstrels and bards,
Rode a lotus-dot elephant, strong as its kind,
With its ichor juice flowing, in a *howdah* of gold.

An umbrella as white as the moon, and a chaplet
That was wrought out of gold dazzled over his head,
And Śakuni, king of Gāndhāra, stood guard
Over him on all sides with his mountain troops.

In front of his host rode ancient Bhīṣma,
With conch, white bow and white umbrella,
And turbaned in white and bannered in white
And drawn by white steeds, like the Snow-White Mountain.

10 All your sons, Dhṛtarāṣṭra, were in his army,
As were Śala with part of the Bāhlīka forces,

ye ca-Ambaṣṭhāḥ kṣatriyā ye ca Sindhau
tathā Sauvīrāḥ Pañcanadāś ca śūrāḥ //
śoṇair hayai rukmaratho mahātmā
Droṇo mahābāhur adīnasattvaḥ /
āste guruḥ prayaśāḥ sarvarājñāṃ
paścāc camūm Indra ivābhirakṣan //
Vārddhakṣatriḥ sarvasainyasya madhye
Bhūriśravāḥ Purumitro Jayaś ca /
Śālvā Matsyāḥ Kekayāś cāpi sarve
gajānīkair bhrātaro yotsyamānāḥ //
Śāradvataś cottaradhūr mahātmā
maheṣvāso Gautamāś citrayodhī /
Śakaiḥ Kirātair Yavanaiḥ Pahlavaiś ca
sārdhaṃ camūm uttarato 'bhipāti //
mahārathair Andhaka-Vṛṣṇi-Bhojaiḥ
Saurāṣṭrakair Nairṛtair āttaśastraiḥ /
bṛhadbalaḥ Kṛtavarmābhigupto
balaṃ tvadīyaṃ dakṣiṇato 'bhipāti //
15 *Saṃśaptakānām ayutaṃ rathānāṃ*
mṛtyur jayo vā-Arjunasyeti sṛṣṭāḥ /
yena-Arjunas tena rājan kṛtāstrāḥ
prayātā vai te Trigartāś ca śūrāḥ //
sāgraṃ śatasahasraṃ tu nāgānāṃ tava Bhārata /
nāge nāge rathaśataṃ śataṃ cāśvā rathe rathe //
aśve 'sve daśa dhānuṣkā dhānuṣke daśa carmiṇaḥ /
evaṃ vyūḍhāny anīkāni Bhīṣmeṇa tava Bhārata //
avyūhan mānuṣaṃ vyūhaṃ daivaṃ gāndharvam āsuram /
divase divase prāpte Bhīṣmaḥ Śāṃtanavo 'graṇīḥ //
mahārathaughavipulaḥ samudra iva parvaṇi /
Bhīṣmeṇa Dhārtarāṣṭrāṇāṃ vyūhaḥ pratyaṅmukho yudhi //
20 *anantarūpā dhvajinī tvadīyā*
narendra bhīmā na tu Pāṇḍavānām /
tāṃ tv eva manye bṛhatīṃ duṣpradhṛṣyāṃ
yasyā netārau Keśavaś ca-Arjunaś ca //

21.1 *Saṃjaya uvāca /*
bṛhatīṃ Dhārtarāṣṭrāṇāṃ dṛṣṭvā senāṃ samudyatām /
viṣādam agamad rājā Kuntīputro Yudhiṣṭhiraḥ //
vyūhaṃ Bhīṣmeṇa cābhedyaṃ kalpitaṃ prekṣya Pāṇḍavaḥ /
abhedyam iva saṃprekṣya viṣaṇṇo 'rjunam abravīt //
Dhanaṃjaya kathaṃ śakyam asmābhir yoddhum āhave /
Dhārtarāṣṭrair mahābāho yeṣāṃ yoddhā pitāmahaḥ //

The Ambaṣṭha barons, and those from the Sindhu,
The Sauvīras and knights from the Land of Five Rivers.

On a chariot of gold with blood-red horses
Stood great-souled, strong-armed, cheerful Droṇa,
Renowned as the teacher of all those kings,
Who like Indra protected the rear of the army.

In the army's center were Vārddhakṣatri,
Purumitra, Jaya, and Bhūriśravas,
The Śālvas, the Matsyas, and Kekayas all,
The warlike brethren, with elephant troops.

Great-souled Śāradvata, northern commander,
Great archer and marvelous fighter himself,
Rode guard on the host from the north with his troops
Of Yavanas, Pahlavas, Kirātas, and Śakas.

The strong Kṛtavarman, protected by warriors
Of the Andhakas, Vṛṣṇis, and Bhojas, as well
As Saurāṣṭras and Nairṛtas drawing their blades,
Rode guard on that army of yours on the south.

15 The ten thousand chariots of the Sworn Warriors
Who were made for Arjuna's triumph or death,
Were ready to strike where Arjuna went,
And there marched the Trigarta champions as well.

You had at least a hundred thousand elephants in the field, Bhārata, and for every elephant a hundred chariots, for every chariot a hundred horsemen, for every horse ten archers, for every archer ten men with shields. Thus had Bhīṣma arrayed the troops, Bhārata. From day to day Bhīṣma Śāṃtanava, your marshal, rearrayed them in formations devised by men, Gods, Gandharvas, and Asuras. And this army of the Dhārtarāṣṭras, billowing like the ocean at full moon, arrayed by Bhīṣma, faced west on the field of battle.

Your fearful, flag-bearing army, O king,
Outnumbered the Pāṇḍavas' army by far,
Yet I think theirs was vast and invincible,
For Kṛṣṇa and Arjuna were its guides.

Saṃjaya said:

21.1 When Kuntī's son Yudhiṣṭhira saw the vast army of the Dhārtarāṣṭras[1] in readiness, the king became discouraged. On seeing the seemingly impenetrable troops marshaled by Bhīṣma and regarding them as in fact impenetrable, he said dispiritedly to Arjuna, "Dhanaṃjaya, how shall we be able to do battle with the Dhārtarāṣṭras whose champion is grandfather himself, strong-armed

akṣobhyo 'yam abhedyaś ca Bhīṣmeṇāmitrakarśinā /
kalpitaḥ śāstradṛṣṭena vidhinā bhūritejasā //
5 *te vayaṃ saṃśayaṃ prāptāḥ sasainyāḥ śatrukarśana /*
katham asmān mahāvyūhād udyānaṃ no bhaviṣyati //
atha-Arjuno 'bravīt Pārthaṃ Yudhiṣṭhiram amitrahā /
viṣaṇṇam abhisaṃprekṣya tava rājann anīkinīm //
prajñayābhyadhikāñ śūrān guṇayuktān bahūn api /
jayanty alpatarā yena tan nibodha viśāṃ pate //
tat tu te kāraṇaṃ rājan pravakṣyāmy anasūyave /
Nāradas tam ṛṣir veda Bhīṣma-Droṇau ca Pāṇḍava //
etam evārtham āśritya yuddhe devāsure 'bravīt /
pitāmahaḥ kila purā Mahendrādīn divaukasaḥ //
10 *na tathā balavīryābhyāṃ vijayante jigīṣavaḥ /*
yathā satyānṛśaṃsyābhyāṃ dharmeṇaivodyamena ca //
tyaktvādharmaṃ ca lobhaṃ ca mohaṃ codyamam āsthitāḥ /
yudhyadhvam anahaṃkārā yato dharmas tato jayaḥ //
evaṃ rājan vijānīhi dhruvo 'smākaṃ raṇe jayaḥ /
yathā me Nāradaḥ prāha yataḥ Kṛṣṇas tato jayaḥ //
guṇabhūto jayaḥ Kṛṣṇe pṛṣṭhato 'nveti Mādhavam /
anyathā vijayaś cāsya saṃnatiś cāparo guṇaḥ //
anantatejā Govindaḥ śatrupūgeṣu nirvyathaḥ /
puruṣaḥ sanātanatamo yataḥ Kṛṣṇas tato jayaḥ //
15 *purā hy eṣa Harir bhūtvā Vaikuṇṭho 'kuṇṭhasāyakaḥ /*
surāsurān avasphūrjann abravīt ke jayantv iti //
anu Kṛṣṇaṃ jayemeti yair uktaṃ tatra tair jitam /
tat prasādād dhi trailokyaṃ prāptaṃ Śakrādibhiḥ suraiḥ //
tasya te na vyathāṃ kāṃcid iha paśyāmi Bhārata /
yasya te jayam āśāste viśvabhuk tridaśeśvaraḥ //

Saṃjaya uvāca /
22.1 *tato Yudhiṣṭhiro rājā svāṃ senāṃ samacodayat /*
prativyūhann anīkāni Bhīṣmasya Bharatarṣabha //
yathoddiṣṭāny anīkāni pratyavyūhanta Pāṇḍavāḥ /
svargaṃ param abhīpsantaḥ suyuddhena Kurūdvahāḥ //
madhye Śikhaṇḍino 'nīkaṃ rakṣitaṃ Savyasācinā /
Dhṛṣṭadyumnasya ca svayaṃ Bhīmena paripālitam //
anīkaṃ dakṣiṇaṃ rājan Yuyudhānena pālitam /
śrīmatā Sātvatāgryeṇa Śakreṇeva dhanuṣmatā //
5 *Mahendrayānapratimaṃ rathaṃ tu*
sopaskaraṃ hāṭakaratnacitram /
Yudhiṣṭhiraḥ kāñcanabhāṇḍayoktraṃ
samāsthito nāgakulasya madhye //
samucchritaṃ dāntaśalākam asya
supāṇḍuraṃ chatram atīva bhāti /

prince? Bhīṣma, plougher of his enemies, who brims with vigor, has
5 made his army unshakable and unbreakable by the rules of scripture.
We and our troops are in danger, plougher of foes! How are we to
escape from this overpowering battle plan?"

Enemy-killer Arjuna replied to Yudhiṣṭhira Pārtha, who was
discouraged by the sight of your army, king, "Listen, lord of your
people, how fewer men triumph over many talented and shrewd
warriors. I shall tell you how, and do not gainsay me. The seer
Nārada knows it, Pāṇḍava, and so do Bhīṣma and Droṇa.

"It is told that Grandfather once said to great Indra and the other
celestials concerning this very issue at the battle of Gods and Asuras,
10 'Those who seek victory win not so much by strength and might as
by truth and mercy, and by Law and enterprise. Abandon lawlessness,
greed, and delusion, be enterprising, and then fight without thought of
self. Where Law goes goes victory!' So know, king, that our victory
is assured, for as Nārada has told me, 'Where Kṛṣṇa goes goes
victory.' Victory is a talent with Kṛṣṇa, and it follows closely behind
the Mādhava. And no less than victory is modesty a virtue with him.
Govinda of infinite splendor strides unconcernedly among the
multitudes of his enemies, the most everlasting man, and 'where
15 Kṛṣṇa goes goes victory.' Once, in his manifestation as Hari Vaikuṇṭha
of the ever-sharp arrows, he said thunderously to Gods and Asuras,
'Who shall win?' And they won who said, 'With Kṛṣṇa we shall win!'
Indeed, it was by his grace that Śakra and the Gods won the Three
Worlds. I see no cause of concern for you at all, Bhārata, when he,
the ruler of the world and the lord of the Thirty, wishes you to
triumph!"

Saṃjaya said:

22.1 Thereupon King Yudhiṣṭhira arrayed his troops against Bhīṣma's
formation, bull of the Bharatas, and he exhorted his army, "The
Pāṇḍavas have now drawn up their ranks in defense according to the
positions assigned them. The scions of Kuru wish for highest heaven
in a good fight!" In the center was Śikhaṇḍin's force protected by the
Left-handed Archer, and that of Dhṛṣṭadyumna himself, who was
guarded by Bhīma. The southern flank of the army was commanded
by Yuyudhāna, sire, the illustrious chief of the Sātvatas, a bowman
like Śakra himself.

5 On a chariot worthy of carrying Indra,
Bright with jewels and gold, filled with weapon gear,
And teamed with horses harnessed in gold,
In the midst of his elephants, Yudhiṣṭhira rode.

His ivory-handled parasol shone
In a luminous haze, quite white and tall,

pradakṣiṇaṃ cainam upācaranti
maharṣayaḥ saṃstutibhir narendram //
purohitāḥ śatruvadhaṃ vadanto
maharṣivṛddhāḥ śrutavanta eva /
japyaiś ca mantraiś ca tathauṣadhībhiḥ
samantataḥ svastyayanaṃ pracakruḥ //
tataḥ sa vastrāṇi tathaiva gāś ca
phalāni puṣpāṇi tathaiva niṣkān /
Kurūttamo brāhmaṇasān mahātmā
kurvan yayau Śakra ivāmarebhyaḥ //
sahasrasūryaḥ śatakiṅkiṇīkaḥ
parārdhyajāmbūnadahemacitraḥ /
ratho 'rjunasyāgnir ivārcimālī
vibhrājate śvetahayaḥ sucakraḥ //
10 *tam āsthitaḥ Keśavasaṃgṛhītaṃ*
kapidhvajaṃ Gāṇḍivabāṇahastaḥ /
dhanurdharo yasya samaḥ pṛthivyāṃ
na vidyate no bhavitā vā kadācit //
udvartayiṣyaṃs tava putrasenām
atīva raudraṃ sa bibharti rūpam /
anāyudho yaḥ subhujo bhujābhyāṃ
narāśvanāgān yudhi bhasma kuryāt //
sa Bhīmasenaḥ sahito yamābhyāṃ
Vṛkodaro vīrarathasya goptā /
taṃ prekṣya mattarṣabhasiṃhakhelaṃ
loke Mahendrapratimānakalpam //
samīkṣya senāgragataṃ durāsadaṃ
pravivyathuḥ paṅkagatā ivoṣṭrāḥ /
Vṛkodaraṃ vāraṇarājadarpaṃ
yodhās tvadīyā bhayavignasattvāḥ //
anīkamadhye tiṣṭhantaṃ rājaputraṃ durāsadam /
abravīd Bharataśreṣṭhaṃ Guḍākeśaṃ Janārdanaḥ //
Vāsudeva uvāca /
15 *ya eṣa goptā pratapan balastho*
yo naḥ senāṃ siṃha ivekṣate ca /
sa eṣa Bhīṣmaḥ Kuruvaṃśaketur
yenāhṛtās triṃśato vājimedhāḥ //
etāny anīkāni mahānubhāvaṃ
gūhanti meghā iva gharmaraśmim /
etāni hatvā puruṣapravīra
kāṅkṣasva yuddhaṃ Bharatarṣabheṇa //

And the seers performed circumambulation
And with litanies lauded the king of men.

The priests who predicted the death of his foes
And the grand old seers who were steeped in the Vedas
Pronounced with prayers, *mantras*, and herbs
Around him the blessings to speed his campaign.

The great-souled chief of the Kurus bestowed
On the brahmins cattle as well as clothes,
And flowers and fruit and breastplates of gold,
And departed like Indra among the Immortals.

With hundreds of bells, and sparkling with fine
Jāmbūnada gold like a thousand suns
Did Arjuna's well-wheeled, white-teamed chariot
Blaze forth like fire with its garland of flames,

10 And the ape-bannered hero, with Keśava[1] driving,
With his Gāṇḍiva bow and arrows in hand,
Advanced, the archer whose equal on earth
Has never been nor shall ever be.

The future destroyer of your sons' army
Who now bore an aspect exceedingly fearsome,
He who strong-armed though unarmed with his bare arms
Burned elephants, horses, and men in a battle:

He Bhīmasena the Wolf-Belly guarded
With the twins the chariot of Arjuna;
And spying him, image of Indra on earth,
A raging bull and a lion in sport,

That fort of a man in front of the army,
Wolf-Belly as proud as an elephant king,
Your warriors felt mettle ebbing in terror
And shivered like camels enmeshed in the mud.

Janārdana said to Bharata chief Guḍākeśa, the unassailable son of a king who stood in the middle of the troops,

Vāsudeva said:

15 There stands he, Bhīṣma, the Kauravas' standard,
The commander ablaze in the midst of his troops,
Who looks like a lion upon our army,
Who thirty times offered the Rite of the Horse.

The majestic man is covered by troops
As rain clouds cover the hot-rayed sun:
Destroy them all, thou hero of men,
And seek to combat that Bharata bull!

Dhṛtarāṣṭra uvāca /
keṣāṃ prahṛṣṭās tatrāgre yodhā yudhyanti Saṃjaya /
udagramanasaḥ ke 'tra ke vā dīnā vicetasaḥ //
ke pūrvaṃ prāharaṃs tatra yuddhe hṛdayakampane /
māmakāḥ Pāṇḍavānāṃ vā tan mamācakṣva Saṃjaya //
kasya senāsamudaye gandhamālyasamudbhavaḥ /
vācaḥ pradakṣiṇāś caiva yodhānām abhigarjatām //
Saṃjaya uvāca /
20 *ubhayoḥ senayos tatra yodhā jahṛṣire mudā /*
sragdhūpapānagandhānām ubhayatra samudbhavaḥ //
saṃhatānām anīkānāṃ vyūḍhānāṃ Bharatarṣabha /
saṃsarpatām udīrṇānāṃ vimardaḥ sumahān abhūt //
vāditraśabdas tumulaḥ śaṅkhabherīvimiśritaḥ /
kuñjarāṇāṃ ca nadatāṃ sainyānāṃ ca prahṛṣyatām //

Dhṛtarāṣṭra uvāca /
23[1].1 *dharmakṣetre Kurukṣetre samavetā yuyutsavaḥ /*
māmakāḥ Pāṇḍavāś caiva kim akurvata Saṃjaya //
Saṃjaya uvāca /
dṛṣṭvā tu Pāṇḍavānīkaṃ vyūḍhaṃ Duryodhanas tadā /
ācāryam upasaṃgamya rājā vacanam abravīt //
paśyaitāṃ Pāṇḍuputrāṇām ācārya mahatīṃ camūm /
vyūḍhāṃ Drupadaputreṇa tava śiṣyeṇa dhīmatā //
atra śūrā maheṣvāsā Bhīma-Arjunasamā yudhi /
Yuyudhāno Virāṭaś ca Drupadaś ca mahārathaḥ //
5 *Dhṛṣṭaketuś Cekitānaḥ Kāśirājaś ca vīryavān /*
Purujit Kuntibhojaś ca Śaibyaś ca narapuṃgavaḥ //
Yudhāmanyuś ca vikrānta Uttamaujāś ca vīryavān /
Saubhadro Draupadeyāś ca sarva eva mahārathāḥ //
asmākaṃ tu viśiṣṭā ye tān nibodha dvijottama /
nāyakā mama sainyasya saṃjñārthaṃ tān bravīmi te //
bhavān Bhīṣmaś ca Karṇaś ca Kṛpaś ca samitiṃjayaḥ /
Aśvatthāmā Vikarṇaś ca Saumadattis tathaiva ca //
anye ca bahavaḥ śūrā madarthe tyaktajīvitāḥ /
nānāśastrapraharaṇāḥ sarve yuddhaviśāradāḥ //
10 *aparyāptaṃ tad asmākaṃ balaṃ Bhīmābhirakṣitam /*
paryāptaṃ tv idam eteṣāṃ balaṃ Bhīṣmābhirakṣitam //
ayaneṣu ca sarveṣu yathābhāgam avasthitāḥ /
Bhīṣmam evābhirakṣantu bhavantaḥ sarva eva hi //
tasya saṃjanayan harṣaṃ Kuruvṛddhaḥ pitāmahaḥ /
siṃhanādaṃ vinadyoccaiḥ śaṅkhaṃ dadhmau pratāpavān //
tataḥ śaṅkhāś ca bheryaś ca paṇavānakagomukhāḥ /
sahasaivābhyahanyanta sa śabdas tumulo 'bhavat //
tataḥ śvetair hayair yukte mahati syandane sthitau /
Mādhavaḥ Pāṇḍavaś caiva divyau śaṅkhau pradadhmatuḥ //

Dhṛtarāṣṭra said:
Whose warriors, Saṃjaya, were the first to give battle exultantly?
Who were in cheerful spirits there? Who lost heart and wits? Who
were the first to strike in that heart-shattering war, my men or the
Pāṇḍavas'? Saṃjaya, tell me! In whose multitudinous army was there
a smell of fragrant flowers, and was the speech of the thunderous
warriors devout?
Saṃjaya said:
20 The warriors in both armies exulted, and in both rose a fragrance
of flowers and incense. The first clash of the massed, marshaled troops
that slowly and proudly advanced was magnificent, and the sound of
music mixed with peals of conches and drums and the noise of roaring
elephants and churning troops were deafening.

Dhṛtarāṣṭra said:
23[1].1 When in the Field of the Kurus, the Field of the Law, my troops
and the Pāṇḍavas had massed belligerently, what did they do,
Saṃjaya?
Saṃjaya said:
When King Duryodhana saw the Pāṇḍava's army arrayed, he
approached the Teacher and said, "Look at that mighty host of the
sons of Pāṇḍu, marshaled by Drupada's son,[1] your sagacious student!
There are champions there, great archers, the likes of Bhīma and
5 Arjuna in battle—Yuyudhāna, Virāṭa, the great warrior Drupada,
Dhṛṣṭaketu, Cekitāna, the gallant king of the Kāśis, Purujit Kuntibhoja,
and the Śaibya, a bull among men, valiant Yudhāmanyu and gallant
Uttamaujas, Saubhadra and the Draupadeyas, all good warriors. But
now hear, best of brahmins, about our outstanding men, the leaders
of my army, I mention them by name: yourself, Bhīṣma, Karṇa, Kṛpa,
Samitiṃjaya, Aśvatthāman, Vikarṇa, the son of Somadatta, and many
other heroes who are laying down their lives for me, all experienced
10 fighters with many kinds of weapons. Their army, protected by Bhīma,
is no match for us, but this army, protected by Bhīṣma, is a match for
them. All of you, stationed at your positions, must defend Bhīṣma at
all passages!"
Then grandfather, the majestic elder of the Kurus, roared loud his
lion's roar, bringing joy to Duryodhana, and blew his conch. On a
sudden, thereupon, conches, kettledrums, cymbals, drums and clarions
were sounded, and there was a terrifying noise. The Mādhava and
Pāṇḍava, standing on their chariot yoked with the four white horses,

15 *Pāñcajanyaṃ Hṛṣīkeśo Devadattaṃ Dhanaṃjayaḥ /*
Pauṇḍraṃ dadhmau mahāśaṅkhaṃ bhīmakarmā Vṛkodaraḥ //
Anantavijayaṃ rājā Kuntīputro Yudhiṣṭhiraḥ /
Nakulaḥ Sahadevaś ca Sughoṣa-Maṇipuṣpakau //
Kāśyaś ca parameṣvāsaḥ Śikhaṇḍī ca mahārathaḥ /
Dhṛṣṭadyumno Virāṭaś ca Sātyakiś cāparājitaḥ //
Drupado Draupadeyāś ca sarvaśaḥ pṛthivīpate /
Saubhadraś ca mahābāhuḥ śaṅkhān dadhmuḥ pṛthak pṛthak //
sa ghoṣo Dhārtarāṣṭrāṇāṃ hṛdayāni vyadārayat /
nabhaś ca pṛthivīṃ caiva tumulo vyanunādayat //
20 *atha vyavasthitān dṛṣṭvā Dhārtarāṣṭrān kapidhvajaḥ /*
pravṛtte śastrasaṃpāte dhanur udyamya Pāṇḍavaḥ //
Hṛṣīkeśaṃ tadā vākyam idam āha mahīpate /
senayor ubhayor madhye rathaṃ sthāpaya me 'cyuta //
yāvad etān nirīkṣe 'haṃ yoddhukāmān avasthitān /
kair mayā saha yoddhavyam asmin raṇasamudyame //
yotsyamānān avekṣe 'haṃ ya ete 'tra samāgatāḥ /
Dhārtarāṣṭrasya durbuddher yuddhe priyacikīrṣavaḥ //
evam ukto Hṛṣīkeśo Guḍākeśena Bhārata /
senayor ubhayor madhye sthāpayitvā rathottamam //
25 *Bhīṣma-Droṇapramukhataḥ sarveṣāṃ ca mahīkṣitām /*
uvāca Pārtha paśyaitān samavetān Kurūn iti //
tatrāpaśyat sthitān Pārthaḥ pitṝn atha pitāmahān /
ācāryān mātulān bhrātṝn putrān pautrān sakhīṃs tathā //
śvaśurān suhṛdaś caiva senayor ubhayor api /
tān samīkṣya sa Kaunteyaḥ sarvān bandhūn avasthitān //
kṛpayā parayāviṣṭo viṣīdann idam abravīt /
Arjuna uvāca /
dṛṣṭvemān svajanān Kṛṣṇa yuyutsūn samavasthitān //
sīdanti mama gātrāṇi mukhaṃ ca pariśuṣyati /
vepathuś ca śarīre me romaharṣaś ca jāyate //
30 *Gāṇḍīvaṃ sraṃsate hastāt tvak caiva paridahyate /*
na ca śaknomy avasthātuṃ bhramatīva ca me manaḥ //
nimittāni ca paśyāmi viparītāni Keśava /
na ca śreyo 'nupaśyāmi hatvā svajanam āhave //
na kāṅkṣe vijayaṃ Kṛṣṇa na ca rājyaṃ sukhāni ca /
kiṃ no rājyena Govinda kiṃ bhogair jīvitena vā //
yeṣām arthe kāṅkṣitaṃ no rājyaṃ bhogāḥ sukhāni ca /
ta eva naḥ sthitā yoddhuṃ prāṇāṃs tyaktvā sudustyajān //
ācāryāḥ pitaraḥ putrās tathaiva ca pitāmahāḥ /
mātulāḥ śvaśurāḥ pautrāḥ syālāḥ saṃbandhinas tathā //
35 *etān na hantum icchāmi ghnato 'pi Madhusūdana /*
api trailokyarājyasya hetoḥ kiṃ nu mahīkṛte //
nihatya Dhārtarāṣṭrān naḥ kā prītiḥ syāj Janārdana /
pāpam evāśrayed asmān hatvaitān ātatāyinaḥ //

15 both blew their conches—Hṛṣīkeśa[2] his Pāñcajanya, Dhanaṃjaya his
Devadatta. Wolf-Belly of the terrible deeds blew his great conch
Pauṇḍra, Nakula and Sahadeva their Sughoṣa and Maṇipuṣpaka. The
Kāśi king, a great archer, the mighty warrior Śikhaṇḍin,
Dhṛṣṭadyumna, Virāṭa and the undefeated Sātyaki, Drupada and all
the Draupadeyas, O king of the earth, and strong-armed Saubhadra,
each blew his conch. The sound rent the hearts of the Dhārtarāṣṭras
and reverberated fearfully through sky and earth.
20 The ape-bannered Pāṇḍava, seeing the Dhārtarāṣṭras in position,
lifted his bow when the clash of arms began, O king, and said to
Hṛṣīkeśa, "Acyuta, station my chariot in between the two armies, far
enough for me to see the eager warriors in position—for, whom am
I to fight in this enterprise of war? I want to see the men who are
about to give battle, who have come together here to do a favor to the
evil-spirited Duryodhana."
At Guḍākeśa's words, O Bhārata, Hṛṣīkeśa stationed the fine chariot
25 between the two armies, before Bhīṣma, Droṇa and all the kings, and
he said to the Pārtha, "Behold the Kurus assembled!" The Pārtha
saw them stand there, fathers, grandfathers, teachers, maternal
uncles, brothers, sons, grandsons, friends, fathers-in-law, and good
companions, in both armies. Watching all his relatives stand arrayed,
he was overcome with the greatest compassion, and he said
despairingly, "Kṛṣṇa, when I see all my family poised for war, my
limbs falter and my mouth goes dry. There is a tremor in my body
30 and my hairs bristle. Gāṇḍīva is slipping from my hand and my skin
is burning, I am not able to hold my ground and my mind seems to
whirl. And I see contrary portents, Keśava, but I see no good to come
from killing my family in battle! I do not wish victory, Keśava, nor
kingship and pleasures. What use is kingship to us, Govinda? What
use are comforts and life? The very men for whose sake we want
kingship, comforts, and joy, stand in line to battle us, forfeiting their
hard-to-relinquish lives! Teachers, fathers, sons, grandfathers,
35 maternal uncles, fathers-in-law, grandsons, brothers-in-law, and other
relatives-in-law—I do not want to kill them, though they be killers,
Madhusūdana, even for the sovereignty of the three worlds, let alone
earth!

"What joy is left, Janārdana, after we have killed the Dhārtarāṣṭras?
Nothing but guilt will accrue to us if we kill these assassins! Therefore

tasmān nārhā vayaṃ hantuṃ Dhārtarāṣṭrān sabāndhavān /
svajanaṃ hi kathaṃ hatvā sukhinaḥ syāma Mādhava //
yady apy ete na paśyanti lobhopahatacetasaḥ /
kulakṣayakṛtaṃ doṣaṃ mitradrohe ca pātakam //
kathaṃ na jñeyam asmābhiḥ pāpād asmān nivartitum /
kulakṣayakṛtaṃ doṣaṃ prapaśyadbhir Janārdana //
40 *kulakṣaye praṇaśyanti kuladharmāḥ sanātanāḥ /*
dharme naṣṭe kulaṃ kṛtsnam adharmo 'bhibhavaty uta //
adharmābhibhavāt Kṛṣṇa praduṣyanti kulastriyaḥ /
strīṣu duṣṭāsu Vārṣṇeya jāyate varṇasaṃkaraḥ //
saṃkaro narakāyaiva kulaghnānāṃ kulasya ca /
patanti pitaro hy eṣāṃ luptapiṇḍodakakriyāḥ //
doṣair etaiḥ kulaghnānāṃ varṇasaṃkarakārakaiḥ /
utsādyante jātidharmāḥ kuladharmāś ca śāśvatāḥ //
utsannakuladharmāṇāṃ manuṣyāṇāṃ Janārdana /
narake niyataṃ vāso bhavatīty anuśuśruma //
45 *aho bata mahat pāpaṃ kartuṃ vyavasitā vayam /*
yad rājyasukhalobhena hantuṃ svajanam udyatāḥ //
yadi mām apratīkāram aśastraṃ śastrapāṇayaḥ /
Dhārtarāṣṭrā raṇe hanyus tan me kṣemataraṃ bhavet //
Saṃjaya uvāca /
evam uktvā-Arjunaḥ saṃkhye rathopastha upāviśat /
visṛjya saśaraṃ cāpaṃ śokasaṃvignamānasaḥ //

Saṃjaya uvāca /
24[2].1 *taṃ tathā kṛpayāviṣṭam aśrupūrṇākulekṣaṇam /*
viṣīdantam idaṃ vākyam uvāca Madhusūdanaḥ //
Śrībhagavān uvāca /
kutas tvā kaśmalam idaṃ viṣame samupasthitam /
anāryajuṣṭam asvargyam akīrtikaram Arjuna //
klaibyaṃ mā sma gamaḥ Pārtha naitat tvayy upapadyate /
kṣudraṃ hṛdayadaurbalyaṃ tyaktvottiṣṭha paraṃtapa //
Arjuna uvāca /
kathaṃ Bhīṣmam ahaṃ saṃkhye Droṇaṃ ca Madhusūdana /
iṣubhiḥ pratiyotsyāmi pūjārhāv arisūdana //
5 *gurūn ahatvā hi mahānubhāvāñ*
śreyo bhoktuṃ bhaikṣam apīha loke /
hatvārthakāmāṃs tu gurūn ihaiva
bhuñjīya bhogān rudhirapradigdhān //
na caitad vidmaḥ kataran no garīyo
yad vā jayema yadi vā no jayeyuḥ /
yān eva hatvā na jijīviṣāmas
te 'vasthitāḥ pramukhe Dhārtarāṣṭrāḥ //

we must not kill the Dhārtarāṣṭras and our kin, for how can we be happy when we have killed family, Mādhava? Even if their minds are so sick with greed that they do not see the evil that is brought on by the destruction of family, and the crime that lurks in the betrayal of friendship, how can *we* fail to know enough to shrink from this crime, we who do see the evil brought on by the destruction of family, Janārdana?

40 "With the destruction of family the eternal family Laws are destroyed. When Law is destroyed, lawlessness besets the entire family. From the prevalence of lawlessness the women of the family become corrupt, Kṛṣṇa; when the women are corrupt, there is class miscegenation, and miscegenation leads to hell for family killers and family. Their ancestors tumble, their rites of riceball and water disrupted. These evils of family killers that bring about class miscegenation cause the sempiternal class Laws and family Laws to be cast aside. For men who have cast aside their family Laws a place in hell is assured, as we have been told.

45 "Woe! We have resolved to commit a great crime as we stand ready to kill family out of greed for kingship and pleasures! It were healthier for me if the Dhārtarāṣṭras, weapons in hand, were to kill me, unarmed and defenseless, on the battlefield!"

Having spoken thus, on that field of battle, Arjuna sat down in the chariot pit, letting go of arrows and bow, his heart anguished with grief.

Saṃjaya said:

24[2].1 Then, to this Arjuna who was so overcome with compassion, despairing, his troubled eyes filled with tears, Madhusūdana said—

The Lord said:

Why has this mood come over you at this bad time, Arjuna, this cowardice unseemly to the noble, not leading to heaven, dishonorable? Do not act like a eunuch, Pārtha, it does not become you! Rid yourself of this vulgar weakness of heart, stand up, enemy-burner!

Arjuna said:

How can I fight back at Bhīṣma with my arrows in battle, or at Droṇa, Madhusūdana? Both deserve my homage, enemy-slayer!

5 It were better that without slaying my gurus
I went begging instead for alms in this land
Than that I by slaying my covetous gurus
Indulge in the joys that are dipped in their blood.

And we do not know what is better for us:
That we defeat them or they defeat us;
Dhṛtarāṣṭra's men are positioned before us,
After killing whom we have nothing to live for.

kārpaṇyadoṣopahatasvabhāvaḥ
pṛcchāmi tvā dharmasaṃmūḍhacetāḥ /
yac chreyaḥ syān niścitaṃ brūhi tan me
śiṣyas te 'haṃ śādhi māṃ tvāṃ prapannam //
na hi prapaśyāmi mamāpanudyād
yac chokam ucchoṣaṇam indriyāṇām /
avāpya bhūmāv asapatnam ṛddhaṃ
rājyaṃ surāṇām api cādhipatyam //
Saṃjaya uvāca /
evam uktvā Hṛṣīkeśaṃ Guḍākeśaḥ paraṃtapa /
na yotsya iti Govindam uktvā tūṣṇīṃ babhūva ha //
10 *tam uvāca Hṛṣīkeśaḥ prahasann iva Bhārata /*
senayor ubhayor madhye viṣīdantam idaṃ vacaḥ //
Śrībhagavān uvāca /
aśocyān anvaśocas tvaṃ prajñāvādāṃś ca bhāṣase /
gatāsūn agatāsūṃś ca nānuśocanti paṇḍitāḥ //
na tv evāhaṃ jātu nāsaṃ na tvaṃ neme janādhipāḥ /
na caiva na bhaviṣyāmaḥ sarve vayam ataḥ param //
dehino 'smin yathā dehe kaumāraṃ yauvanaṃ jarā /
tathā dehāntaraprāptir dhīras tatra na muhyati //
mātrāsparśās tu Kaunteya śītoṣṇasukhaduḥkhadāḥ /
āgamāpāyino 'nityās tāṃs titikṣasva Bhārata //
15 *yaṃ hi na vyathayanty ete puruṣaṃ puruṣarṣabha /*
samaduḥkhasukhaṃ dhīraṃ so 'mṛtatvāya kalpate //
nāsato vidyate bhāvo nābhāvo vidyate sataḥ /
ubhayor api dṛṣṭo 'ntas tv anayos tattvadarśibhiḥ //
avināśi tu tad viddhi yena sarvam idaṃ tatam /
vināśam avyayasyāsya na kaścit kartum arhati //
antavanta ime dehā nityasyoktāḥ śarīriṇaḥ /
anāśino 'prameyasya tasmād yudhyasva Bhārata //
ya enaṃ vetti hantāraṃ yaś cainaṃ manyate hatam /
ubhau tau na vijānīto nāyaṃ hanti na hanyate //
20 *na jāyate mriyate vā kadācin*
nāyaṃ bhūtvā bhavitā vā na bhūyaḥ /
ajo nityaḥ śāśvato 'yaṃ purāṇo
na hanyate hanyamāne śarīre //
vedāvināśinaṃ nityaṃ ya enam ajam avyayam /
kathaṃ sa puruṣaḥ Pārtha kaṃ ghātayati hanti kam //
vāsāṃsi jīrṇāni yathā vihāya
navāni gṛhṇāti naro 'parāṇi /

My nature afflicted with the vice of despair,
My mind confused over what is the Law,
I ask, what is better? Pray tell me for sure,
Pray guide me, your student who asks for your help!

There is nothing I see that might dispel
This sorrow that desiccates my senses,
If on earth I were to obtain without rivals
A kingdom, nay even the reign of the Gods!

Saṃjaya said:

Having spoken thus to Hṛṣīkeśa, enemy-burner Guḍākeśa said to Govinda, "I will not fight!" and fell silent. And with a hint of laughter Hṛṣīkeśa spoke to him who sat forlorn between the two armies, O Bhārata—

The Lord said:

You sorrow over men you should not be sorry for, and yet you speak to sage issues. The wise are not sorry for either the living or the dead. Never was there a time when I did not exist, or you, or these kings, nor shall any of us cease to exist hereafter. Just as creatures with bodies pass through childhood, youth, and old age in their bodies, so there is a passage to another body, and a wise man is not confused about it. The contacts of the senses with their objects, which produce sensations of cold and heat, comfort and discomfort, come and go without staying, Kaunteya. Endure them, Bhārata. The wise man whom they do not trouble, for whom happiness and unhappiness are the same, is fit for immortality.

There is no becoming of what did not already exist, there is no unbecoming of what does exist: those who see the principles see the boundary between the two.[1] But know that that on which all this world is strung is imperishable: no one can bring about the destruction of this indestructible. What ends of this unending embodied, indestructible, and immeasurable being is just its bodies—therefore fight, Bhārata! He who thinks that this being is a killer and he who imagines that it is killed do neither of them know. It is not killed nor does it kill.

It is never born nor does it die;
Nor once that it is will it ever not be;
Unborn, unending, eternal, and ancient
It is not killed when the body is killed.

The man who knows him for what he is—indestructible, eternal, unborn, without end—how does he kill whom or have whom killed, Pārtha?

As a man discards his worn-out clothes
And puts on different ones that are new,

tathā śarīrāṇi vihāya jīrṇāny
anyāni saṃyāti navāni dehī //
nainaṃ chindanti śastrāṇi nainaṃ dahati pāvakaḥ /
na cainaṃ kledayanty āpo na śoṣayati mārutaḥ //
acchedyo 'yam adāhyo 'yam akledyo 'śoṣya eva ca /
nityaḥ sarvagataḥ sthāṇur acalo 'yaṃ sanātanaḥ //
25 *avyakto 'yam acintyo 'yam avikāryo 'yam ucyate /*
tasmād evaṃ viditvainaṃ nānuśocitum arhasi //
atha cainaṃ nityajātaṃ nityaṃ vā manyase mṛtam /
tathāpi tvaṃ mahābāho nainaṃ śocitum arhasi //
jātasya hi dhruvo mṛtyur dhruvaṃ janma mṛtasya ca /
tasmād aparihārye 'rthe na tvaṃ śocitum arhasi //
avyaktādīni bhūtāni vyaktamadhyāni Bhārata /
avyaktanidhanāny eva tatra kā paridevanā //
āścaryavat paśyati kaścid enam
āścaryavad vadati tathaiva cānyaḥ /
āścaryavac cainam anyaḥ śṛṇoti
śrutvāpy enaṃ veda na caiva kaścit //
30 *dehī nityam avadhyo 'yaṃ dehe sarvasya Bhārata /*
tasmāt sarvāṇi bhūtāni na tvaṃ śocitum arhasi //
svadharmam api cāvekṣya na vikampitum arhasi /
dharmyād dhi yuddhāc chreyo 'nyat kṣatriyasya na vidyate //
yadṛcchayā copapannaṃ svargadvāram apāvṛtam /
sukhinaḥ kṣatriyāḥ Pārtha labhante yuddham īdṛśam //
atha cet tvam imaṃ dharmyaṃ saṃgrāmaṃ na kariṣyasi /
tataḥ svadharmaṃ kīrtiṃ ca hitvā pāpam avāpsyasi //
akīrtiṃ cāpi bhūtāni kathayiṣyanti te 'vyayām /
saṃbhāvitasya cākīrtir maraṇād atiricyate //
35 *bhayād raṇād uparataṃ maṃsyante tvāṃ mahārathāḥ /*
yeṣāṃ ca tvaṃ bahumato bhūtvā yāsyasi lāghavam //
avācyavādāṃś ca bahūn vadiṣyanti tavāhitāḥ /
nindantas tava sāmarthyaṃ tato duḥkhataraṃ nu kim //
hato vā prāpsyasi svargaṃ jitvā vā bhokṣyase mahīm /
tasmād uttiṣṭha Kaunteya yuddhāya kṛtaniścayaḥ //
sukhaduḥkhe same kṛtvā lābhālābhau jayājayau /
tato yuddhāya yujyasva naivaṃ pāpam avāpsyasi //
eṣā te 'bhihitā sāṃkhye buddhir yoge tv imāṃ śṛṇu /
buddhyā yukto yayā Pārtha karmabandhaṃ prahāsyasi //
40 *nehābhikramanāśo 'sti pratyavāyo na vidyate /*
svalpam apy asya dharmasya trāyate mahato bhayāt //
vyavasāyātmikā buddhir ekeha Kurunandana /
bahuśākhā hy anantāś ca buddhayo 'vyavasāyinām //
yām imāṃ puṣpitāṃ vācaṃ pravadanty avipaścitaḥ /
vedavādaratāḥ Pārtha nānyad astīti vādinah //

> So the one in the body discards aged bodies
> And joins with other ones that are new.

Swords do not cut him, fire does not burn him, water does not wet
him, wind does not parch him. He cannot be cut, he cannot be
burned, wetted, or parched, for he is eternal, ubiquitous, stable,
25 unmoving, and forever. He is the unmanifest, beyond thought, he is
said to be beyond transformation; therefore if you know him as such,
you have no cause for grief.

Or suppose you hold that he is constantly born and constantly
dead, you still have no cause to grieve over him, strong-armed prince,
for to the born death is assured, and birth is assured to the dead;
therefore there is no cause for grief, if the matter is inevitable.
Bhārata, with creatures their beginnings are unclear, their middle
periods are clear, and their ends are unclear—why complain about it?

> It is by a rare chance that a man does see him,
> It's a rarity too if another proclaims him,
> A rare chance that someone else will hear him,
> And even if hearing him no one knows him.

30 This embodied being is in anyone's body forever beyond killing,
Bhārata; therefore you have no cause to sorrow over any creatures.
Look to your Law and do not waver, for there is nothing more
salutary for a baron than a war that is lawful. It is an open door to
heaven, happily happened upon; and blessed are the warriors,
Pārtha, who find a war like that!

Or suppose you will not engage in this lawful war: then you give
up your Law and honor, and incur guilt. Creatures will tell of your
undying shame, and for one who has been honored dishonor is worse
35 than death. The warriors will think that you shrank from the battle
out of fear, and those who once esteemed you highly will hold you of
little account. Your ill-wishers will spread many unspeakable tales
about you, condemning your skill—and what is more miserable than
that?

Either you are killed and will then attain to heaven, or you triumph
and will enjoy the earth. Therefore rise up, Kaunteya, resolved upon
battle! Holding alike happiness and unhappiness, gain and loss, victory
and defeat, yoke yourself to the battle, and so do not incur evil.

This is the spirit[2] according to theory;[3] now hear how this spirit
applies in practice,[4] yoked with which you will cut away the bondage
40 of the act. In this there is no forfeiture of effort, nor an obstacle to
completion;[5] even very little of *this* Law[6] saves from great peril. This
one spirit is defined here as singleness of purpose, scion of Kuru,
whereas the spirits of those who are not purposeful are countless and
many-branched.[7] This flowering language which the unenlightened
expound,[8] they who delight in the disputations[9] on the Veda, holding

kāmātmānaḥ svargaparā janmakarmaphalapradām /
kriyāviśeṣabahulāṃ bhogaiśvaryagatiṃ prati //
bhogaiśvaryaprasaktānāṃ tayāpahṛtacetasām /
vyavasāyātmikā buddhiḥ samādhau na vidhīyate //
45 *traiguṇyaviṣayā vedā nistraiguṇyo bhava-Arjuna /*
nirdvaṃdvo nityasattvastho niryogakṣema ātmavān //
yāvān artha udapāne sarvataḥ saṃplutodake /
tāvān sarveṣu vedeṣu brāhmaṇasya vijānataḥ //
karmaṇy evādhikāras te mā phaleṣu kadācana /
mā karmaphalahetur bhūr mā te saṅgo 'stv akarmaṇi //
yogasthaḥ kuru karmāṇi saṅgaṃ tyaktvā Dhanaṃjaya /
siddhyasiddhyoḥ samo bhūtvā samatvaṃ yoga ucyate //
dūreṇa hy avaraṃ karma buddhiyogād Dhanaṃjaya /
buddhau śaraṇam anviccha kṛpaṇāḥ phalahetavaḥ //
50 *buddhiyukto jahātīha ubhe sukṛtaduṣkṛte /*
tasmād yogāya yujyasva yogaḥ karmasu kauśalam //
karmajaṃ buddhiyuktā hi phalaṃ tyaktvā manīṣiṇaḥ /
janmabandhavinirmuktāḥ padaṃ gacchanty anāmayam //
yadā te mohakalilaṃ buddhir vyatitariṣyati /
tadā gantāsi nirvedaṃ śrotavyasya śrutasya ca //
śrutivipratipannā te yadā sthāsyati niścalā /
samādhāv acalā buddhis tadā yogam avāpsyasi //
Arjuna uvāca /
sthitaprajñasya kā bhāṣā samādhisthasya Keśava /
sthitadhīḥ kiṃ prabhāṣeta kim āsīta vrajeta kim //
Śrībhagavān uvāca /
55 *prajahāti yadā kāmān sarvān Pārtha manogatān /*
ātmany evātmanā tuṣṭaḥ sthitaprajñas tadocyate //
duḥkheṣv anudvignamanāḥ sukheṣu vigataspṛhaḥ /
vītarāgabhayakrodhaḥ sthitadhīr munir ucyate //
yaḥ sarvatrānabhisnehas tat tat prāpya śubhāśubham /
nābhinandati na dveṣṭi tasya prajñā pratiṣṭhitā //
yadā saṃharate cāyaṃ kūrmo 'ṅgānīva sarvaśaḥ /
indriyāṇīndriyārthebhyas tasya prajñā pratiṣṭhitā //
viṣayā vinivartante nirāhārasya dehinaḥ /
rasavarjaṃ raso 'py asya paraṃ dṛṣṭvā nivartate //

that there is nothing more, Pārtha, inspired by desires, set upon heaven—this language that brings on rebirth as the result of acts and abounds in a variety of rituals aimed at the acquisition of pleasures and power, robs those addicted to pleasures and power of their minds; and on them this spirit, this singleness of purpose in concentration, is not enjoined.[10] The domain of the Vedas is the world of the three *guṇas*:[11] transcend that domain, Arjuna, beyond the pairs of opposites, always abiding in purity, beyond acquisition and conservation, the master of yourself. As much use as there is in a well when water overflows on all sides,[12] so much use is there in all Vedas for the enlightened brahmin.

Your entitlement is only to the rite, not ever at all to its fruits.[13] Be not motivated by the fruits of acts, but also do not purposely seek to avoid acting.[14] Abandon self-interest, Dhanaṃjaya, and perform the acts while applying this singlemindedness. Remain equable in success and failure—this equableness is called the application;[15] for the act as such is far inferior to the application of singleness of purpose to it, Dhanaṃjaya. Seek shelter in this singlemindedness—pitiful are those who are motivated by fruits! Armed with this singleness of purpose, a man relinquishes here both good and evil *karman*.[16] Therefore yoke yourself to this application—this application is the capacity to act.[17] The enlightened who are armed with this singleness of purpose rid themselves of the fruits that follow upon acts; and, set free from the bondage of rebirth,[18] go on to a state of bliss. When you have the desire to cross over this quagmire of delusion, then you will become disenchanted with what is supposed to be revealed, and the revealed itself.[19] When your spirit of purposiveness stands unshaken at cross-purposes with the revealed truth, and immobile in concentration, then you will have achieved the application.

Arjuna said:

What describes the man who stands in concentration, Keśava? What does the one whose insight is firm say? How does he sit? How does he walk?

The Lord said:

A man is called one whose insight is firm when he forsakes all the desirable objects that come to his mind, Pārtha, and is sufficient unto himself. Not distressed in adversities, without craving for pleasures, innocent of passion, fear and anger, he is called a sage whose insight is firm. Firm stands the insight of him who has no preference for anything, whether he meets good or evil, and neither welcomes nor hates either one. When he entirely withdraws his senses from their objects[20] as a tortoise withdraws its limbs, his insight stands firm. For an embodied man who does not eat,[21] the sense objects fade away, except his taste for them; his taste, too, fades when he has seen the highest.

60 *yatato hy api Kaunteya puruṣasya vipaścitaḥ /*
indriyāṇi pramāthīni haranti prasabhaṃ manaḥ //
tāni sarvāṇi saṃyamya yukta āsīta matparaḥ /
vaśe hi yasyendriyāṇi tasya prajñā pratiṣṭhitā //
dhyāyato viṣayān puṃsaḥ saṅgas teṣūpajāyate /
saṅgāt sañjāyate kāmaḥ kāmāt krodho 'bhijāyate //
krodhād bhavati saṃmohaḥ saṃmohāt smṛtivibhramaḥ /
smṛtibhraṃśād buddhināśo buddhināśāt praṇaśyati //
rāgadveṣaviyuktais tu viṣayān indriyaiś caran /
ātmavaśyair vidheyātmā prasādam adhigacchati //
65 *prasāde sarvaduḥkhānāṃ hānir asyopajāyate /*
prasannacetaso hy āśu buddhiḥ paryavatiṣṭhate //
nāsti buddhir ayuktasya na cāyuktasya bhāvanā /
na cābhāvayataḥ śāntir aśāntasya kutaḥ sukham //
indriyāṇāṃ hi caratāṃ yan mano 'nuvidhīyate /
tad asya harati prajñāṃ vāyur nāvam ivāmbhasi //
tasmād yasya mahābāho nigṛhītāni sarvaśaḥ /
indriyāṇīndriyārthebhyas tasya prajñā pratiṣṭhitā //
yā niśā sarvabhūtānāṃ tasyāṃ jāgarti saṃyamī /
yasyāṃ jāgrati bhūtāni sā niśā paśyato muneḥ //
70 *āpūryamāṇam acalapratiṣṭhaṃ*
samudram āpaḥ praviśanti yadvat /
tadvat kāmā yaṃ praviśanti sarve
sa śāntim āpnoti na kāmakāmī //
vihāya kāmān yaḥ sarvān pumāṃś carati niḥspṛhaḥ /
nirmamo nirahaṃkāraḥ sa śāntim adhigacchati //
eṣā brāhmī sthitiḥ Pārtha naināṃ prāpya vimuhyati /
sthitvāsyām antakāle 'pi brahmanirvāṇam ṛcchati //

Arjuna uvāca /
25[3].1 *jyāyasī cet karmaṇas te matā buddhir Janārdana /*
tat kiṃ karmaṇi ghore māṃ niyojayasi Keśava //
vyāmiśreṇaiva vākyena buddhiṃ mohayasīva me /
tad ekaṃ vada niścitya yena śreyo 'ham āpnuyām //
Śrībhagavān uvāca /
loke 'smin dvividhā niṣṭhā purā proktā mayānagha /
jñānayogena sāṃkhyānāṃ karmayogena yoginām //
na karmaṇām anārambhān naiṣkarmyaṃ puruṣo 'śnute /
na ca saṃnyasanād eva siddhiṃ samadhigacchati //
5 *na hi kaścit kṣaṇam api jātu tiṣṭhaty akarmakṛt /*
kāryate hy avaśaḥ karma sarvaḥ prakṛtijair guṇaiḥ //
karmendriyāṇi saṃyamya ya āste manasā smaran /

60 Even of a wise man who tries, Kaunteya, the whirling senses carry
off the mind by force. One should sit down, controlling one's senses,
yoked, and intent on me, for firm stands the insight of him who has
his senses under control. When a man thinks about sense objects, an
interest in them develops. From this interest grows desire, from desire
anger; from anger rises delusion, from delusion loss of memory, from
loss of memory the death of the spirit, and from the death of the
spirit one perishes. When he experiences the objects with senses that
neither love nor hate and are under his control, and thus has himself
under control, he attains to serenity. In a state of serenity all his
65 sufferings cease, for in one whose mind is serene, singleness of purpose
is soon fixed. The one who is not yoked has no singleness of purpose;
the one who is not yoked has no power to bring things about; and he
who does not bring things about knows no serenity—and how can a
man without serenity know happiness? For a mind that is amenable
to the ranging senses carries off a man's capacity for insight, as the
wind a ship at sea. Therefore the insight of him is firm who keeps his
senses entirely away from their objects, strong-armed prince. The
controlled man wakes in what is night for all creatures, as it is night
for the seer of vision when the other creatures are awake.

70 If all objects of wishes flow into a man
As rivers flow into the ocean bed
Which, while being filled, stays unmoved to its depths,
He becomes serene, not the one who desires them.

The man who forsakes all objects of desire and goes about without cravings, possessiveness, and self-centeredness becomes serene.

This is the stance on *brahman*, Pārtha: having achieved it one is not deluded. Maintaining this stance even in his last hour, he attains to the *nirvāṇa* that is *brahman*.[22]

Arjuna said:

25[3].1 If you hold that insight is superior to action, Janārdana, why then
do you urge me on to fearful action? With quite contradictory words
you seem to confuse my own insight. Therefore tell me definitively
which is the course by which I will attain to the supreme good.

The Lord said:

I have of old propounded, prince sans blame, that in this world
there is a twofold position to take: for those who uphold insight
through a discipline of knowledge, for those who uphold action
through a discipline of action. A person does not avoid incurring
karman just by not performing acts,[1] nor does he achieve success by
5 giving up acts. For no one lives even for a moment without doing
some act, for the three forces[2] of nature cause everyone to act, willy-
nilly. He who, while curbing the faculties of action, yet in his mind

indriyārthān vimūḍhātmā mithyācāraḥ sa ucyate //
yas tv indriyāṇi manasā niyamyārabhate 'rjuna /
karmendriyaiḥ karmayogam asaktaḥ sa viśiṣyate //
niyataṃ kuru karma tvaṃ karma jyāyo hy akarmaṇaḥ /
śarīrayātrāpi ca te na prasidhyed akarmaṇaḥ //
yajñārthāt karmaṇo 'nyatra loko 'yaṃ karmabandhanaḥ /
tadarthaṃ karma Kaunteya muktasaṅgaḥ samācara //
10 *sahayajñāḥ prajāḥ sṛṣṭvā purovāca Prajāpatiḥ /*
anena prasaviṣyadhvam eṣa vo 'stv iṣṭakāmadhuk //
devān bhāvayatānena te devā bhāvayantu vaḥ /
parasparaṃ bhāvayantaḥ śreyaḥ param avāpsyatha //
iṣṭān bhogān hi vo devā dāsyante yajñabhāvitāḥ /
tair dattān apradāyaibhyo yo bhuṅkte stena eva saḥ //
yajñaśiṣṭāśinaḥ santo mucyante sarvakilbiṣaiḥ /
bhuñjate te tv aghaṃ pāpā ye pacanty ātmakāraṇāt //
annād bhavanti bhūtāni parjanyād annasaṃbhavaḥ /
yajñād bhavati parjanyo yajñaḥ karmasamudbhavaḥ //
15 *karma brahmodbhavaṃ viddhi brahmākṣarasamudbhavam /*
tasmāt sarvagataṃ brahma nityaṃ yajñe pratiṣṭhitam //
evaṃ pravartitaṃ cakraṃ nānuvartayatīha yaḥ /
aghāyur indriyārāmo moghaṃ Pārtha sa jīvati //
yas tv ātmaratir eva syād ātmatṛptaś ca mānavaḥ /
ātmany eva ca saṃtuṣṭas tasya kāryaṃ na vidyate //
naiva tasya kṛtenārtho nākṛteneha kaścana /
na cāsya sarvabhūteṣu kaścid arthavyapāśrayaḥ //
tasmād asaktaḥ satataṃ kāryaṃ karma samācara /
asakto hy ācaran karma param āpnoti pūruṣaḥ //
20 *karmaṇaiva hi saṃsiddhim āsthitā Janakādayaḥ /*
lokasaṃgraham evāpi saṃpaśyan kartum arhasi //
yad yad ācarati śreṣṭhas tat tad evetaro janaḥ /
sa yat pramāṇaṃ kurute lokas tad anuvartate //
na me Pārthāsti kartavyaṃ triṣu lokeṣu kiṃcana /
nānavāptam avāptavyaṃ varta eva ca karmaṇi //
yadi hy ahaṃ na varteyaṃ jātu karmaṇy atandritaḥ /
mama vartmānuvartante manuṣyāḥ Pārtha sarvaśaḥ //
utsīdeyur ime lokā na kuryāṃ karma ced aham /
saṃkarasya ca kartā syām upahanyām imāḥ prajāḥ //
25 *saktāḥ karmaṇy avidvāṃso yathā kurvanti Bhārata /*
kuryād vidvāṃs tathāsaktaś cikīrṣur lokasaṃgraham //
na buddhibhedaṃ janayed ajñānāṃ karmasaṅginām /
joṣayet sarvakarmāṇi vidvān yuktaḥ samācaran //
prakṛteḥ kriyamāṇāni guṇaiḥ karmāṇi sarvaśaḥ /
ahaṃkāravimūḍhātmā kartāham iti manyate //

indulges his memories of sense objects is called a self-deceiving
hypocrite. But he who curbs his senses with his mind, Arjuna, and
then disinterestedly undertakes the discipline of action with his action
faculties, stands out. Carry out the fixed acts, for action is better than
failure to act: even the mere maintenance of your body does not
succeed without acting.

All the world is in bondage to the *karman*[3] of action, except for
action for purposes of sacrifice:[4] therefore engage in action for that
10 purpose, disinterestedly, Kaunteya. Prajāpati, after creating creatures
and sacrifice together, said in the beginning: "Ye shall multiply by it,
it shall be the cow that yields your desires. Give ye the Gods being
with it, and the Gods shall give ye being. And thus giving each other
being ye shall attain to the highest good. Themselves enhanced in their
being with sacrifice, the Gods shall give ye the pleasures ye desire: he
who enjoys their gifts without return to them is but a thief." The
strict who eat only what is left over after sacrificing are cleansed of all
taints, while the wicked who cook for themselves alone eat filth.

Creatures exist by food, food grows from rain, rain springs from
15 sacrifice, sacrifice arises from action. This ritual action, you must
know, originates from the *brahman* of the Veda,[5] and this *brahman*
itself issues from the Syllable *OṂ*.[6] Therefore the ubiquitous *brahman*[7]
is forever based upon sacrifice. He who does not keep rolling the
wheel that has been set in motion, indulging his senses in a lifespan
of evil, lives for nothing, Pārtha. On the other hand, a man who
delights in the self, is satiated with the self, is completely contented
with the self alone, has nothing left to do. He has no reason at all to
do anything or not to do anything, nor does he have any incentive
of personal interest in any creature at all. Therefore pursue the daily
tasks disinterestedly, for, while performing his acts without self-
interest, a person obtains the highest good. For it was by acting alone[8]
20 that Janaka and others achieved success, so you too must act while
only looking to what holds together the world.[9] People do whatever
the superior man does: people follow what he sets up as the standard.

I have no task at all to accomplish in these three worlds, Pārtha. I
have nothing to obtain that I do not have already. Yet I move in
action. If I were not to move in action, untiringly, at all times, Pārtha,
people all around would follow my lead. These people would collapse
if I did not act; I would be the author of miscegenation; I would
25 assassinate these creatures. The wise, disinterested man should do his
acts in the same way as the ignorant do, but only to hold the world
together, Bhārata. One should not sow dissension in the minds of the
ignorant, who are interested in their actions: the wise man should
take kindly to all acts, but himself do them in a disciplined fashion.

At any rate, actions are performed by the three forces of nature,
but, deluded by self-attribution, one thinks: "I did it!" But he who

tattvavit tu mahābāho guṇakarmavibhāgayoḥ /
guṇā guṇeṣu vartanta iti matvā na sajjate //
prakṛter guṇasaṃmūḍhāḥ sajjante guṇakarmasu /
tān akṛtsnavido mandān kṛtsnavin na vicālayet //
30 mayi sarvāṇi karmāṇi saṃnyasyādhyātmacetasā /
nirāśīr nirmamo bhūtvā yudhyasva vigatajvaraḥ //
ye me matam idaṃ nityam anutiṣṭhanti mānavāḥ /
śraddhāvanto 'nasūyanto mucyante te 'pi karmabhiḥ //
ye tv etad abhyasūyanto nānutiṣṭhanti me matam /
sarvajñānavimūḍhāṃs tān viddhi naṣṭān acetasaḥ //
sadṛśaṃ ceṣṭate svasyāḥ prakṛter jñānavān api /
prakṛtiṃ yānti bhūtāni nigrahaḥ kiṃ kariṣyati //
indriyasyendriyasyārthe rāgadveṣau vyavasthitau /
tayor na vaśam āgacchet tau hy asya paripanthinau //
35 śreyān svadharmo viguṇaḥ paradharmāt svanuṣṭhitāt /
svadharme nidhanaṃ śreyaḥ paradharmodayād api //
Arjuna uvāca /
atha kena prayukto 'yaṃ pāpaṃ carati pūruṣaḥ /
anicchann api Vārṣṇeya balād iva niyojitaḥ //
Śrībhagavān uvāca /
kāma eṣa krodha eṣa rajoguṇasamudbhavaḥ /
mahāśano mahāpāpmā viddhy enam iha vairiṇam //
dhūmenāvriyate vahnir yathādarśo malena ca /
yatholbenāvṛto garbhas tathā tenedam āvṛtam //
āvṛtaṃ jñānam etena jñānino nityavairiṇā /
kāmarūpeṇa Kaunteya duṣpūreṇānalena vā //
40 indriyāṇi mano buddhir asyādhiṣṭhānam ucyate /
etair vimohayaty eṣa jñānam āvṛtya dehinam //
tasmāt tvam indriyāṇy ādau niyamya Bharatarṣabha /
pāpmānaṃ prajahi hy enaṃ jñānavijñānanāśanam //
indriyāṇi parāṇy āhur indriyebhyaḥ paraṃ manaḥ /
manasas tu parā buddhir yo buddheḥ paratas tu saḥ //
evaṃ buddheḥ paraṃ buddhvā saṃstabhyātmānam ātmanā /
jahi śatruṃ mahābāho kāmarūpaṃ durāsadam //

Śrībhagavān uvāca /
26[4].1 imaṃ Vivasvate yogaṃ proktavān aham avyayam /
Vivasvān Manave prāha Manur Ikṣvākave 'bravīt //
evaṃ paraṃparāprāptam imaṃ rājarṣayo viduḥ /
sa kāleneha mahatā yogo naṣṭaḥ paraṃtapa //
sa evāyaṃ mayā te 'dya yogaḥ proktaḥ purātanaḥ /
bhakto 'si me sakhā ceti rahasyaṃ hy etad uttamam //

knows the principles that govern the distribution of those forces and their actions knows that the forces are operating on the forces, and he takes no interest in actions. Because they are confused about these forces of nature, people identify with the actions of these forces, and he who knows it all has no reason to upset the slow-witted who do not.[10]

30 Leaving all actions to me,[11] with your mind intent upon the universal self, be without personal aspirations or concern for possessions, and fight unconcernedly. They who always follow this view of mine, believing it without disputing it, are freed from their *karman*. But those who do dispute and fail to follow my view, deluded in all they know, they, to be sure, are witless and lost.

Even the man of knowledge behaves according to his nature—creatures follow their natures: who will stop them? Love and hatred lie waiting in the sense and its object: one should not fall into their power, for they ambush one.

35 It is more salutary to carry out your own Law poorly than another's Law well; it is better to die in your own Law than to prosper in another's.

Arjuna said:

What is it that drives a man to commit evil, Vārṣṇeya, however reluctantly, as though propelled by force?

The Lord said:

It is desire, it is anger, which springs from the force of *rajas*, the
great devourer, the great evil: know that that is the enemy here. This
world is clouded by it as fire by smoke, as a mirror by dust, as an
embryo by the caul. The knowledge of the conscient is covered by this
eternal enemy desire, Kaunteya, as by an insatiable fire. The senses,
40 the mind, and the spirit are said to be its lair: by means of them it
clouds knowledge and leads into delusion the one within the body.
Therefore, bull of the Bharatas, first control your senses, then kill off
that evil which destroys insight and knowledge.

The senses, they say, are superior to their objects; the mind is higher than the senses; the spirit is higher than the mind; and beyond the spirit is he. Thus knowing the one beyond the spirit, pull yourself together and kill desire, your indomitable enemy, strong-armed prince!

The Lord said:

26[4].1 I propounded this imperishable Yoga to Vivasvat. Vivasvat transmitted it to Manu; Manu told it to Ikṣvāku. Thus came down the tradition of Yoga which the royal seers knew. Over a long span of time this Yoga was lost on earth, enemy-burner. What I have propounded to you today is this same ancient Yoga, treating you in so doing as my loyal follower and friend, for this is the ultimate mystery.

Arjuna uvāca /
aparaṃ bhavato janma paraṃ janma Vivasvataḥ /
katham etad vijānīyāṃ tvam ādau proktavān iti //
Śrībhagavān uvāca /
5 *bahūni me vyatītāni janmāni tava ca-Arjuna /*
tāny ahaṃ veda sarvāṇi na tvaṃ vettha paraṃtapa //
ajo 'pi sann avyayātmā bhūtānām īśvaro 'pi san /
prakṛtiṃ svām adhiṣṭhāya saṃbhavāmy ātmamāyayā //
yadā yadā hi dharmasya glānir bhavati Bhārata /
abhyutthānam adharmasya tadātmānaṃ sṛjāmy aham //
paritrāṇāya sādhūnāṃ vināśāya ca duṣkṛtām /
dharmasaṃsthāpanārthāya saṃbhavāmi yuge yuge //
janma karma ca me divyam evaṃ yo vetti tattvataḥ /
tyaktvā dehaṃ punarjanma naiti mām eti so 'rjuna //
10 *vītarāgabhayakrodhā manmayā mām upāśritāḥ /*
bahavo jñānatapasā pūtā madbhāvam āgatāḥ //
ye yathā māṃ prapadyante tāṃs tathaiva bhajāmy aham /
mama vartmānuvartante manuṣyāḥ Pārtha sarvaśaḥ //
kāṅkṣantaḥ karmaṇāṃ siddhiṃ yajanta iha devatāḥ /
kṣipraṃ hi mānuṣe loke siddhir bhavati karmajā //
cāturvarṇyaṃ mayā sṛṣṭaṃ guṇakarmavibhāgaśaḥ /
tasya kartāram api māṃ viddhy akartāram avyayam //
na māṃ karmāṇi limpanti na me karmaphale spṛhā /
iti māṃ yo 'bhijānāti karmabhir na sa badhyate //
15 *evaṃ jñātvā kṛtaṃ karma pūrvair api mumukṣubhiḥ /*
kuru karmaiva tasmāt tvaṃ pūrvaiḥ pūrvataraṃ kṛtam //
kiṃ karma kim akarmeti kavayo 'py atra mohitāḥ /
tat te karma pravakṣyāmi yaj jñātvā mokṣyase 'śubhāt //
karmaṇo hy api boddhavyaṃ boddhavyaṃ ca vikarmaṇaḥ /
akarmaṇaś ca boddhavyaṃ gahanā karmaṇo gatiḥ //
karmaṇy akarma yaḥ paśyed akarmaṇi ca karma yaḥ /
sa buddhimān manuṣyeṣu sa yuktaḥ kṛtsnakarmakṛt //
yasya sarve samārambhāḥ kāmasaṃkalpavarjitāḥ /
jñānāgnidagdhakarmāṇaṃ tam āhuḥ paṇḍitaṃ budhāḥ //
20 *tyaktvā karmaphalāsaṅgaṃ nityatṛpto nirāśrayaḥ /*
karmaṇy abhipravṛtto 'pi naiva kiṃcit karoti saḥ //
nirāśīr yatacittātmā tyaktasarvaparigrahaḥ /
śārīraṃ kevalaṃ karma kurvan nāpnoti kilbiṣam //
yadṛcchālābhasaṃtuṣṭo dvaṃdvātīto vimatsaraḥ /

Arjuna said:

But your birth is recent; Vivasvat's birth belongs to the distant past! How am I to understand that you "propounded it in the beginning"?

The Lord said:

I have known many past births, and so have you, Arjuna. I remember them all, while you do not, enemy-burner. Although indeed I am unborn and imperishable, although I am the lord of the creatures, I do resort to nature, which is mine,[1] and take on birth by my own wizardry. For whenever the Law languishes, Bhārata, and lawlessness flourishes, I create myself. I take on existence from eon to eon, for the rescue of the good and the destruction of the evil, in order to reestablish the Law. He who knows thus the divinity, as in fact it is, of my birth and work, no more returns to rebirth when he dies—he returns to me, Arjuna. There have been many who, rid of passions, fears, and angers, and made pure by the austerities of insight, have immersed themselves in me, resorted to me, and become of one being with me. I share in them in the manner in which they turn to me; for in all their various ways men do follow my trail, Pārtha.

People offer up sacrifices to deities when they want their actions to be crowned with success; for in this world of men the success that follows action follows swiftly. I have created the society of the four classes with due regard for the various distribution of the *guṇas* and the range of their workings: know that I am its author, and that I am forever without *karman*. Actions do not stick to me, for I have no yearning for the fruits of my actions: he who understands me in this way is himself no longer bound by his own actions. The ancient aspirants to release also performed their acts in this same spirit; therefore you too must perform the same act which the ancients performed long ago.

Even wise men are confused about what is "action" and what is "nonaction"—let me tell you what "action" is, and when you know it you shall be free of evil. For one should know about action, know about misaction, and know about nonaction—the course of "action" *is* complex. He is possessed of the right spirit who is able to discern that there is no *karman* in action,[2] while there is *karman* in nonaction; if he among all men is yoked with this spirit[3] he can perform any act. The wise call that man a sage all of whose undertakings are devoid of the intention to achieve an object of desire,[4] for his *karman*[5] has been burned off by the fire of insight. If one engages in an act while forgetting about its fruit, being already fully satisfied and in need of nothing, one does not incur any *karman* at all. He is not polluted when he does only bodily acts, without any expectations,[6] keeping mind and self controlled, and renounces all possessions. Contented with anything that comes his way,[7] beyond the pairs of opposites,

samaḥ siddhāv asiddhau ca kṛtvāpi na nibadhyate //
gatasaṅgasya muktasya jñānāvasthitacetasaḥ /
yajñāyācarataḥ karma samagraṃ pravilīyate //
brahmārpaṇaṃ brahma havir brahmāgnau brahmaṇā hutam /
brahmaiva tena gantavyaṃ brahmakarmasamādhinā //
25 *daivam evāpare yajñaṃ yoginaḥ paryupāsate /*
brahmāgnāv apare yajñaṃ yajñenaivopajuhvati //
śrotrādīnīndriyāṇy anye saṃyamāgniṣu juhvati /
śabdādīn viṣayān anya indriyāgniṣu juhvati //
sarvāṇīndriyakarmāṇi prāṇakarmāṇi cāpare /
ātmasaṃyamayogāgnau juhvati jñānadīpite //
dravyayajñās tapoyajñā yogayajñās tathāpare /
svādhyāyajñānayajñāś ca yatayaḥ saṃśitavratāḥ //
apāne juhvati prāṇaṃ prāṇe 'pānaṃ tathāpare /
prāṇāpānagatī ruddhvā prāṇāyāmaparāyaṇāḥ //
30 *apare niyatāhārāḥ prāṇān prāṇeṣu juhvati /*
sarve 'py ete yajñavido yajñakṣapitakalmaṣāḥ //
yajñaśiṣṭāmṛtabhujo yānti brahma sanātanam /
nāyaṃ loko 'sty ayajñasya kuto 'nyaḥ Kurusattama //
evaṃ bahuvidhā yajñā vitatā brahmaṇo mukhe /
karmajān viddhi tān sarvān evaṃ jñātvā vimokṣyase //
śreyān dravyamayād yajñāj jñānayajñaḥ paraṃtapa /
sarvaṃ karmākhilaṃ Pārtha jñāne parisamāpyate //
tad viddhi praṇipātena paripraśnena sevayā /
upadekṣyanti te jñānaṃ jñāninas tattvadarśinaḥ //
35 *yaj jñātvā na punar moham evaṃ yāsyasi Pāṇḍava /*
yena bhūtāny aśeṣeṇa drakṣyasy ātmany atho mayi //
api ced asi pāpebhyaḥ sarvebhyaḥ pāpakṛttamaḥ /
sarvaṃ jñānaplavenaiva vṛjinaṃ saṃtariṣyasi //
yathaidhāṃsi samiddho 'gnir bhasmasāt kurute 'rjuna /
jñānāgniḥ sarvakarmāṇi bhasmasāt kurute tathā //
na hi jñānena sadṛśaṃ pavitram iha vidyate /
tat svayaṃ yogasaṃsiddhaḥ kālenātmani vindati //
śraddhāvāṃl labhate jñānaṃ tatparaḥ saṃyatendriyaḥ /
jñānaṃ labdhvā parāṃ śāntim acireṇādhigacchati //
40 *ajñaś cāśraddadhānaś ca saṃśayātmā vinaśyati /*
nāyaṃ loko 'sti na paro na sukhaṃ saṃśayātmanaḥ //
yogasaṃnyastakarmāṇaṃ jñānasaṃchinnasaṃśayam /
ātmavantaṃ na karmāṇi nibadhnanti Dhanaṃjaya //
tasmād ajñānasaṃbhūtaṃ hṛtsthaṃ jñānāsinātmanaḥ /
chittvainaṃ saṃśayaṃ yogam ātiṣṭhottiṣṭha Bhārata //

without envy, and equable in success and failure, he is not bound,
even though he acts.

All the *karman* of one who acts sacrificially dissolves when he is
disinterested and freed, and has steadied his thoughts with insight.
Brahman[8] is the offering, *brahman* is the oblation that is poured into
the *brahman* fire by *brahman*: he who thus contemplates the act as
25 nothing but *brahman* must reach *brahman*. There are yogins[9] who
regard sacrifice as directed to deities;[10] others offer up sacrifice by
sacrificing into the fire that is *brahman*. Others offer the senses[11] of
hearing and so forth into the fires of restraint, while others sacrifice
the objects[12] of sound, etc., into the fires of the senses. Others again
offer up all the actions of the senses and those of the vital faculties
into the wisdom-kindled fire of the yoga of self-restraint. There are
sacrificers who offer with substances, others with austerities, others
with yoga, others with knowledge and Vedic study—ascetics all and
strict in their vows. Some sacrifice *prāṇa* into *apāna*[13] and *apāna* into
prāṇa, blocking the passage of *prāṇa* and *apāna* as they practice breath
30 control. Others limit their meals and offer *prāṇas* into *prāṇas*.[14] All of
them know the meaning of sacrifice and destroy their evil with
sacrifice. Living on the elixir that is the remnants of their sacrifice,
they go to the eternal *brahman*. This world is not of him who fails to
sacrifice—could then the higher world be his, best of Kurus?

Thus sacrifices of many kinds are strung in the mouth of
brahman:[15] know that they all spring from action, and knowing this
you shall be free. The sacrifice of knowledge[16] is higher than a
sacrifice of substances, enemy-burner, but all action culminates in
knowledge, Pārtha. Know this: The men of wisdom who see the truth
shall teach you their knowledge, if you submit to them, put questions
35 to them and attend to them. Armed with their knowledge you will no
more fall victim to confusion, and through it you will see all creatures
without exception within yourself and then within me. Even if you
are the worst criminal of them all, you will cross over all villainy
with just your lifeboat of knowledge. Just as a blazing fire reduces its
kindling to ashes, Arjuna, so the fire of knowledge makes ashes of all
karman. For there is no means of purification the like of knowledge;
and in time one will find that knowledge within oneself, when one is
oneself perfected by yoga. The believer who is directed to it and has
40 mastered his senses obtains the knowledge; and having obtained it he
soon finds the greatest peace. The ignorant and unbelieving man who
is riven with doubts perishes: for the doubter there is neither this
world nor the next; nor is there happiness.

Acts do not bind him who has renounced his *karman* through yoga,
cut down his doubts with knowledge, and mastered himself,
Dhanaṃjaya. Therefore cut away this doubt in your heart, which
springs from ignorance, with the sword of knowledge: rise to this yoga
and stand up, Bhārata!

Arjuna uvāca /
27[5].1 *saṃnyāsaṃ karmaṇāṃ Kṛṣṇa punar yogaṃ ca śaṃsasi /*
yac chreya etayor ekaṃ tan me brūhi suniścitaṃ //
Śrībhagavān uvāca /
saṃnyāsaḥ karmayogaś ca niḥśreyasakarāv ubhau /
tayos tu karmasaṃnyāsāt karmayogo viśiṣyate //
jñeyaḥ sa nityasaṃnyāsī yo na dveṣṭi na kāṅkṣati /
nirdvaṃdvo hi mahābāho sukhaṃ bandhāt pramucyate //
sāṃkhyayogau pṛthag bālāḥ pravadanti na paṇḍitāḥ /
ekam apy āsthitaḥ samyag ubhayor vindate phalam //
5 *yat sāṃkhyaiḥ prāpyate sthānaṃ tad yogair api gamyate /*
ekaṃ sāṃkhyaṃ ca yogaṃ ca yaḥ paśyati sa paśyati //
saṃnyāsas tu mahābāho duḥkham āptum ayogataḥ /
yogayukto munir brahma nacireṇādhigacchati //
yogayukto viśuddhātmā vijitātmā jitendriyaḥ /
sarvabhūtātmabhūtātmā kurvann api na lipyate //
naiva kiṃcit karomīti yukto manyeta tattvavit /
paśyañ śṛṇvan spṛśañ jighrann aśnan gacchan svapañ śvasan //
pralapan visṛjan gṛhṇann unmiṣan nimiṣann api /
indriyāṇīndriyārtheṣu vartanta iti dhārayan //
10 *brahmaṇy ādhāya karmāṇi saṅgaṃ tyaktvā karoti yaḥ /*
lipyate na sa pāpena padmapatram ivāmbhasā //
kāyena manasā buddhyā kevalair indriyair api /
yoginaḥ karma kurvanti saṅgaṃ tyaktvātmaśuddhaye //
yuktaḥ karmaphalaṃ tyaktvā śāntim āpnoti naiṣṭhikīm /
ayuktaḥ kāmakāreṇa phale sakto nibadhyate //
sarvakarmāṇi manasā saṃnyasyāste sukhaṃ vaśī /
navadvāre pure dehī naiva kurvan na kārayan //
na kartṛtvaṃ na karmāṇi lokasya sṛjati prabhuḥ /
na karmaphalasaṃyogaṃ svabhāvas tu pravartate //
15 *nādatte kasyacit pāpaṃ na caiva sukṛtaṃ vibhuḥ /*
ajñānenāvṛtaṃ jñānaṃ tena muhyanti jantavaḥ //
jñānena tu tad ajñānaṃ yeṣāṃ nāśitam ātmanaḥ /
teṣām ādityavaj jñānaṃ prakāśayati tat param //
tadbuddhayas tadātmānas tanniṣṭhās tatparāyaṇāḥ /
gacchanty apunarāvṛttiṃ jñānanirdhūtakalmaṣāḥ //

Arjuna said:

27[5].1 You praise the relinquishment of acts[1] and at the same time the practice of them, Kṛṣṇa. Now tell me decidedly which is the better of the two.

The Lord said:

Both the renunciation and the practice of acts lead to the supreme good; but of these two the practice of acts is higher than the renunciation of acts. He is to be counted a perpetual renouncer[2] who neither hates nor desires, for, strong-armed prince, if one transcends the pairs of opposites, one is easily freed from bondage. Only fools propound that insight and the practice of acts are different things, not the wise: by undertaking one you find the full fruit of both.

5 The adepts of insight and the adepts of practice reach one and the same goal: he sees truly who sees that insight and practice are one and the same. True renunciation is hard to accomplish without the practice of yoga,[3] but armed with yoga the sage soon attains to *brahman*. Armed with yoga, pure of soul, master of self and senses, identifying himself with the selves of all creatures, he is not tainted even though he acts. The man of yoga, knowing the truth, knows that while seeing, hearing, touching, smelling, eating, walking, sleeping, breathing, speaking, eliminating, grasping, opening and closing his eyes, he does in fact do nothing,[4] as he realizes that it is only the senses operating on their objects.

10 If one places all *karman*[5] on *brahman* and acts disinterestedly, he is no more stained by evil than a lotus petal by muddy water. Yogins do their acts with body, mind, spirit, and even the senses disengaged, in order to purify the self, without any interest in the acts themselves. The man of yoga, renouncing the fruits of his acts, reaches the peace of the ultimate foundation, while the undisciplined man, who acts on his desires because he is interested in fruits, is fettered by *karman*. Having renounced all *karman* with the mind, the soul dwells, happy and masterful, in its nine-gated fortress,[6] neither doing nor causing acts.

The Lord has not created into people either authorship of acts, or
the acts themselves, or the concatenation of act and fruit: that is the
15 doing of Nature.[7] The lord[8] does not take on any act's evil or good
karman; ignorance obscures insight—that is why people get confused.[9]
Of those, however, who have destroyed this ignorance about the self
with true knowledge, this knowledge illumines like a sun that supreme
reality. Their spirits directed to it, their selves into it, founded on it,
devoted to it, they no more go to return again, for their knowledge
has cleansed away the taints.

vidyāvinayasaṃpanne brāhmaṇe gavi hastini /
śuni caiva śvapāke ca paṇḍitāḥ samadarśinaḥ //
ihaiva tair jitaḥ sargo yeṣāṃ sāmye sthitaṃ manaḥ /
nirdoṣaṃ hi samaṃ brahma tasmād brahmaṇi te sthitāḥ //
20 *na prahṛṣyet priyaṃ prāpya nodvijet prāpya cāpriyam /*
sthirabuddhir asaṃmūḍho brahmavid brahmaṇi sthitaḥ //
bāhyasparśeṣv asaktātmā vindaty ātmani yat sukham /
sa brahmayogayuktātmā sukham akṣayam aśnute //
ye hi saṃsparśajā bhogā duḥkhayonaya eva te /
ādyantavantaḥ Kaunteya na teṣu ramate budhaḥ //
śaknotīhaiva yaḥ soḍhuṃ prāk śarīravimokṣaṇāt /
kāmakrodhodbhavaṃ vegaṃ sa yuktaḥ sa sukhī naraḥ //
yo 'ntaḥsukho 'ntarārāmas tathāntarjyotir eva yaḥ /
sa yogī brahmanirvāṇaṃ brahmabhūto 'dhigacchati //
25 *labhante brahmanirvāṇam ṛṣayaḥ kṣīṇakalmaṣāḥ /*
chinnadvaidhā yatātmānaḥ sarvabhūtahite ratāḥ //
kāmakrodhaviyuktānāṃ yatīnāṃ yatacetasām /
abhito brahmanirvāṇaṃ vartate viditātmanām //
sparśān kṛtvā bahir bāhyāṃś cakṣuś caivāntare bhruvoḥ /
prāṇāpānau samau kṛtvā nāsābhyantaracāriṇau //
yatendriyamanobuddhir munir mokṣaparāyaṇaḥ /
vigatecchābhayakrodho yaḥ sadā mukta eva saḥ //
bhoktāraṃ yajñatapasāṃ sarvalokamaheśvaram /
suhṛdaṃ sarvabhūtānāṃ jñātvā māṃ śāntim ṛcchati //

Śrībhagavān uvāca /
28[6].1 *anāśritaḥ karmaphalaṃ kāryaṃ karma karoti yaḥ /*
sa saṃnyāsī ca yogī ca na niragnir na cākriyaḥ //
yaṃ saṃnyāsam iti prāhur yogaṃ taṃ viddhi Pāṇḍava /
na hy asaṃnyastasaṃkalpo yogī bhavati kaścana //
ārurukṣor muner yogaṃ karma kāraṇam ucyate /
yogārūḍhasya tasyaiva śamaḥ kāraṇam ucyate //
yadā hi nendriyārtheṣu na karmasv anuṣajjate /
sarvasaṃkalpasaṃnyāsī yogārūḍhas tadocyate //
5 *uddhared ātmanātmānaṃ nātmānam avasādayet /*
ātmaiva hy ātmano bandhur ātmaiva ripur ātmanaḥ //
bandhur ātmātmanas tasya yenātmaivātmanā jitaḥ /
anātmanas tu śatrutve vartetātmaiva śatruvat //
jitātmanaḥ praśāntasya param ātmā samāhitaḥ /

Wise are they who see no difference between a learned, well-mannered brahmin, a cow, an elephant, a dog, and an eater of dogs. In this very world they have conquered creation whose minds are rooted in disinterest. For *brahman* is without flaws and indifferent,[10] and therefore they are rooted in *brahman*.
20 He should not rejoice upon finding pleasure, nor sadden when
meeting the unpleasant: the knower of *brahman* who stands upon
brahman is steady of spirit and harbors no delusions. Disinterested in
outer sense impressions, he finds the happiness that is in himself; his
spirit yoked with the yoga[11] of *brahman*, he tastes a happiness that is
permanent. Indeed, the pleasures that spring from sense impressions
are sources of unhappiness, because they have beginnings and ends,
Kaunteya, so the wise man does not indulge in them. The man who
in this very life, before he is freed from his body, is able to withstand
the driving force that gathers from craving and anger, is yoked, is
happy. When he finds happiness within, joy within, light within, this
man of yoga becomes *brahman*, attains to the beatitude that is
25 *brahman*. This beatitude that is *brahman* is achieved by the seers whose
evil has been cast off, whose doubts have been resolved, who have mastered themselves and are dedicated to the well being of all creatures. The beatitude that is *brahman* lies before the ascetics who are rid of craving and anger, who have tamed their thinking and know themselves. Keeping outside the impressions from the outside world, centering the gaze between the eyebrows, evening out inhalation and exhalation within the nostrils, controlling senses, mind, and spirit, totally devoted to release, with no trace left of desire, fear, or anger, the seer is released forever. Knowing that I am the recipient of sacrifices and austerities, the great lord of all the world, the friend of all creatures, he attains serenity.

The Lord said:

28[6].1 He who performs the task set for him without interest in its fruit
is the true renouncer and yogin, not the one who does not maintain
the fire and fails to perform the rites.[1] Know, Pāṇḍava, that what they
proclaim as "renunciation" is precisely this discipline,[2] for no one
becomes a man of discipline without abandoning the intention of
fruits. When a sage wishes to rise to this discipline, action is called his
means; when he has risen to this discipline, serenity is called his
means. For he is said to have risen to the discipline only when he is
interested no longer in sense objects, no longer in his acts, but has
5 renounced all intentions.[3] Let him by himself save himself and not
lower himself, for oneself alone is one's friend, oneself alone one's
enemy. To him his self is a friend who by himself has conquered
himself;[4] but when the man who has not mastered himself is hostile,
he acts as his own enemy. To him who has mastered himself and has

śītoṣṇasukhaduḥkheṣu tathā mānāvamānayoḥ //
jñānavijñānatṛptātmā kūṭastho vijitendriyaḥ /
yukta ity ucyate yogī samaloṣṭāśmakāñcanaḥ //
suhṛnmitrāryudāsīnamadhyasthadveṣyabandhuṣu /
sādhuṣv api ca pāpeṣu samabuddhir viśiṣyate //
10 *yogī yuñjīta satatam ātmānaṃ rahasi sthitaḥ /*
ekākī yatacittātmā nirāśīr aparigrahaḥ //
śucau deśe pratiṣṭhāpya sthiram āsanam ātmanaḥ /
nātyucchritaṃ nātinīcaṃ cailājinakuśottaram //
tatraikāgraṃ manaḥ kṛtvā yatacittendriyakriyaḥ /
upaviśyāsane yuñjyād yogam ātmaviśuddhaye //
samaṃ kāyaśirogrīvaṃ dhārayann acalaṃ sthiraḥ /
saṃprekṣya nāsikāgraṃ svaṃ diśaś cānavalokayan //
praśāntātmā vigatabhīr brahmacārivrate sthitaḥ /
manaḥ saṃyamya maccitto yukta āsīta matparaḥ //
15 *yuñjann evaṃ sadātmānaṃ yogī niyatamānasaḥ /*
śāntiṃ nirvāṇaparamāṃ matsaṃsthām adhigacchati //
nātyaśnatas tu yogo 'sti na caikāntam anaśnataḥ /
na cātisvapnaśīlasya jāgrato naiva ca-Arjuna //
yuktāhāravihārasya yuktaceṣṭasya karmasu /
yuktasvapnāvabodhasya yogo bhavati duḥkhahā //
yadā viniyataṃ cittam ātmany evāvatiṣṭhate /
niḥspṛhaḥ sarvakāmebhyo yukta ity ucyate tadā //
yathā dīpo nivātastho neṅgate sopamā smṛtā /
yogino yatacittasya yuñjato yogam ātmanaḥ //
20 *yatroparamate cittaṃ niruddhaṃ yogasevayā /*
yatra caivātmanātmānaṃ paśyann ātmani tuṣyati //
sukham ātyantikaṃ yat tad buddhigrāhyam atīndriyam /
vetti yatra na caivāyaṃ sthitaś calati tattvataḥ //
yaṃ labdhvā cāparaṃ lābhaṃ manyate nādhikaṃ tataḥ /
yasmin sthito na duḥkhena guruṇāpi vicālyate //
taṃ vidyād duḥkhasaṃyogaviyogaṃ yogasaṃjñitam /
sa niścayena yoktavyo yogo 'nirviṇṇacetasā //
saṃkalpaprabhavān kāmāṃs tyaktvā sarvān aśeṣataḥ /
manasaivendriyagrāmaṃ viniyamya samantataḥ //
25 *śanaiḥ śanair uparamed buddhyā dhṛtigṛhītayā /*
ātmasaṃsthaṃ manaḥ kṛtvā na kiṃcid api cintayet //
yato yato niścarati manaś cañcalam asthiram /
tatas tato niyamyaitad ātmany eva vaśaṃ nayet //
praśāntamanasaṃ hy enaṃ yoginaṃ sukham uttamam /

become serene, the higher self is completely stable, in cold and heat,
in happiness and unhappiness, in honor or abuse. Contented in his
insight and knowledge, firm on his peak, master of his senses, looking
with the same eyes on a lump of clay, a rock, or a piece of gold, he is
called a yogin who is truly "yoked." He is set apart by his equanimity
before friends, allies, enemies, uninvolved parties, neutrals, hateful
folk, and relatives, before good men and evil ones.

10 Let the yogin[5] yoke himself at all times, while remaining in retreat,
solitary, in control of his thoughts, without expectations and without
encumbrances. Let him set up for himself a firm stool in a pure spot,
neither too high nor too low, with a cover of cloth, deerskin, or *kuśa*
grass. As he sits on his seat, let him pinpoint his mind, so that the
workings of mind and senses are under control, and yoke himself to
yoga for the cleansing of his self. Holding body, head, and neck
straight and immobile, let him steadily gaze at the tip of his nose,
without looking anywhere else. Serene, fearless, faithful to his vow of
chastity, and restraining his thinking, let him sit yoked, his thought
15 on me, his intention focused on me. When he thus yokes himself
continuously, the yogin of restrained thought attains to the peace that
lies in me, beyond *nirvāṇa*.[6]

Yoga is neither for him who eats too much or not at all, nor for
him who sleeps too much or keeps himself awake, Arjuna. Sorrow-dispelling yoga is his who has curbed his meals and diversions, curbed
his motions in activities, curbed his sleeping and waking. He is called
"yoked" when his restrained mind has come to rest upon his self
alone and he is without craving for any object of desire. Just as a
candle flame outside a draft does not flicker[7] —that is the well-known
metaphor of a yogin of restrained mind who yokes himself to the yoga
of the self.

20 When thought ceases, curbed by the practice of yoga, when he
himself looks upon himself and is contented with himself, when he
knows a total bliss beyond sensual pleasure, which can be grasped by
the spirit alone, and when he knows it and, once fixed upon it, does
not truly stray from it, when he has acquired it and can think of no
greater acquisition, when firm on it he cannot be swayed even by
profound grief—then he knows that this is the unbinding of his bond
with sorrow, which is called "yoga," and that this yoga must be
yoked on him decisively with undespairing heart.

Renouncing without exception all objects of desire that are rooted
in intentions, taming the village of his senses all around with his
25 mind, he should little by little *cease*, while he holds his spirit with
fortitude, merges his mind in the self, and thinks of nothing at all.
Wherever his volatile mind might stray unsteadily, he halts it and
subdues it in the self. For a higher bliss engulfs the yogin whose mind

upaiti śāntarajasaṃ brahmabhūtam akalmaṣam //
yuñjann evaṃ sadātmānaṃ yogī vigatakalmaṣaḥ /
sukhena brahmasaṃsparśam atyantaṃ sukham aśnute //
sarvabhūtastham ātmānaṃ sarvabhūtāni cātmani /
īkṣate yogayuktātmā sarvatra samadarśanaḥ //
30 *yo māṃ paśyati sarvatra sarvaṃ ca mayi paśyati /*
tasyāhaṃ na praṇaśyāmi sa ca me na praṇaśyati //
sarvabhūtasthitaṃ yo māṃ bhajaty ekatvam āsthitaḥ /
sarvathā vartamāno 'pi sa yogī mayi vartate //
ātmaupamyena sarvatra samaṃ paśyati yo 'rjuna /
sukhaṃ vā yadi vā duḥkhaṃ sa yogī paramo mataḥ //
Arjuna uvāca /
yo 'yaṃ yogas tvayā proktaḥ sāmyena Madhusūdana /
etasyāhaṃ na pasyāmi cañcalatvāt sthitiṃ sthirām //
cañcalaṃ hi manaḥ Kṛṣṇa pramāthi balavad dṛḍham /
tasyāhaṃ nigrahaṃ manye vāyor iva suduṣkaram //
Śrībhagavān uvāca /
35 *asaṃśayaṃ mahābāho mano durnigrahaṃ calam /*
abhyāsena tu Kaunteya vairāgyeṇa ca gṛhyate //
asaṃyatātmanā yogo duṣprāpa iti me matiḥ /
vaśyātmanā tu yatatā śakyo 'vāptum upāyataḥ //
Arjuna uvāca /
ayatiḥ śraddhayopeto yogāc calitamānasaḥ /
aprāpya yogasaṃsiddhiṃ kāṃ gatiṃ Kṛṣṇa gacchati //
kaccin nobhayavibhraṣṭaś chinnābhram iva naśyati /
apratiṣṭho mahābāho vimūḍho brahmaṇaḥ pathi //
etan me saṃśayaṃ Kṛṣṇa chettum arhasy aśeṣataḥ /
tvadanyaḥ saṃśayasyāsya chettā na hy upapadyate //
Śrībhagavān uvāca /
40 *pārtha naiveha nāmutra vināśas tasya vidyate /*
na hi kalyāṇakṛt kaścid durgatiṃ tāta gacchati //
prāpya puṇyakṛtāṃl lokān uṣitvā śāśvatīḥ samāḥ /
śucīnāṃ śrīmatāṃ gehe yogabhraṣṭo 'bhijāyate //
atha vā yoginām eva kule bhavati dhīmatām /
etad dhi durlabhataraṃ loke janma yad īdṛśam //
tatra taṃ buddhisaṃyogaṃ labhate paurvadehikam /
yatate ca tato bhūyaḥ saṃsiddhau Kurunandana //
pūrvābhyāsena tenaiva hriyate hy avaśo 'pi saḥ /
jijñāsur api yogasya śabdabrahmātivartate //
45 *prayatnād yatamānas tu yogī saṃśuddhakilbiṣaḥ /*
anekajanmasaṃsiddhas tato yāti parāṃ gatim //
tapasvibhyo 'dhiko yogī jñānibhyo 'pi mato 'dhikaḥ /
karmibhyaś cādhiko yogī tasmād yogī bhava-Arjuna //

is at peace, whose passions are appeased—who has become *brahman*,
with no more taints.
Yoking himself always in this manner, the taintless yogin
effortlessly savors the infinite bliss that is the touch of *brahman*. Yoked
in yoga, he sees himself in all creatures, all creatures in himself—he
sees everything the same.
30 When he sees me in everything and sees everything in me, I will
not be lost to him and he will not be lost to me. He who shares in me
as living in all creatures and thus becomes one with me, he is a
yogin who, however he moves, moves in me. He is deemed the
ultimate yogin, Arjuna, who, by comparing everything with himself,
sees the same in everything, whether it be blissful or wretched.
Arjuna said:
Madhusūdana, this yoga you propound as equanimity, I cannot see
how it would stay stable, because we are changeful: for, Kṛṣṇa, the
mind is always changing, whirling, domineering, and tough—I see it
as no more susceptible to control than wind itself!
The Lord said:
35 No doubt at all, strong-armed prince, the mercurial mind is hard
to hold down. Yet, Kaunteya, it *can* be held, with tenacity and
dispassion. While I agree that this yoga is hard to achieve for one
who is not master of himself, it can be achieved with the right means
by a self-controlled man who makes the effort.
Arjuna said:
Still, Kṛṣṇa, a non-ascetic who, while having faith, allows his mind
to stray from this yoga before he achieves the ultimate success of yoga
—what becomes of him? Does he not, like a shredded cloud, fade
away, a failure either way,[8] strong-armed lord, without foundation
and astray on the path to *brahman*? Pray resolve this doubt of mine
completely, Kṛṣṇa, for no one can resolve this doubt but you.
The Lord said:
40 No, Pārtha, neither here nor hereafter is he lost, for no one who
does good can go wrong, my friend. He goes to the worlds which are
gained by merit, and when he has dwelled there for years without
end, this "failed yogin" is born high in the house of pure and
prosperous folk, or in the family of wise yogins: indeed, such a birth
is quite rare in this world. There he will recover the purposiveness of
his previous life, scion of Kuru, and strive once more to perfect it. For
a person is sustained, even involuntarily, by his previous application:
desirous of knowing the yoga he proceeds beyond the *brahman* that is
45 the Veda. Then this vigorously striving yogin goes the ultimate
journey, cleansed of evil and perfected in numerous lives. The yogin
surpasses the ascetics, surpasses even the sages who know, surpasses
the workers who merely act. Therefore, Arjuna, become a yogin. Him

yogināṃ api sarveṣāṃ madgatenāntarātmanā /
śraddhāvān bhajate yo māṃ sa me yuktatamo mataḥ //

Śrībhagavān uvāca /
29[7]1. *mayy āsaktamanāḥ Pārtha yogaṃ yuñjan madāśrayaḥ /*
asaṃśayaṃ samagraṃ māṃ yathā jñāsyasi tac chṛṇu //
jñānaṃ te 'haṃ savijñānam idaṃ vakṣyāmy aśeṣataḥ /
yaj jñātvā neha bhūyo 'nyaj jñātavyam avaśiṣyate //
manuṣyāṇāṃ sahasreṣu kaścid yatati siddhaye /
yatatām api siddhānāṃ kaścin māṃ vetti tattvataḥ //
bhūmir āpo 'nalo vāyuḥ khaṃ mano buddhir eva ca /
ahaṃkāra itīyaṃ me bhinnā prakṛtir aṣṭadhā //
5 *apareyam itas tv anyāṃ prakṛtiṃ viddhi me parām /*
jīvabhūtāṃ mahābāho yayedaṃ dhāryate jagat //
etadyonīni bhūtāni sarvāṇīty upadhāraya /
ahaṃ kṛtsnasya jagataḥ prabhavaḥ pralayas tathā //
mattaḥ parataraṃ nānyat kiṃcid asti Dhanaṃjaya /
mayi sarvam idaṃ protaṃ sūtre maṇigaṇā iva //
raso 'ham apsu Kaunteya prabhāsmi śaśisūryayoḥ /
praṇavaḥ sarvavedeṣu śabdaḥ khe pauruṣaṃ nṛṣu //
puṇyo gandhaḥ pṛthivyāṃ ca tejaś cāsmi vibhāvasau /
jīvanaṃ sarvabhūteṣu tapaś cāsmi tapasviṣu //
10 *bījaṃ māṃ sarvabhūtānāṃ viddhi Pārtha sanātanam /*
buddhir buddhimatām asmi tejas tejasvinām aham //
balaṃ balavatāṃ cāhaṃ kāmarāgavivarjitam /
dharmāviruddho bhūteṣu kāmo 'smi Bharatarṣabha //
ye caiva sāttvikā bhāvā rājasās tāmasāś ca ye /
matta eveti tān viddhi na tv ahaṃ teṣu te mayi //
tribhir guṇamayair bhāvair ebhiḥ sarvam idaṃ jagat /
mohitaṃ nābhijānāti mām ebhyaḥ param avyayam //
daivī hy eṣā guṇamayī mama māyā duratyayā /
mām eva ye prapadyante māyām etāṃ taranti te //
15 *na māṃ duṣkṛtino mūḍhāḥ prapadyante narādhamāḥ /*
māyayāpahṛtajñānā āsuraṃ bhāvam āśritāḥ //
caturvidhā bhajante māṃ janāḥ sukṛtino 'rjuna /
ārto jijñāsur arthārthī jñānī ca Bharatarṣabha //
teṣāṃ jñānī nityayukta ekabhaktir viśiṣyate /
priyo hi jñānino 'tyartham ahaṃ sa ca mama priyaḥ //
udārāḥ sarva evaite jñānī tv ātmaiva me matam /
āsthitaḥ sa hi yuktātmā mām evānuttamāṃ gatim //
bahūnāṃ janmanām ante jñānavān māṃ prapadyate /
vāsudevaḥ sarvam iti sa mahātmā sudurlabhaḥ //
20 *kāmais tais tair hṛtajñānāḥ prapadyante 'nyadevatāḥ /*

I deem the most accomplished man of yoga among all yogins who shares in me[9] in good faith, with his inner self absorbed in me.

The Lord said:
29[7].1 Hear how you, fixing your mind on me and finding shelter in me,
shall know me entirely beyond doubt, while practicing this yoga,
Pārtha. I shall propound to you fully that insight and knowledge, after
acquiring which nothing more remains to be known in this world.
Among thousands of people there is perhaps one who strives toward
success, and even among those who have striven successfully, perhaps
only one really knows me.
My material nature[1] is eightfold, comprising the order of earth,
5 water, fire, wind, ether, mind, spirit, and ego. This is my lower nature,
but know that I have another, higher nature[2] which comprises the
order of souls: it is by the latter that this world is sustained, strong-
armed prince. Realize that all creatures have their source therein: I
am the origin of this entire universe and its dissolution. There is
nothing at all that transcends me, Dhanaṃjaya: all this is strung on
me as strands of pearls are strung on a string. In water I am the
taste, Kaunteya, in sun and moon the light, in all the Vedas the
syllable *OṂ*, in ether the sound,[3] in men their manhood. In earth I
am its fragrance, in the sun its fire, in all creatures their vitality, in
10 the ascetics their austerity. Know, Pārtha, that I am the eternal seed
of all beings, I am the thought of the thinkers, the splendor of the
splendid. I am the strength of the strong, but strength without
ambition and passion. In the beings I am that desire that does not run
counter to the Law, bull of the Bharatas. Know that all conditions of
being, whether influenced by *sattva*, *rajas*, and *tamas*, come from me;
but I am not in them: they are in me.
This entire world is deluded by these three conditions of being
which derive from the *guṇas*,[4] and thus it fails to recognize me who
am in all eternity beyond the *guṇas*. For this miraculous world of my
illusion which consists in the three *guṇas* is hard to escape: only those
15 who resort to me overcome this illusion. The evil, deluded, vile men
who do not resort to me lose their wits to this illusion, and they are
reduced to the condition of demons.
Four kinds of good men seek my love,[5] Arjuna: the suffering, the
seekers for knowledge, the seekers for wealth, and the adepts,[6] bull of
the Bharatas. Among them stands out the adept, who is loyal to me
exclusively[7] and is always yoked, for I am unutterably dear to him,
and he is dear to me. All four are people of stature, but the adept I
count as myself, for through his discipline he comes to me as his
incomparable destination. Only after many a birth does the adept
attain to me, knowing "Vāsudeva is everything," and a man of such
20 great spirit is rare to find. Robbed of all true knowledge by this desire

taṃ taṃ niyamam āsthāya prakṛtyā niyatāḥ svayā //
yo yo yāṃ yāṃ tanuṃ bhaktaḥ śraddhayārcitum icchati /
tasya tasyācalāṃ śraddhāṃ tām eva vidadhāmy aham //
sa tayā śraddhayā yuktas tasyārādhanam īhate /
labhate ca tataḥ kāmān mayaiva vihitān hi tān //
antavat tu phalaṃ teṣāṃ tad bhavaty alpamedhasām /
devān devayajo yānti madbhaktā yānti mām api //
avyaktaṃ vyaktim āpannaṃ manyante mām abuddhayaḥ /
paraṃ bhāvam ajānanto mamāvyayam anuttamam //
25 *nāhaṃ prakāśaḥ sarvasya yogamāyāsamāvṛtaḥ /*
mūḍho 'yaṃ nābhijānāti loko mām ajam avyayam //
vedāhaṃ samatītāni vartamānāni ca-Arjuna /
bhaviṣyāṇi ca bhūtāni māṃ tu veda na kaścana //
icchādveṣasamutthena dvaṃdvamohena Bhārata /
sarvabhūtāni saṃmohaṃ sarge yānti paraṃtapa //
yeṣāṃ tv antagataṃ pāpaṃ janānāṃ puṇyakarmaṇām /
te dvaṃdvamohanirmuktā bhajante māṃ dṛḍhavratāḥ //
jarāmaraṇamokṣāya mām āśritya yatanti ye /
te brahma tad viduḥ kṛtsnam adhyātmaṃ karma cākhilam //
30 *sādhibhūtādhidaivaṃ māṃ sādhiyajñaṃ ca ye viduḥ /*
prayāṇakāle 'pi ca māṃ te vidur yuktacetasaḥ //

Arjuna uvāca /
30[8].1 *kiṃ tad brahma kim adhyātmaṃ kiṃ karma Puruṣottama /*
adhibhūtaṃ ca kiṃ proktam adhidaivaṃ kim ucyate //
adhiyajñaḥ kathaṃ ko 'tra dehe 'smin Madhusūdana /
prayāṇakāle ca kathaṃ jñeyo 'si niyatātmabhiḥ //
Śrībhagavān uvāca /
akṣaraṃ brahma paramaṃ svabhāvo 'dhyātmam ucyate /
bhūtabhāvodbhavakaro visargaḥ karmasaṃjñitaḥ //
adhibhūtaṃ kṣaro bhāvaḥ puruṣaś cādhidaivatam /
adhiyajño 'ham evātra dehe dehabhṛtāṃ vara //
5 *antakāle ca mām eva smaran muktvā kalevaram /*
yaḥ prayāti sa madbhāvaṃ yāti nāsty atra saṃśayaḥ //
yaṃ yaṃ vāpi smaran bhāvaṃ tyajaty ante kalevaram /
taṃ tam evaiti Kaunteya sadā tadbhāvabhāvitaḥ //
tasmāt sarveṣu kāleṣu mām anusmara yudhya ca /
mayy arpitamanobuddhir mām evaiṣyasy asaṃśayaḥ //
abhyāsayogayuktena cetasā nānyagāminā /
paramaṃ puruṣaṃ divyaṃ yāti Pārthānucintayan //

or that, the others resort to other deities, while observing this or that
restraint but themselves remaining constrained only by their own
natures. Yet, whatever may be the divine body that any loyal[8] person
seeks to worship with faith, it is I who make his faith in that body
unshakable. Armed with that faith he aspires to propitiate that deity
and obtains from it his desires—desires for which I in fact provide.
However, the rewards of those of little wit are ephemeral: God-
worshipers go to the Gods, but my loyal followers go to me.

To the unenlightened I am some unseen entity that has become
manifest, for they are ignorant of my transcendent being, which is
25 eternal and incomparable. Since they are clouded by the illusion of my
yoga, I am opaque to all, and the muddled world does not recognize
me as unborn and immortal.

Arjuna, I know the creatures of past, present, and future, but no
one knows me. Confused by the conflicts that spring from desire and
hatred, all creatures in creation are duped into total delusion,
Bhārata, enemy-burner. But when finally the evil *karman* of righteous
men has faded away, and they are freed from the confusions of
conflict, they devote themselves to me, firm in their vows. They who
strive toward freedom from old age and death by resorting to me,
know that *brahman* which is universal as well as specific to every
30 person: they know the act entire. They who know me as "elemental,"
as "divine," and as "sacrificial," until their final hour, know me truly,
with their spirits yoked.

Arjuna said:

30[8].1 What is that *brahman*? What is the individual self? What is act,
Supreme Person? What is called "elemental," and what "divine?"
Who in this body is the "sacrificial" one, and how is he so,
Madhusūdana? And how are you to be known by the disciplined in
their final hour?

The Lord said:

The supreme *brahman* is the imperishable. The individual self is
called nature.[1] And the outpouring that brings about the origination
of the being of the creatures is called act. The "elemental" is
transitory being;[2] the spirit[3] is the "divine," and I myself am the
5 "sacrificial"[4] here in this body, O best of the embodied. He who leaves
his body and departs this life while thinking of me alone in his final
hour, rejoins my being—of that there can be no doubt. A person
always becomes whatever being he thinks of when he at last
relinquishes the body, Kaunteya, for one is given being from its
being.[5] Therefore think of me at all times and fight: with mind and
spirit fixed on me you shall beyond a doubt come to me. While
thinking of the divine Supreme Person with a mind that is yoked to
a discipline of practice and does not stray away from him, he goes to

kaviṃ purāṇam anuśāsitāram
aṇor aṇīyāṃsam anusmared yaḥ /
sarvasya dhātāram acintyarūpam
ādityavarṇaṃ tamasaḥ parastāt //
10 *prayāṇakāle manasācalena*
bhaktyā yukto yogabalena caiva /
bhruvor madhye prāṇam āveśya samyak
sa taṃ paraṃ puruṣam upaiti divyam //
yad akṣaraṃ vedavido vadanti
viśanti yad yatayo vītarāgāḥ /
yad icchanto brahmacaryaṃ caranti
tat te padaṃ saṃgraheṇa pravakṣye //
sarvadvārāṇi saṃyamya mano hṛdi nirudhya ca /
mūrdhny ādhāyātmanaḥ prāṇam āsthito yogadhāraṇām //
OM ity ekākṣaraṃ brahma vyāharan mām anusmaran /
yaḥ prayāti tyajan dehaṃ sa yāti paramāṃ gatim //
ananyacetāḥ satataṃ yo māṃ smarati nityaśaḥ /
tasyāhaṃ sulabhaḥ Pārtha nityayuktasya yoginaḥ //
15 *mām upetya punarjanma duḥkhālayam aśāśvatam /*
nāpnuvanti mahātmānaḥ saṃsiddhiṃ paramāṃ gatāḥ //
ā brahmabhuvanāl lokāḥ punarāvartino 'rjuna /
mām upetya tu Kaunteya punarjanma na vidyate //
sahasrayugaparyantam ahar yad Brahmaṇo viduḥ /
rātriṃ yugasahasrāntāṃ te 'horātravido janāḥ //
avyaktād vyaktayaḥ sarvāḥ prabhavanty aharāgame /
rātryāgame pralīyante tatraivāvyaktasaṃjñake //
bhūtagrāmaḥ sa evāyaṃ bhūtvā bhūtvā pralīyate /
rātryāgame 'vaśaḥ Pārtha prabhavaty aharāgame //
20 *paras tasmāt tu bhāvo 'nyo 'vyakto 'vyaktāt sanātanaḥ /*
yaḥ sa sarveṣu bhūteṣu naśyatsu na vinaśyati //
avyakto 'kṣara ity uktas tam āhuḥ paramāṃ gatim /
yaṃ prāpya na nivartante tad dhāma paramaṃ mama //
puruṣaḥ sa paraḥ Pārtha bhaktyā labhyas tv ananyayā /
yasyāntaḥsthāni bhūtāni yena sarvam idaṃ tatam //
yatra kāle tv anāvṛttim āvṛttiṃ caiva yoginaḥ /
prayātā yānti taṃ kālaṃ vakṣyāmi Bharatarṣabha //
agnir jyotir ahaḥ śuklaḥ ṣaṇmāsā uttarāyaṇam /
tatra prayātā gacchanti brahma brahmavido janāḥ //
25 *dhūmo rātris tathā kṛṣṇaḥ ṣaṇmāsā dakṣiṇāyanam /*
tatra cāndramasaṃ jyotir yogī prāpya nivartate //

him, Pārtha.

The Sage and Preceptor primordial,
More minute than an atom, creator of all,
Of form unimaginable, hued like the sun
At the back of the night—who thus thinks of him

10 In his final hour with unshaken mind,
Armed with his devotion and power of yoga,
With his breath ensconced between his eyebrows,
Attains to the Person Supreme and Divine.

The abode that the Veda-wise call the eternal,
And the aspirants enter with passions shed,
And in search of which they practice the *brahman*,
I shall now propound to you summarily.

Closing all the doors of the senses and blocking the mind in the
heart and holding within the head the breath of the soul, one embarks
upon the retention of yoga. He reaches the highest goal who
relinquishes the body and departs life while uttering the one-syllabled
brahman that is *OṂ* and thinking of me. He who thinks of me
continuously without ever straying in thought to another, that ever-
15 yoked yogin finds me easy to reach, Pārtha. When the great-spirited
travelers to the ultimate perfection reach me, they do not return to
rebirth, that impermanent domain of misery. All the worlds, as far as
the World of Brahmā, return eternally,[6] but once I have been reached
there is no more rebirth.

They know of days and nights who know the Day of Brahmā that
lasts thousands of eons, and the Night that ends after thousands of
eons. At the dawning of the Day all manifestations emerge from the
unmanifest; at the falling of the Night they dissolve in that self-same
unmanifest. This village of creatures helplessly comes into being again
and again and dissolves at the fall of Night, Pārtha, only to be reborn
20 again at the dawn of Day. But there is a being beyond that being, an
eternal Unmanifest beyond the unmanifest,[7] which, while all beings
perish, does not itself perish.

This Unmanifest, also called Akṣara, they declare to be that ultimate goal upon reaching which souls no more return—it is my supreme domain. It is the Supreme Person,[8] attainable only through exclusive devotion, Pārtha, in whom the creatures inhere, the one on whom all this is strung.

I shall set forth the times at which the yogins departing life return
or do not return. The scholars of *brahman* who depart life by fire, by
sunshine, by day, in the bright fortnight, and during the six months
25 after the winter solstice go to *brahman*. The yogin who reaches the
light of the moon by smoke, by night, in the dark fortnight, and

śuklakṛṣṇe gatī hy ete jagataḥ śāśvate mate /
ekayā yāty anāvṛttim anyayāvartate punaḥ //
naite sṛtī Pārtha jānan yogī muhyati kaścana /
tasmāt sarveṣu kāleṣu yogayukto bhava-Arjuna //
vedeṣu yajñeṣu tapaḥsu caiva
dāneṣu yat puṇyaphalaṃ pradiṣṭam /
atyeti tat sarvam idaṃ viditvā
yogī paraṃ sthānam upaiti cādyam //

Śrībhagavān uvāca /
31[9].1 *idaṃ tu te guhyatamaṃ pravakṣyāmy anasūyave /*
jñānaṃ vijñānasahitaṃ yaj jñātvā mokṣyase 'śubhāt //
rājavidyā rājaguhyaṃ pavitram idam uttamam /
pratyakṣāvagamaṃ dharmyaṃ susukhaṃ kartum avyayam //
aśraddadhānāḥ puruṣā dharmasyāsya paraṃtapa /
aprāpya māṃ nivartante mṛtyusaṃsāravartmani //
mayā tatam idaṃ sarvaṃ jagad avyaktamūrtinā /
matsthāni sarvabhūtāni na cāhaṃ teṣv avasthitaḥ //
5 *na ca matsthāni bhūtāni paśya me yogam aiśvaram /*
bhūtabhṛn na ca bhūtastho mamātmā bhūtabhāvanaḥ //
yathākāśasthito nityaṃ vāyuḥ sarvatrago mahān /
tathā sarvāṇi bhūtāni matsthānīty upadhāraya //
sarvabhūtāni Kaunteya prakṛtiṃ yānti māmikām /
kalpakṣaye punas tāni kalpādau visṛjāmy aham //
prakṛtiṃ svām avaṣṭabhya visṛjāmi punaḥ punaḥ /
bhūtagrāmam imaṃ kṛtsnam avaśaṃ prakṛter vaśāt //
na ca māṃ tāni karmāṇi nibadhnanti Dhanaṃjaya /
udāsīnavad āsīnam asaktaṃ teṣu karmasu //
10 *mayādhyakṣeṇa prakṛtiḥ sūyate sacarācaram /*
hetunānena Kaunteya jagad viparivartate //
avajānanti māṃ mūḍhā mānuṣīṃ tanum āśritam /
paraṃ bhāvam ajānanto mama bhūtamaheśvaram //
moghāśā moghakarmāṇo moghajñānā vicetasaḥ /
rākṣasīm āsurīṃ caiva prakṛtiṃ mohinīṃ śritāḥ //
mahātmānas tu māṃ Pārtha daivīṃ prakṛtim āśritāḥ /
bhajanty ananyamanaso jñātvā bhūtādim avyayam //
satataṃ kīrtayanto māṃ yatantaś ca dṛḍhavratāḥ /
namasyantaś ca māṃ bhaktyā nityayuktā upāsate //
15 *jñānayajñena cāpy anye yajanto mām upāsate /*
ekatvena pṛthaktvena bahudhā viśvatomukham //
ahaṃ kratur ahaṃ yajñaḥ svadhāham aham auṣadham /
mantro 'ham aham evājyam aham agnir ahaṃ hutam //

during the six months after the summer solstice returns.[9] These two are considered to be the two routes of the world: the white and the black; by the former one does not return, by the latter one does return. No yogin who knows these two routes is confused about them, Pārtha; therefore be at all times yoked to yoga, Arjuna.

What reward of merit has been assigned
To rituals, Vedas, austerities, gifts,
All that merit the yogin who knows transcends
To attain the supreme, primordial place.

The Lord said:

31[9].1 I shall proclaim to you, who do not demur, this most mysterious
insight accompanied by knowledge which will set you free of evil. It
is the royal wisdom, the royal mystery, the ultimate purification,
which is learned from immediate evidence, conforms to the Law, is
easy to accomplish, and permanent. Men who do not believe in this
doctrine of Law, enemy-burner, fail to reach me and they return to the
runaround of deaths.
All this world is strung on me in the form of the Unmanifest; all
5 creatures exist in me, but I do not exist in them.[1] And again, the
creatures do not exist in me[2] —behold my supernal yoga![3] While
sustaining the creatures and giving them being, my self does not exist
in them. Just as the vast wind which goes everywhere is yet always
contained within space, so, realize this, all creatures are contained in
me. All creatures return to my nature at the end of the eon, Kaunteya,
and at the beginning of the eon I create them again. Resting on my
own nature I create, again and again, this entire aggregate of
creatures involuntarily by the force of my nature.[4]
No acts bind me, Dhanaṃjaya, for I remain disinterested and
10 detached from all acts. Nature gives birth to the standing and moving
creatures under my tutelage, Kaunteya, and for that reason does the
world revolve.
The deluded disregard me in my human form, being ignorant of my
higher nature as the great lord of the creatures. Mindless and futile
in their expectations, actions and knowledge, they abandon themselves
to the deluding nature of Asuras and Rākṣasas. But men of great
spirit who accept my divine nature venerate me uniquely, Pārtha,
knowing that I am the eternal source of the creatures. There are those
who, always yoked to devotion, adore me and glorify me, while
15 exerting themselves with fortitude, and pay homage to me. Others
venerate me, while sacrificing to me with the sacrifice that is
knowledge, as one, or several, or many, in my universal manifestations.
I am the rite, I am the sacrifice, I am the libation to the ancestors, I
am the herb,[5] I am the formula, I am the butter, I am the fire, I am

pitāham asya jagato mātā dhātā pitāmahaḥ /
vedyaṃ pavitram oṃkāra ṛk sāma yajur eva ca //
gatir bhartā prabhuḥ sākṣī nivāsaḥ śaraṇaṃ suhṛt /
prabhavaḥ pralayaḥ sthānaṃ nidhānaṃ bījam avyayam //
tapāmy aham ahaṃ varṣaṃ nigṛhṇāmy utsṛjāmi ca /
amṛtaṃ caiva mṛtyuś ca sad asac cāham Arjuna //
20 *traividyā māṃ somapāḥ pūtapāpā*
yajñair iṣṭvā svargatiṃ prārthayante /
te puṇyamāsādya surendralokam
aśnanti divyān divi devabhogān //
te taṃ bhuktvā svargalokaṃ viśālaṃ
kṣīṇe puṇye martyalokaṃ viśanti /
evaṃ trayīdharmam anuprapannā
gatāgataṃ kāmakāmā labhante //
ananyāś cintayanto māṃ ye janāḥ paryupāsate /
teṣāṃ nityābhiyuktānāṃ yogakṣemaṃ vahāmy aham //
ye 'py anyadevatābhaktā yajante śraddhayānvitāḥ /
te 'pi mām eva Kaunteya yajanty avidhipūrvakam //
ahaṃ hi sarvayajñānāṃ bhoktā ca prabhur eva ca /
na tu mām abhijānanti tattvenātaś cyavanti te //
25 *yānti devavratā devān pitṝn yānti pitṛvratāḥ /*
bhūtāni yānti bhūtejyā yānti madyājino 'pi mām //
patraṃ puṣpaṃ phalaṃ toyaṃ yo me bhaktyā prayacchati /
tad ahaṃ bhaktyupahṛtam aśnāmi prayatātmanaḥ //
yat karoṣi yad aśnāsi yaj juhoṣi dadāsi yat /
yat tapasyasi Kaunteya tat kuruṣva madarpaṇam //
śubhāśubhaphalair evaṃ mokṣyase karmabandhanaiḥ /
saṃnyāsayogayuktātmā vimukto mām upaiṣyasi //
samo 'haṃ sarvabhūteṣu na me dveṣyo 'sti na priyaḥ /
ye bhajanti tu māṃ bhaktyā mayi te teṣu cāpy aham //
30 *api cet sudurācāro bhajate mām ananyabhāk /*
sādhur eva sa mantavyaḥ samyagvyavasito hi saḥ //
kṣipraṃ bhavati dharmātmā śaśvac chāntiṃ nigacchati /
Kaunteya pratijānīhi na me bhaktaḥ praṇaśyati //
māṃ hi Pārtha vyapāśritya ye 'pi syuḥ pāpayonayaḥ /
striyo vaiśyās tathā śūdrās te 'pi yānti parāṃ gatim //
kiṃ punar brāhmaṇāḥ puṇyā bhaktā rājarṣayas tathā /
anityam asukhaṃ lokam imaṃ prāpya bhajasva mām //
manmanā bhava madbhakto madyājī māṃ namaskuru /
mām evaiṣyasi yuktvaivam ātmānaṃ matparāyaṇaḥ //
Śrībhagavān uvāca /
32[10].1 *bhūya eva mahābāho śṛṇu me paramaṃ vacaḥ /*

the offering. I am the father of this world, its mother, the Placer and Grandfather, the object of knowledge, the strainer, the syllable *OṂ*, the *ṛc*, *sāman*, and *yajus*; goal, master, lord, witness, abode, refuge, friend, source and destruction and continuity, container, imperishable seed. I shine and withhold rain or pour it out, I am immortality and death, the existent and the nonexistent, Arjuna.

20 The purified Vedic drinkers of Soma
Seek me with oblations to win their heaven;
And on reaching the blessed domain of Indra
Enjoy the celestial joys of the Gods.

But upon enjoying the vast world of heaven,
Their merit exhausted, they rejoin the mortals;
Thus following devoutly the Law of the Vedas
And craving desires they come and they go.

But to those who serve me while thinking only of me and none
other, who are always yoked, to them I bring felicity. Even they who
in good faith devote themselves to other deities really offer up their
sacrifices to me alone, Kaunteya, be it without proper rite.[6] For I am
the recipient of all sacrifices and their master, though they do not
25 really recognize me and therefore slip. To the Gods go they who are
avowed to the Gods, to the ancestors go they who are avowed to the
ancestors, to the ghouls[7] go they who are avowed to the ghouls, to
me go they who sacrifice to me.

If one disciplined soul proffers to me with love a leaf, a flower, fruit,
or water,[8] I accept this offering of love from him. Whatever you do, or
eat, or offer, or give, or mortify, Kaunteya, make it an offering to me,
and I shall undo the bonds of *karman*, the good and evil fruits. He
whose spirit is yoked to the yoga of renunciation shall come to me. I
am equable to all creatures, no one is hateful to me or dear—but
30 those who share me with love are in me and I am in them. Even a
hardened criminal who loves me and none other is to be deemed a
saint, for he has the right conviction; he soon becomes Law-minded
and finds peace forever. Understand this, Kaunteya: no servitor of
mine is lost. Even people of low origins, women, *vaiśyas*, nay *śūdras*, go
the highest course if they rely on me, Pārtha. So how much more
readily holy brahmins and devoted royal seers! Reduced to this passing
world of unhappiness, embrace me! May your thoughts be toward
me, your love toward me, your sacrifice toward me, your homage
toward me, and you shall come to me, having thus yoked yourself to
me as your highest goal.

The Lord said:

32[10].1 Again, strong-armed prince, listen to my supreme word which,

yat te 'haṃ prīyamāṇāya vakṣyāmi hitakāmyayā //
na me viduḥ suragaṇāḥ prabhavaṃ na maharṣayaḥ /
aham ādir hi devānāṃ maharṣīṇāṃ ca sarvaśaḥ //
yo mām ajam anādiṃ ca vetti lokamaheśvaram /
asaṃmūḍhaḥ sa martyeṣu sarvapāpaiḥ pramucyate //
buddhir jñānam asaṃmohaḥ kṣamā satyaṃ damaḥ śamaḥ /
sukhaṃ duḥkhaṃ bhavo 'bhāvo bhayaṃ cābhayam eva ca //
5 *ahiṃsā samatā tuṣṭis tapo dānaṃ yaśo 'yaśaḥ /*
bhavanti bhāvā bhūtānāṃ matta eva pṛthagvidhāḥ //
maharṣayaḥ sapta pūrve catvāro manavas tathā /
madbhāvā mānasā jātā yeṣāṃ loka imāḥ prajāḥ //
etāṃ vibhūtiṃ yogaṃ ca mama yo vetti tattvataḥ /
so 'vikampena yogena yujyate nātra saṃśayaḥ //
ahaṃ sarvasya prabhavo mattaḥ sarvaṃ pravartate /
iti matvā bhajante māṃ budhā bhāvasamanvitāḥ //
maccittā madgataprāṇā bodhayantaḥ parasparam /
kathayantaś ca māṃ nityaṃ tuṣyanti ca ramanti ca //
10 *teṣāṃ satatayuktānāṃ bhajatāṃ prītipūrvakam /*
dadāmi buddhiyogaṃ taṃ yena mām upayānti te //
teṣām evānukampārtham aham ajñānajaṃ tamaḥ /
nāśayāmy ātmabhāvastho jñānadīpena bhāsvatā //
Arjuna uvāca /
paraṃ brahma paraṃ dhāma pavitraṃ paramaṃ bhavān /
puruṣaṃ śāśvataṃ divyam ādidevam ajaṃ vibhum //
āhus tvām ṛṣayaḥ sarve devarṣir Nāradas tathā /
Asito Devalo Vyāsaḥ svayaṃ caiva bravīṣi me //
sarvam etad ṛtaṃ manye yan māṃ vadasi Keśava /
na hi te Bhagavan vyaktiṃ vidur devā na Dānavāḥ //
15 *svayam evātmanātmānaṃ vettha tvaṃ puruṣottama /*
bhūtabhāvana bhūteśa devadeva jagatpate //
vaktum arhasy aśeṣeṇa divyā hy ātmavibhūtayaḥ /
yābhir vibhūtibhir lokān imāṃs tvaṃ vyāpya tiṣṭhasi //
kathaṃ vidyām ahaṃ yogiṃs tvāṃ sadā paricintayan /
keṣu keṣu ca bhāveṣu cintyo 'si Bhagavan mayā //
vistareṇātmano yogaṃ vibhūtiṃ ca Janārdana /
bhūyaḥ kathaya tṛptir hi śṛṇvato nāsti me 'mṛtam //
Śrībhagavān uvāca /
hanta te kathayiṣyāmi divyā hy ātmavibhūtayaḥ /
prādhānyataḥ Kuruśreṣṭha nāsty anto vistarasya me //
20 *aham ātmā Guḍākeśa sarvabhūtāśayasthitaḥ /*
aham ādiś ca madhyaṃ ca bhūtānām anta eva ca //
Ādityānām ahaṃ Viṣṇur jyotiṣāṃ ravir aṃśumān /
Marīcir Marutām asmi nakṣatrāṇām ahaṃ śaśī //
vedānāṃ sāmavedo 'smi devānām asmi Vāsavaḥ /
indriyāṇāṃ manaś cāsmi bhūtānām asmi cetanā //

for your benefit I shall pronounce to you who love me. Neither the hosts of Gods nor the great seers themselves know my origin, for I am the beginning of Gods and great seers all. He who knows me as the unborn, beginningless great lord of the world, he among mortals is undeluded and freed from all evil taints.

Insight, knowledge, lack of delusion, forbearance, veracity, self-
control, serenity, happiness, unhappiness, becoming and unbecoming,
5 fear and fearlessness, nonviolence, equableness, contentment,
austerity, liberality, renown, and dishonor—all the creatures' various
modes of life spring from me alone. The ancient seven seers and the
four Manus[1] from whom the creatures in the world have issued were
born of my being from my mind. He who truly knows this ubiquity
and yoga[2] of mine is himself yoked to unshakable yoga, no doubt of
that. The wise, who are filled with being, love me in the knowledge
that I am the source of everything and that everything comes forth
from me. With their thoughts on me, their very lives devoted to me,
enlightening one another and always recounting my stories, they are
10 full of contentment and delight. To those who, always yoked, love me
joyfully I grant the singleness of mind by which they attain to me.
Residing in their own very being I compassionately dispel the darkness
of their ignorance with the shining lamp of knowledge.

Arjuna said:

The divine seer Nārada[3] and all the seers declare that you are the
supreme *brahman*, the supreme abode, the supreme means of
sanctification, the divine and eternal Person, the primordial God,
unborn and ubiquitous. So declare Asita Devala and Vyāsa,[4] and you
yourself tell me so, Keśava, I know that all this is true; indeed neither
15 Gods nor Dānavas know your true manifestation, O lord. You yourself
know yourself, Supreme Person, you who give being to the creatures,
lord of the creatures, God of Gods, master of the world! Pray tell me
of all your divine ubiquities,[5] by means of which you permeate these
worlds. How may I know you, yogin, in my constant meditations? In
what various modes of being may I meditate on you, my lord? Tell
me again fully of your yoga and ubiquity, Janārdana, for I am not
sated of listening to your Elixir!

The Lord said:

Well then, I shall recount to you my divine ubiquities, best of
Kurus, the chief ones, for there is no end to my plenitude.

20 I am the self that dwells in all beings, Guḍākeśa, I am the
beginning, the middle, and the end of the beings. Of the Ādityas I am
Viṣṇu, of the celestial lights the shining sun, of the Maruts I am
Marīci, to the constellations I am the moon.[6] Of the Vedas, I am the
Sāmaveda, of the Gods I am Vāsava, of the senses the mind, of the
creatures the consciousness. Of the Rudras I am Śaṃkara, the God of

Rudrāṇāṃ Śaṃkaraś cāsmi Vitteśo Yakṣa-Rakṣasām /
Vasūnāṃ pāvakaś cāsmi Meruḥ śikhariṇām aham //
purodhasāṃ ca mukhyaṃ māṃ viddhi Pārtha Bṛhaspatim /
senānīnām ahaṃ Skandaḥ sarasām asmi sāgaraḥ //
25 *maharṣīṇāṃ Bhṛgur ahaṃ girām asmy ekam akṣaram /*
yajñānāṃ japayajño 'smi sthāvarāṇāṃ Himālayaḥ //
Aśvatthaḥ sarvavṛkṣāṇāṃ devarṣīṇāṃ ca Nāradaḥ /
Gandharvāṇāṃ Citrarathaḥ siddhānāṃ Kapilo muniḥ //
Uccaiḥśravasam aśvānāṃ viddhi mām amṛtodbhavam /
Airāvataṃ gajendrāṇāṃ narāṇāṃ ca narādhipam //
āyudhānām ahaṃ vajraṃ dhenūnām asmi kāmadhuk /
prajanaś cāsmi Kandarpaḥ sarpāṇām asmi Vāsukiḥ //
Anantaś cāsmi Nāgānāṃ Varuṇo yādasām aham /
Pitṝṇām Aryamā cāsmi Yamaḥ saṃyamatām aham //
30 *Prahlādaś cāsmi Daityānāṃ Kālaḥ kalayatām aham /*
mṛgāṇāṃ ca mṛgendro 'haṃ Vainateyaś ca pakṣiṇām //
pavanaḥ pavatām asmi Rāmaḥ śastrabhṛtām aham /
jhaṣāṇāṃ makaraś cāsmi srotasām asmi Jāhnavī //
sargāṇām ādir antaś ca madhyaṃ caivāham Arjuna /
adhyātmavidyā vidyānāṃ vādaḥ pravadatām aham //
akṣarāṇām akāro 'smi dvaṃdvaḥ sāmāsikasya ca /
aham evākṣayaḥ kālo dhātāhaṃ viśvatomukhaḥ //
mṛtyuḥ sarvaharaś cāham udbhavaś ca bhaviṣyatām /
kīrtiḥ śrīr vāk ca nārīṇāṃ smṛtir medhā dhṛtiḥ kṣamā //
35 *bṛhatsāma tathā sāmnāṃ gāyatrī chandasām aham /*
māsānāṃ mārgaśīrṣo 'ham ṛtūnāṃ kusumākaraḥ //
dyūtaṃ chalayatām asmi tejas tejasvinām aham /
jayo 'smi vyavasāyo 'smi sattvaṃ sattvavatām aham //
Vṛṣṇīnāṃ Vāsudevo 'smi Pāṇḍavānāṃ Dhanaṃjayaḥ /
munīnām apy ahaṃ Vyāsaḥ kavīnām Uśanā kaviḥ //
daṇḍo damayatām asmi nītir asmi jigīṣatām /
maunaṃ caivāsmi guhyānāṃ jñānaṃ jñānavatām aham //
yac cāpi sarvabhūtānāṃ bījaṃ tad aham Arjuna /
na tad asti vinā yat syān mayā bhūtaṃ carācaram //
40 *nānto 'sti mama divyānāṃ vibhūtīnāṃ paraṃtapa /*
eṣa tūddeśataḥ prokto vibhūter vistaro mayā //
yad yad vibhūtimat sattvaṃ śrīmad ūrjitam eva vā /
tat tad evāvagaccha tvaṃ mama tejo'ṃśasaṃbhavam //
atha vā bahunaitena kiṃ jñātena tava-Arjuna /
viṣṭabhyāham idaṃ kṛtsnam ekāṃśena sthito jagat //

Arjuna uvāca /
33[11].1 *madanugrahāya paramaṃ guhyam adhyātmasaṃjñitam /*
yat tvayoktaṃ vacas tena moho 'yaṃ vigato mama //
bhavāpyayau hi bhūtānāṃ śrutau vistaraśo mayā /

Riches am I to Yakṣas and Rākṣasas, of the Vasus I am the fire, of the
mountains the Meru. Know that of the priests I am their chief
Bṛhaspati, Pārtha, of marshals Skanda,[7] of the waters I am the ocean.
25 Of the great seers I am Bhṛgu, of words the One Syllable, of sacrifices
the prayer, of standing creatures the Himālaya.

Among all trees I am the Aśvattha, of the divine seers Nārada, of the
Gandharvas Citraratha, of the Siddhas the hermit Kapila. Know that
among horses I am Uccaiḥśravas born from the Elixir,[8] Airāvata
among grand elephants, the king among his people. Of weapons I am
the thunderbolt, of cows the Cow of Plenty, I am Kandarpa[9] in
procreation, I am Vāsuki of the snakes. I am Ananta among the
Serpents, Varuṇa among sea creatures, Aryaman among the Fathers,
30 Yama among those who tame.[10] Of the Daityas I am Prahlāda, Kāla
among things that count,[11] the lion among wild animals, Garuḍa
among birds.

Of the means of purification I am the wind, among armsmen Rāma,
among sea monsters the crocodile, among rivers the Ganges. I am the
beginning, middle, and end of the creations, Arjuna, the wisdom of
the self among all wisdom, the debate of the disputers. I am the *a*
among syllables,[12] the *dvaṃdva*[13] among compounds, I am everlasting
Time, the Placer who looks everywhere, I am all-snatching Death, and
the Source of things yet to be. Of feminines I am Fame, Beauty,
35 Speech, Recollection, Wisdom, Fortitude, and Patience. Of the Sāmans
I am the Bṛhat, of meters the Gāyatrī, of months Mārgaśīrṣa,[14] of
seasons Spring. Of gamblers I am the dicing game, of the splendid the
splendor; I am the victory, the resolution, the courage of the
courageous.

Among the Vṛṣṇis I am Vāsudeva, among the Pāṇḍavas Arjuna, of
the hermits I am Vyāsa, of sages Kavi Uśanas.[15] I am the stick of those
who chastise, the statesmanship of those who seek to triumph, the
taciturnity of the mysteries,[16] the wisdom of the wise.

I am whatever is the seed of all creatures, Arjuna. Not a being,
40 standing or moving, can exist without me. There is no limit to my
divine ubiquities, enemy-burner: the full extent of my ubiquity I have
here merely indicated. Whatever beings have transcending power,
luster and might, know that each and every one of them has its
source in a particle of my splendor. But what is the point to you of
knowing this much, Arjuna? I support this entire universe with but a
single portion of mine!

Arjuna said:

33[11].1 This ultimate mystery bearing upon the soul, which you have
propounded to me as a favor, has dispelled my delusion. I have heard
from you in all detail the becoming and unbecoming of the creatures,

tvattaḥ kamalapatrākṣa māhātmyam api cāvyayam //
evam etad yathāttha tvam ātmānaṃ parameśvara /
draṣṭum icchāmi te rūpam aiśvaraṃ puruṣottama //
manyase yadi tac chakyaṃ mayā draṣṭum iti prabho /
yogeśvara tato me tvaṃ darśayātmānam avyayam //
Śrībhagavān uvāca /
5 *paśya me Pārtha rūpāṇi śataśo 'tha sahasraśaḥ /*
nānāvidhāni divyāni nānāvarṇākṛtīni ca //
paśya-Ādityān Vasūn Rudrān Aśvinau Marutas tathā /
bahūny adṛṣṭapūrvāṇi paśyāścaryāṇi Bhārata //
ihaikasthaṃ jagat kṛtsnaṃ paśyādya sacarācaram /
mama dehe Guḍākeśa yac cānyad draṣṭum icchasi //
na tu māṃ śakyase draṣṭum anenaiva svacakṣuṣā /
divyaṃ dadāmi te cakṣuḥ paśya me yogam aiśvaram //
Saṃjaya uvāca /
evam uktvā tato rājan mahāyogeśvaro Hariḥ /
darśayām āsa Pārthāya paramaṃ rūpam aiśvaram //
10 *anekavaktranayanam anekādbhutadarśanam /*
anekadivyābharaṇaṃ divyānekodyatāyudham //
divyamālyāmbaradharaṃ divyagandhānulepanam /
sarvāścaryamayaṃ devam anantaṃ viśvatomukham //
divi sūryasahasrasya bhaved yugapad utthitā /
yadi bhāḥ sadṛśī sā syād bhāsas tasya mahātmanaḥ //
tatraikasthaṃ jagat kṛtsnaṃ pravibhaktam anekadhā /
apaśyad devadevasya śarīre Pāṇḍavas tadā //
tataḥ sa vismayāviṣṭo hṛṣṭaromā Dhanaṃjayaḥ /
praṇamya śirasā devaṃ kṛtāñjalir abhāṣata //
Arjuna uvāca /
15 *paśyāmi devāṃs tava deva dehe*
sarvāṃs tathā bhūtaviśeṣasaṃghān /
Brahmāṇam Īśaṃ kamalāsanastham
ṛṣīṃś ca sarvān uragāṃś ca divyān //
anekabāhūdaravaktranetraṃ
paśyāmi tvā sarvato 'nantarūpam /
nāntaṃ na madhyaṃ na punas tavādiṃ
paśyāmi viśveśvara viśvarūpa //
kirīṭinaṃ gadinaṃ cakriṇaṃ ca
tejorāśiṃ sarvato dīptimantam /
paśyāmi tvāṃ durnirīkṣyaṃ samantād
dīptānalārkadyutim aprameyam //
tvam akṣaraṃ paramaṃ veditavyaṃ
tvam asya viśvasya paraṃ nidhānam /
tvam avyayaḥ śāśvatadharmagoptā
sanātanas tvaṃ puruṣo mato me //

lotus-eyed one, and your own indestructible greatness. Now I wish to set eye on your real, supernal form, just as you have described yourself, sovereign lord, Supreme Person! If you think that I shall be able to look upon it, lord, master of Yoga,[1] display to me your imperishable person.

The Lord said:

Pārtha, behold my hundreds and thousands of shapes, of many
5 kinds, divine, in manifold colors and figures. Behold the Ādityas, Vasus, Rudras, Aśvins, Maruts;[2] behold, Bhārata, many marvels that have never been witnessed before. Behold the entire universe with standing and moving creatures centered here in this body of mine—and whatever else you desire to see. But you shall not be able to look upon me with just your ordinary eyes: I shall give you divine sight: behold my sovereign Yoga!

Saṃjaya said:

Having thus spoken, Hari, the great sovereign of Yoga, revealed to
10 the Pārtha his supreme supernal form, with countless mouths and eyes, displaying multitudes of marvels, wearing numbers of divine ornaments, and raising divine weapons beyond count. And this form wore celestial garlands and robes, it was anointed with the perfumes of the Gods—it was God himself, infinite and universal, containing all miracles.[3]

If in the sky the light of a thousand suns were to rise at once, it would be the likeness of the light of that great-spirited One. In that body of the God of Gods the Pāṇḍava saw the entire universe centered, in its infinite differentiations. Dhanaṃjaya was stunned, and he shivered. He folded his hands, bowed his head and said—

Arjuna said:

15 I see all Gods in your body, O God,
And all creatures in all their varieties—
On his lotus seat the sovereign Brahmā,
The seers all and the snakes divine.

Your own infinitude stretching away,
Many arms, eyes, bellies, and mouths do I see,
No end do I see, no beginning, no middle,
In you, universal in power and form.

With diadem, mace, and discus endowed,
A mass of light ablaze on all sides,
I see you, so rare to behold, all around
Immeasurably burning like sun or the fire.

You are *Akṣara*, highest of truths to be known,[4]
The highest foundation of all this world,
Undying protector of Law sempiternal,
The Person Eternal I hold you to be.

anādimadhyāntam anantavīryam
anantabāhuṃ śaśisūryanetram /
paśyāmi tvāṃ dīptahutāśavaktraṃ
svatejasā viśvam idaṃ tapantam //
20 *dyāvāpṛthivyor idam antaraṃ hi*
vyāptaṃ tvayaikena diśaś ca sarvāḥ /
dṛṣṭvādbhutaṃ rūpam idaṃ tavograṃ
lokatrayaṃ pravyathitaṃ mahātman //
amī hi tvā surasaṃghā viśanti
kecid bhītāḥ prāñjalayo gṛṇanti /
svastīty uktvā maharṣisiddhasaṃghāḥ
stuvanti tvāṃ stutibhiḥ puṣkalābhiḥ //
Rudra-Ādityā Vasavo ye ca Sādhyā
Viśve 'śvinau Marutaś coṣmapāś ca /
Gandharva-Yakṣa-Asura-Siddhasaṃghā
vīkṣante tvā vismitāś caiva sarve //
rūpaṃ mahat te bahuvaktranetraṃ
mahābāho bahubāhūrupādam /
bahūdaraṃ bahudaṃṣṭrākarālaṃ
dṛṣṭvā lokāḥ pravyathitās tathāham //
nabhaḥspṛśaṃ dīptam anekavarṇaṃ
vyāttānanaṃ dīptaviśālanetram /
dṛṣṭvā hi tvāṃ pravyathitāntarātmā
dhṛtiṃ na vindāmi śamaṃ ca Viṣṇo //
25 *daṃṣṭrākarālāni ca te mukhāni*
dṛṣṭvaiva kālānalasaṃnibhāni /
diśo na jāne na labhe ca śarma
prasīda deveśa jagannivāsa //
amī ca tvāṃ Dhṛtarāṣṭrasya putrāḥ
sarve sahaivāvanipālasaṃghaiḥ /
Bhīṣmo Droṇaḥ Sūtaputras tathāsau
sahāsmadīyair api yodhamukhyaiḥ //
vaktrāṇi te tvaramāṇā viśanti
daṃṣṭrākarālāni bhayānakāni /
kecid vilagnā daśanāntareṣu
saṃdṛśyante cūrṇitair uttamāṅgaiḥ //
yathā nadīnāṃ bahavo 'mbuvegāḥ
samudram evābhimukhā dravanti /
tathā tavāmī naralokavīrā
viśanti vaktrāṇy abhivijvalanti //

Beginningless, middleless, endless, almighty,
Many-armed, with eyes that are sun and moon,
I see you with mouths that are blazing fires
Setting fire to this world with your incandescence.

20 All space that extends between heaven and earth,
All horizons are filled by you alone;
Having seen your dreadful and wondrous form
The three worlds shudder, great-spirited One!

For yonder the hosts of the Gods go into you—
Some laud you in fear with folded hands,
The throngs of the seers and Siddhas say Hail!
And sing your praise in long litanies.

Ādityas and Rudras, Vasus and Sādhyas,
The All-Gods, Asvins, Maruts and Fathers,
Gandharvas and Asuras, Yakṣas and Siddhas
Behold you amazed in all their numbers.

At the sight of your mass with its eyes and mouths,
Multitudinous arms, thighs, bellies, and feet,
Strong-armed One, and maws that are spiky with tusks
The worlds are in panic and so am I!

At the aspect of you who are brushing the sky,
Ablaze, many-hued, maws gaping, and eyes
Asparkle and wide, my innards are quaking,
And, Viṣṇu, I find neither firmness nor peace.

25 Just watching your mouths that bristle with fangs
And resemble the fire at the end of the eon,
I know no directions and find no shelter—
Have mercy, great God, repose of the world!

And yonder all sons of Dhṛtarāṣṭra
Along with the hosts of the kings of the earth,
Like Bhīṣma, Droṇa, that son of a *sūta*,[5]
Along with our own chief warriors too

Are hastening into your numerous mouths[6]
That are spiky with tusks and horrifying—
There are some who are dangling between your teeth,
Their heads already crushed to bits.

As many a river in spate ever faster
Streams oceanward in a headlong rush,
So yonder heroic rulers of earth
Are streaming into your flame-licked mouths.

yathā pradīptaṃ jvalanaṃ pataṃgā
viśanti nāśāya samṛddhavegāḥ /
tathaiva nāśāya viśanti lokās
tavāpi vaktrāṇi samṛddhavegāḥ //
30 *lelihyase grasamānaḥ samantāl*
lokān samagrān vadanair jvaladbhiḥ /
tejobhir āpūrya jagat samagraṃ
bhāsas tavogrāḥ pratapanti Viṣṇo //
ākhyāhi me ko bhavān ugrarūpo
namo 'stu te devavara prasīda /
vijñātum icchāmi bhavantam ādyaṃ
na hi prajānāmi tava pravṛttim //
Śrībhagavān uvāca /
kālo 'smi lokakṣayakṛt pravṛddho
lokān samāhartum iha pravṛttaḥ /
ṛte 'pi tvā na bhaviṣyanti sarve
ye 'vasthitāḥ pratyanīkeṣu yodhāḥ //
tasmāt tvam uttiṣṭha yaśo labhasva
jitvā śatrūn bhuṅkṣva rājyaṃ samṛddham /
mayaivaite nihatāḥ pūrvam eva
nimittamātraṃ bhava savyasācin //
Droṇaṃ ca Bhīṣmaṃ ca Jayadrathaṃ ca
Karṇaṃ tathānyān api yodhavīrān /
mayā hatāṃs tvaṃ jahi mā vyathiṣṭhā
yudhyasva jetāsi raṇe sapatnān //
Saṃjaya uvāca /
35 *etac chrutvā vacanaṃ Keśavasya*
kṛtāñjalir vepamānaḥ Kirīṭī /
namaskṛtvā bhūya evāha Kṛṣṇaṃ
sagadgadaṃ bhītabhītaḥ praṇamya //
Arjuna uvāca /
sthāne Hṛṣīkeśa tava prakīrtyā
jagat prahṛṣyaty anurajyate ca /
Rakṣāṃsi bhītāni diśo dravanti
sarve namasyanti ca Siddhasaṃghāḥ //
kasmāc ca te na nameran mahātman
garīyase Brahmaṇo 'py ādikartre /
ananta deveśa jagannivāsa
tvam akṣaraṃ sad asat tatparaṃ yat //
tvam ādidevaḥ puruṣaḥ purāṇas
tvam asya viśvasya paraṃ nidhānam /

As moths on the wing ever faster will aim
For a burning fire and perish in it,
Just so do these men increasing their speed
Make haste to your mouths to perish in them.

30 You are greedily licking your lips to devour
These worlds entire with your flickering mouths:
Your dreadful flames are filling with fire,
And burn to its ends this universe, Viṣṇu![7]

Reveal to me, who are you so dread?
Obeisance to you, have mercy, good God!
I seek to encompass you who are primeval,
For I comprehend not the course you are taking.

The Lord said:

I am Time grown old to destroy the world,
Embarked on the course of world annihilation:
Except for yourself none of these will survive,
Of these warriors arrayed in opposite armies.

Therefore raise yourself now and reap rich fame,
Rule the plentiful realm by defeating your foes!
I myself have doomed them ages ago:
Be merely my hand in this, Left-handed Archer!

Slay Droṇa and Bhīṣma and Jayadratha,
And Karṇa as well as other fine warriors—
My victims—destroy them and tarry not!
Wage war! You shall trounce your rivals in battle!

Saṃjaya said:

35 Upon hearing these words from Keśava
The Diademed Arjuna folded his hands,
And trembling he bowed and responded to Kṛṣṇa
In a stammer, prostrate, and terror-struck—

Arjuna said:

It is meet, Hṛṣīkeśa, that, hearing you praised,
The world is enraptured and flooded with love:
The terrified Rākṣasas flee to all regions,
The throngs of the Siddhas proffer their homage.

And why should they fail to bow down, great-souled One,
Creator more worthy of honor than Brahmā?
Unending Lord God, repose of the world,
You're what is and is not and what is beyond it.

The Original God, the Person Eternal,
You are of this world the ultimate support,

vettāsi vedyaṃ ca paraṃ ca dhāma
tvayā tataṃ viśvam anantarūpa //
Vāyur Yamo 'gnir Varuṇaḥ Śaśāṅkaḥ
Prajāpatis tvaṃ prapitāmahaś ca /
namo namas te 'stu sahasrakṛtvaḥ
punaś ca bhūyo 'pi namo namas te //
40 *namaḥ purastād atha pṛṣṭhatas te*
namo 'stu te sarvata eva sarva /
anantavīryāmitavikramas tvaṃ
sarvaṃ samāpnoṣi tato 'si sarvaḥ //
sakheti matvā prasabhaṃ yad uktaṃ
he Kṛṣṇa he Yādava he sakheti /
ajānatā mahimānaṃ tavedaṃ
mayā pramādāt praṇayena vāpi //
yac cāvahāsārtham asatkṛto 'si
vihāraśayyāsanabhojaneṣu /
eko 'tha vāpy Acyuta tatsamakṣaṃ
tat kṣāmaye tvām aham aprameyam //
pitāsi lokasya carācarasya
tvam asya pūjyaś ca gurur garīyān /
na tvatsamo 'sty abhyadhikaḥ kuto 'nyo
lokatraye 'py apratimaprabhāva //
tasmāt praṇamya praṇidhāya kāyaṃ
prasādaye tvām aham īśam īḍyam /
piteva putrasya sakheva sakhyuḥ
priyaḥ priyāyārhasi deva soḍhum //
45 *adṛṣṭapūrvaṃ hṛṣito 'smi dṛṣṭvā*
bhayena ca pravyathitaṃ mano me /
tad eva me darśaya deva rūpaṃ
prasīda deveśa jagannivāsa //
kirīṭinaṃ gadinaṃ cakrahastam
icchāmi tvāṃ draṣṭum ahaṃ tathaiva /
tenaiva rūpeṇa caturbhujena
sahasrabāho bhava viśvamūrte //
Śrībhagavān uvāca /
mayā prasannena tava-Arjunedaṃ
rūpaṃ paraṃ darśitam ātmayogāt /
tejomayaṃ viśvam anantam ādyaṃ
yan me tvadanyena na dṛṣṭapūrvam //

The knower, the known, the final abode—
All is strung upon you, of infinite form:

Moon, wind, fire, Varuṇa, Yama are you,
Prajāpati are you, the great-grandfather,
I praise thee, I praise thee a thousandfold,
Once more and again I praise thee, I praise thee,

40 I praise thee in front, I praise thee in back,
I praise thee on every side, O All!
Of infinite vigor, of measureless might,
You encompass it all and therefore are all.

If, thinking you friend, I have too boldly
Cried, "Yādava! Kṛṣṇa! Come here, my good friend!"[8]
Not knowing of this your magnificence,
Out of absence of mind or sheer affection,

If perchance I have slighted you—merely in jest—
In matters of sport, bed, seating, or meal,[9]
In privacy, Acyuta, or before others—
I ask your indulgence, immeasurable One!

Of the quick and the firm you are the begetter,
By all to be honored the worthiest guru;
No one is your equal, still less then your better,
For in all three worlds your might has no bounds.

Therefore I bow low, prostrating my body,
And ask your forgiveness, worshipful Lord!
Pray bear with me, God, as a father with son,
As a friend with friend, as a lover with loved one.

45 At the sight of this unwitnessed marvel I thrill
While a sense of dread unsettles my mind:
Please show me, O God, the body I've known,
Have mercy, Lord God, repose of the world!

I wish now to see you again as before,
With your diadem, mace, and discus in hand,
Assume once again your four-armed form,
O thousand-armed One, embodied in all!

The Lord said:
Out of grace for you, Arjuna, have I revealed
By my power of Yoga my highest form,
Full of fire, universal, primeval, unending,
Which no one but you has ever beheld.

na vedayajñādhyayanair na dānair
na ca kriyābhir na tapobhir ugraiḥ /
evaṃrūpaḥ śakya ahaṃ nṛloke
draṣṭuṃ tvadanyena Kurupravīra //
mā te vyathā mā ca vimūḍhabhāvo
dṛṣṭvā rūpaṃ ghoram īdṛṅ mamedam /
vyapetabhīḥ prītamanāḥ punas tvaṃ
tad eva me rūpam idaṃ prapaśya //
Saṃjaya uvāca /
50 *ity Arjunaṃ Vāsudevas tathoktvā*
svakaṃ rūpaṃ darśayām āsa bhūyaḥ /
āśvāsayām āsa ca bhītam enaṃ
bhūtvā punaḥ saumyavapur mahātmā //
Arjuna uvāca /
dṛṣṭvedaṃ mānuṣaṃ rūpaṃ tava saumyaṃ Janārdana /
idānīm asmi saṃvṛttaḥ sacetāḥ prakṛtiṃ gataḥ //
Śrībhagavān uvāca /
sudurdarśam idaṃ rūpaṃ dṛṣṭavān asi yan mama /
devā apy asya rūpasya nityaṃ darśanakāṅkṣiṇaḥ //
nāhaṃ vedair na tapasā na dānena na cejyayā /
śakya evaṃvidho draṣṭuṃ dṛṣṭavān asi māṃ yathā //
bhaktyā tv ananyayā śakya aham evaṃvidho 'rjuna /
jñātuṃ draṣṭuṃ ca tattvena praveṣṭuṃ ca paraṃtapa //
55 *matkarmakṛn matparamo madbhaktaḥ saṅgavarjitaḥ /*
nirvairaḥ sarvabhūteṣu yaḥ sa mām eti Pāṇḍava //

Arjuna uvāca /
34[12].1 *evaṃ satatayuktā ye bhaktās tvāṃ paryupāsate /*
ye cāpy akṣaram avyaktaṃ teṣāṃ ke yogavittamāḥ //
Śrībhagavān uvāca /
mayy āveśya mano ye māṃ nityayuktā upāsate /
śraddhayā parayopetās te me yuktatamā matāḥ //
ye tv akṣaram anirdeśyam avyaktaṃ paryupāsate /
sarvatragam acintyaṃ ca kūṭastham acalaṃ dhruvam //
saṃniyamyendriyagrāmaṃ sarvatra samabuddhayaḥ /
te prāpnuvanti mām eva sarvabhūtahite ratāḥ //
5 *kleśo 'dhikataras teṣām avyaktāsaktacetasām /*
avyaktā hi gatir duḥkhaṃ dehavadbhir avāpyate //
ye tu sarvāṇi karmāṇi mayi saṃnyasya matparāḥ /
ananyenaiva yogena māṃ dhyāyanta upāsate //
teṣām ahaṃ samuddhartā mṛtyusaṃsārasāgarāt /
bhavāmi nacirāt Pārtha mayy āveśitacetasām //

Not with Veda or rites, not with study or gifts,
Not with sacrifice or with awesome *tapas*
Can I in this world be beheld in this form
By any but you, great hero of Kuru.

Have no more fear, be no longer bemused
By the sight of this form of me so awe-inspiring;
Your terror gone, your heart again pleased,
Set eyes once more on the body you know!

Saṃjaya said:

50 Quoth Vāsudeva to Arjuna
And showed him once more his form of before,
And put that terrified man to rest
By becoming again his gentle old self.

Arjuna said:

Now that I see your gentle human shape, Janārdana, I have come to my senses and my normal tenor is restored!

The Lord said:

You have seen this rarely revealed form that is mine: even the
Gods always yearn for a glimpse of this form. Thus, as I am and as
you have seen me, I cannot be seen with the aid of the Vedas,
austerities, gifts, and sacrifices. Only through exclusive *bhakti*[10] can I
be seen thus, Arjuna, and known as I really am, and entered into,
55 enemy-tamer. Only he comes to me, Pāṇḍava, who acts for me, who
holds me as the highest, who is devoted to me without self-interest
and without any animosity against any creature.

Arjuna said:

34[12].1 Who are the foremost adepts of yoga: those who attend on you with the devotion they constantly practice, or those who seek out the imperishable that is unmanifest?[1]

The Lord said:

Those I deem the most adept at yoga who fix their minds on me
and in constant yoga and with complete faith attend on me. But those
who attend on the inexpressible unmanifest Imperishable, omnipresent,
inconceivable, standing on the peak,[2] immovable, and fixed, while
they master their senses and remain equably disposed to everyone and
everything and have the well-being of all creatures at heart, those
5 reach me too. But it requires greater toil for those whose minds are
directed to the Unmanifest, for their goal is not manifest and the
embodied attain it with hardship. On the other hand, those who,
absorbed in me, resign all their acts to me and contemplatively attend
on me with exclusive yoga,[3] soon find in me their savior from the
ocean that is the run-around of deaths, Pārtha, for their minds are
conducted to enter into me.

mayy eva mana ādhatsva mayi buddhiṃ niveśaya /
nivasiṣyasi mayy eva ata ūrdhvaṃ na saṃśayaḥ //
atha cittaṃ samādhātuṃ na śaknoṣi mayi sthiram /
abhyāsayogena tato mām icchāptuṃ Dhanaṃjaya //
10 *abhyāse 'py asamartho 'si matkarmaparamo bhava /*
madartham api karmāṇi kurvan siddhim avāpsyasi //
athaitad apy aśakto 'si kartuṃ madyogam āśritaḥ /
sarvakarmaphalatyāgaṃ tataḥ kuru yatātmavān //
śreyo hi jñānam abhyāsāj jñānād dhyānaṃ viśiṣyate /
dhyānāt karmaphalatyāgas tyāgāc chāntir anantaram //
adveṣṭā sarvabhūtānāṃ maitraḥ karuṇa eva ca /
nirmamo nirahaṃkāraḥ samaduḥkhasukhaḥ kṣamī //
saṃtuṣṭaḥ satataṃ yogī yatātmā dṛḍhaniścayaḥ /
mayy arpitamanobuddhir yo madbhaktaḥ sa me priyaḥ //
15 *yasmān nodvijate loko lokān nodvijate ca yaḥ /*
harṣāmarṣabhayodvegair mukto yaḥ sa ca me priyaḥ //
anapekṣaḥ śucir dakṣa udāsīno gatavyathaḥ /
sarvārambhaparityāgī yo madbhaktaḥ sa me priyaḥ //
yo na hṛṣyati na dveṣṭi na śocati na kāṅkṣati /
śubhāśubhaparityāgī bhaktimān yaḥ sa me priyaḥ //
samaḥ śatrau ca mitre ca tathā mānāvamānayoḥ /
śītoṣṇasukhaduḥkheṣu samaḥ saṅgavivarjitaḥ //
tulyanindāstutir maunī saṃtuṣṭo yena kenacit /
aniketaḥ sthiramatir bhaktimān me priyo naraḥ //
20 *ye tu dharmyāmṛtam idaṃ yathoktaṃ paryupāsate /*
śraddadhānā matparamā bhaktās te 'tīva me priyāḥ //

Śrībhagavān uvāca /
35[13].1 *idaṃ śarīraṃ Kaunteya kṣetram ity abhidhīyate /*
etad yo vetti taṃ prāhuḥ kṣetrajña iti tadvidaḥ //
kṣetrajñaṃ cāpi māṃ viddhi sarvakṣetreṣu Bhārata /
kṣetrakṣetrajñayor jñānaṃ yat taj jñānaṃ mataṃ mama //
tat kṣetraṃ yac ca yādṛk ca yadvikāri yataś ca yat /
sa ca yo yatprabhāvaś ca tat samāsena me śṛṇu //
ṛṣibhir bahudhā gītaṃ chandobhir vividhaih pṛthak /
brahmasūtrapadaiś caiva hetumadbhir viniścitaiḥ //
5 *mahābhūtāny ahaṃkāro buddhir avyaktam eva ca /*
indriyāṇi daśaikaṃ ca pañca cendriyagocarāḥ //
icchā dveṣaḥ sukhaṃ duḥkhaṃ saṃghātaś cetanā dhṛtiḥ /
etat kṣetraṃ samāsena savikāram udāhṛtam //
amānitvam adambhitvam ahiṃsā kṣāntir ārjavam /
ācāryopāsanaṃ śaucaṃ sthairyam ātmavinigrahaḥ //
indriyārtheṣu vairāgyam anahaṃkāra eva ca /

Fix your mind on me alone, let your spirit enter into me, and ever
after you shall dwell within myself, no doubt of that. Or if at first you
cannot hold your spirit firmly fixed on me, still cherish the desire to
10 reach me by repeated yoga, Dhanaṃjaya. Even if you are incapable of
this repeated application, be intent on acting for me, for by doing acts
for my sake you will also attain success. Or even if you are incapable
of acting thus, though you are inclined to me, at least restrain yourself
and renounce the fruit of all your actions. Knowledge is higher than
study, contemplation transcends knowledge, the relinquishment of the
fruits of acts surpasses contemplation, and upon resignation follows
serenity.[4]

Without hatred of any creature, friendly and compassionate
without possessiveness and self-pride, equable in happiness and
unhappiness, forbearing, contented, always yoked, mastering himself,
resolute in decisions, with his mind and spirit dedicated to me—such
15 a devotee of mine is beloved of me. Beloved of me is he who does not
vex the world and is not vexed by it, and who is free from joy,
intolerance, fear, and vexation. Beloved of me is the devotee who is
dependent on nothing, pure, capable, disinterested, unworried, and
who renounces all undertakings.[5] Beloved of me is the devotee who
neither hates nor rejoices, does not mourn or hanker, and relinquishes
both good and evil.

A man who remains the same toward friend or foe, in honor or
dishonor, in heat or cold, in happiness and misery, devoid of all self-
interest, equable when praised or blamed, taciturn, contented with
anything whatever, homeless, firm of mind, and devoted—such a man
20 is dear to me. Beloved above all are they who, faithful and absorbed
in me, attend to this elixir of Law I have set forth to you.

The Lord said:

35[13].1 This body, Kaunteya, is called "the field," and the ones who know
this call the one who knows this "field" the "guide" to this field.[1]
Know, Bhārata, that I too am such a guide, but to all the fields; this
knowledge of guide and field I deem knowledge indeed. Hear from me
in summary what this field is, what defines it, how it evolves and
whence, and who the guide is and what power he has. The seers have
chanted about them severally in various meters[2] as well as in definite
statements corroborated by arguments in the *Brahmasūtras*.[3]
5 The Elements, the *ahaṃkāra*, the *buddhi*, the Unmanifest, the ten
Faculties, the five Realms of these faculties, attraction, aversion,
pleasure and displeasure, the bodily organism, consciousness and
continuity: this enumeration is quoted in brief as constituting the field
and its evolutes.[4] Lack of pride, lack of display, lack of injury,
forbearance, uprightness, respect for one's teacher, purity, fortitude,
self-mastery, dispassion toward sense objects, lack of self-pride,

janmamṛtyujarāvyādhiduḥkhadoṣānudarśanam //
asaktir anabhiṣvaṅgaḥ putradāragṛhādiṣu /
nityaṃ ca samacittatvam iṣṭāniṣṭopapattiṣu //
10 *mayi cānanyayogena bhaktir avyabhicāriṇī /*
viviktadeśasevitvam aratir janasaṃsadi //
adhyātmajñānanityatvaṃ tattvajñānārthadarśanam /
etaj jñānam iti proktam ajñānaṃ yad ato 'nyathā //
jñeyaṃ yat tat pravakṣyāmi yaj jñātvāmṛtam aśnute /
anādimat paraṃ brahma na sat tan nāsad ucyate //
sarvataḥpāṇipādaṃ tat sarvato'kṣiśiromukham /
sarvataḥśrutimal loke sarvam āvṛtya tiṣṭhati //
sarvendriyaguṇābhāsaṃ sarvendriyavivarjitam /
asaktaṃ sarvabhṛc caiva nirguṇaṃ guṇabhoktṛ ca //
15 *bahir antaś ca bhūtānām acaraṃ caram eva ca /*
sūkṣmatvāt tad avijñeyaṃ dūrasthaṃ cāntike ca tat //
avibhaktaṃ ca bhūteṣu vibhaktam iva ca sthitam /
bhūtabhartṛ ca taj jñeyaṃ grasiṣṇu prabhaviṣṇu ca //
jyotiṣām api taj jyotis tamasaḥ param ucyate /
jñānaṃ jñeyaṃ jñānagamyaṃ hṛdi sarvasya viṣṭhitam //
iti kṣetraṃ tathā jñānaṃ jñeyaṃ coktaṃ samāsataḥ /
madbhakta etad vijñāya madbhāvāyopapadyate //
prakṛtiṃ puruṣaṃ caiva viddhy anādī ubhāv api /
vikārāṃś ca guṇāṃś caiva viddhi prakṛtisaṃbhavān //
20 *kāryakāraṇakartṛtve hetuḥ prakṛtir ucyate /*
puruṣaḥ sukhaduḥkhānāṃ bhoktṛtve hetur ucyate //
puruṣaḥ prakṛtistho hi bhuṅkte prakṛtijān guṇān /
kāraṇaṃ guṇasaṅgo 'sya sadasadyonijanmasu //
upadraṣṭānumantā ca bhartā bhoktā maheśvaraḥ /
paramātmeti cāpy ukto dehe 'smin puruṣaḥ paraḥ //
ya evaṃ vetti puruṣaṃ prakṛtiṃ ca guṇaiḥ saha /
sarvathā vartamāno 'pi na sa bhūyo 'bhijāyate //
dhyānenātmani paśyanti kecid ātmānam ātmanā /
anye sāṃkhyena yogena karmayogena cāpare //
25 *anye tv evam ajānantaḥ śrutvānyebhya upāsate /*
te 'pi cātitaranty eva mṛtyuṃ śrutiparāyaṇāḥ //
yāvat saṃjāyate kiṃcit sattvaṃ sthāvarajaṅgamam /
kṣetrakṣetrajñasaṃyogāt tad viddhi Bharatarṣabha //
samaṃ sarveṣu bhūteṣu tiṣṭhantaṃ parameśvaram/
vinaśyatsv avinaśyantaṃ yaḥ paśyati sa paśyati //

awareness of the faults inherent in birth, death, old age, sickness, and
unhappiness, lack of attachments, lack of involvement with sons, wife,
home, etc., constant equanimity whether pleasing or displeasing events
10 befall, unstraying devotion to me through exclusive yoga,[5] seeking
out a secluded spot, ungregariousness, constancy of knowledge
concerning the self, and insight into the import of knowledge of real
things—all this is declared to be knowledge, and ignorance is its
opposite.

I shall set forth to you that object of knowledge by knowing which
one attains to the beginningless *brahman*,[6] which is called neither
existent nor nonexistent. Its hands and feet stretching everywhere, its
head and face looking in every direction, its ears reaching out every
way, it covers all in the universe. While devoid of all the senses, it
appears[7] to have the qualities of all of them; while disinterested, it
15 sustains all; while beyond the *guṇas*, it experiences the *guṇas*. While
within and outside the creatures, it is both that which moves and that
which stands; it is hard to know because of its subtleness; and it is
both far away and nearby. Although undistributed, it appears
distributed among the creatures. It should be conceived of as at once
sustaining, bringing forth, and devouring the creatures. It is called the
light of lights beyond the darkness,[8] the knowledge, the object of
knowledge and the goal of knowledge that abides in the heart of
everyone. Thus in short has been expounded the field, and the
knowledge that is to be had of it: my devotee who achieves this
knowledge is fit to share in my being.

Know that Prakṛti and Puruṣa are both beginningless, and that
20 Prakṛti is the source of the evolutes and the *guṇas*. Prakṛti is stated to
be a cause inasmuch as it is the agency in the production of products,[9]
while Puruṣa is stated to be a cause in that he experiences happiness
and unhappiness. For Puruṣa residing within Prakṛti experiences the
guṇas that spring from Prakṛti: his involvement with the *guṇas* is the
cause of births in either high wombs or low ones. The Great Lord,
also called Supreme Soul, is that transcendent Puruṣa who is spectator,
consenter, sustainer, and experiencer. He who thus knows Puruṣa,
Prakṛti, and *guṇas* is not born again, in whatever way he now exists.

There are those who by themselves see that soul in themselves by
means of introspection.[10] Others do so by means of the yoga of
25 acquired insight.[11] Still others by means of the yoga of action. And
then there are those who, albeit ignorant, hear of it from others and
believe in it: they too, true believers in what they hear, do overcome
death.

Whatever creature is born, whether moving or standing, springs from the union of "field" and "guide"—realize that, bull of the Bharatas. He who sees the Supreme Lord equally present in all creatures, not perishing while these creatures perish, he sees indeed.

samaṃ paśyan hi sarvatra samavasthitam īśvaram /
na hinasty ātmanātmānaṃ tato yāti parāṃ gatim //
prakṛtyaiva ca karmāṇi kriyamāṇāni sarvaśaḥ /
yaḥ paśyati tathātmānam akartāraṃ sa paśyati //
30 *yadā bhūtapṛthagbhāvam ekastham anupaśyati /*
tata eva ca vistāraṃ brahma saṃpadyate tadā //
anāditvān nirguṇatvāt paramātmāyam avyayaḥ /
śarīrastho 'pi Kaunteya na karoti na lipyate //
yathā sarvagataṃ saukṣmyād ākāśaṃ nopalipyate /
sarvatrāvasthito dehe tathātmā nopalipyate //
yathā prakāśayaty ekaḥ kṛtsnaṃ lokam imaṃ raviḥ /
kṣetraṃ kṣetrī tathā kṛtsnaṃ prakāśayati Bhārata //
kṣetrakṣetrajñayor evam antaraṃ jñānacakṣuṣā /
bhūtaprakṛtimokṣaṃ ca ye vidur yānti te param //

Śrībhagavān uvāca /
36[14].1 *paraṃ bhūyaḥ pravakṣyāmi jñānānāṃ jñānam uttamam /*
yaj jñātvā munayaḥ sarve parāṃ siddhim ito gatāḥ //
idaṃ jñānam upāśritya mama sādharmyam āgatāḥ /
sarge 'pi nopajāyante pralaye na vyathanti ca //
mama yonir mahad brahma tasmin garbhaṃ dadhāmy aham /
saṃbhavaḥ sarvabhūtānāṃ tato bhavati Bhārata //
sarvayoniṣu Kaunteya mūrtayaḥ saṃbhavanti yāḥ /
tāsāṃ brahma mahad yonir ahaṃ bījapradaḥ pitā //
5 *sattvaṃ rajas tama iti guṇāḥ prakṛtisaṃbhavāḥ /*
nibadhnanti mahābāho dehe dehinam avyayam //
tatra sattvaṃ nirmalatvāt prakāśakam anāmayam /
sukhasaṅgena badhnāti jñānasaṅgena cānagha //
rajo rāgātmakaṃ viddhi tṛṣṇāsaṅgasamudbhavam /
tan nibadhnāti Kaunteya karmasaṅgena dehinam //
tamas tv ajñānajaṃ viddhi mohanaṃ sarvadehinām /
pramādālasyanidrābhis tan nibadhnāti Bhārata //
sattvaṃ sukhe sañjayati rajaḥ karmaṇi Bhārata /
jñānam āvṛtya tu tamaḥ pramāde sañjayaty uta //
10 *rajas tamaś cābhibhūya sattvaṃ bhavati Bhārata /*
rajaḥ sattvaṃ tamaś caiva tamaḥ sattvaṃ rajas tathā //
sarvadvāreṣu dehe 'smin prakāśa upajāyate /
jñānaṃ yadā tadā vidyād vivṛddhaṃ sattvam ity uta //
lobhaḥ pravṛttir ārambhaḥ karmaṇām aśamaḥ spṛhā /
rajasy etāni jāyante vivṛddhe Bharatarṣabha //
aprakāśo 'pravṛttiś ca pramādo moha eva ca /
tamasy etāni jāyante vivṛddhe Kurunandana //

When he sees the lord equally present everywhere, he himself no
longer hurts the self[12] and then goes the supreme journey. He who
sees that all actions are performed by Prakṛti alone and that the self
30 does not act at all, sees indeed. When he perceives that the variety of
beings have one center from which all expand, then he is at one with
brahman.

This imperishable self is transcendent because of its beginninglessness and its being beyond the *guṇas*. Although present in the body, Kaunteya, it does not act nor is it affected. Just as all-pervading space is not affected because it is too subtle, so this self, while present in every body, is not affected. Even as the one sun illumines the entire world, thus the owner of the field illumines the entire field, Bhārata. Those who with the eye of insight realize the boundary of field and guide, and the mode of separation from the Prakṛti of beings, attain the ultimate.

The Lord said:

36[14].1 Again I shall instruct you in the highest import of all knowledge,
the knowledge through which all hermits have acquired supreme
success. By absorbing this knowledge they have reached my order of
being and at periodic creation are not reborn, nor do they suffer at the
time of dissolution.

The Large Brahman is womb to me: in it I plant the seed, and
thence the origination of all beings takes effect, Bhārata. The Large
Brahman is the original womb from which the forms that are born
from any wombs ultimately issue, Kaunteya, while I am the father
5 who bestows the fruit. The *guṇas* called *sattva, rajas,* and *tamas* are
born from Prakṛti, and they fetter the eternal embodied souls to their
bodies, strong-armed one. Among these *guṇas, sattva,* which because
of its spotlessness is illumining and salubrious, binds the soul by means
of an attachment to joy and an attachment to knowledge, prince sans
blame. Know that *rajas* is characterized by passion and arises from an
attachment to craving; it binds the embodied soul by an attachment
to action, Kaunteya. Know, on the other hand, that *tamas* arises from
ignorance and deludes the embodied souls; it binds through
absentmindedness, sloth, and sleep, Bhārata. *Sattva* attaches one to
joy, *rajas* to activity, Bhārata; *tamas* attaches one to negligence by
obfuscating knowledge.

10 *Sattva* predominates by suppressing *rajas* and *tamas*, Bhārata; *rajas*
by suppressing *sattva* and *tamas, tamas* by suppressing *sattva* and
rajas. When in all the faculties in the body the light of knowledge
shines forth, then one knows that *sattva* is in full strength. When *rajas*
predominates, there arise greed, vigorous activity, enterprise,
restlessness, and passion, bull among Bharatas. Obscurity, indolence,
neglect, and delusion arise when *tamas* prevails, joy of the Kurus. If

yadā sattve pravṛddhe tu pralayaṃ yāti dehabhṛt /
tadottamavidāṃ lokān amalān pratipadyate //
15 *rajasi pralayaṃ gatvā karmasaṅgiṣu jāyate /*
tathā pralīnas tamasi mūḍhayoniṣu jāyate //
karmaṇaḥ sukṛtasyāhuḥ sāttvikaṃ nirmalaṃ phalam /
rajasas tu phalaṃ duḥkham ajñānaṃ tamasaḥ phalam //
sattvāt saṃjāyate jñānaṃ rajaso lobha eva ca /
pramādamohau tamaso bhavato 'jñānam eva ca //
ūrdhvaṃ gacchanti sattvasthā madhye tiṣṭhanti rājasāḥ /
jaghanyaguṇavṛttasthā adho gacchanti tāmasāḥ //
nānyaṃ guṇebhyaḥ kartāraṃ yadā draṣṭānupaśyati /
guṇebhyaś ca paraṃ vetti madbhāvaṃ so 'dhigacchati //
20 *guṇān etān atītya trīn dehī dehasamudbhavān /*
janmamṛtyujarāduḥkhair vimukto 'mṛtam aśnute //
Arjuna uvāca /
kair liṅgais trīn guṇān etān atīto bhavati prabho /
kimācāraḥ kathaṃ caitāṃs trīn guṇān ativartate //
Śrībhagavān uvāca /
prakāśaṃ ca pravṛttiṃ ca moham eva ca Pāṇḍava /
na dveṣṭi saṃpravṛttāni na nivṛttāni kāṅkṣati //
udāsīnavad āsīno guṇair yo na vicālyate /
guṇā vartanta ity eva yo 'vatiṣṭhati neṅgate //
samaduḥkhasukhaḥ svasthaḥ samaloṣṭāśmakāñcanaḥ /
tulyapriyāpriyo dhīras tulyanindātmasaṃstutiḥ //
25 *mānāvamānayos tulyas tulyo mitrāripakṣayoḥ /*
sarvārambhaparityāgī guṇātītaḥ sa ucyate //
māṃ ca yo 'vyabhicāreṇa bhaktiyogena sevate /
sa guṇān samatītyaitān brahmabhūyāya kalpate //
brahmaṇo hi pratiṣṭhāham amṛtasyāvyayasya ca /
śāśvatasya ca dharmasya sukhasyaikāntikasya ca //

Śrībhagavān uvāca /
37[15].1 *ūrdhvamūlam adhaḥśākham Aśvatthaṃ prāhur avyayam /*
chandāṃsi yasya parṇāni yas taṃ veda sa vedavit //
adhaś cordhvaṃ prasṛtās tasya śākhā
guṇapravṛddhā viṣayapravālāḥ /
adhaś ca mūlāny anusaṃtatāni
karmānubandhīni manuṣyaloke //

the embodied soul dies when *sattva* reigns, he attains to the pure
15 worlds[1] of those who have the highest knowledge. The one dying in
rajas is reborn among people who are given to acting; while one
expiring in *tamas* is born among the witless.
They say that the pure reward of correct action has the nature of
sattva, that the fruit of *rajas* is unhappiness, and of *tamas* ignorance.
From *sattva* rises knowledge, from *rajas* greed, from *tamas* negligence,
delusion, and ignorance. Those abiding in *sattva* go upward, those in
rajas stay in the middle, those who abide in the function of *tamas*, the
lowest of the *guṇas*, go downward.
When a man of insight perceives that no one but the *guṇas* acts
and knows the one who transcends the *guṇas*, he ascends to my being.
20 By transcending these three *guṇas*, which are the sources of the body,[2]
the embodied soul rids himself of the miseries of birth, death, and old
age and becomes immortal.
Arjuna said:
My lord, what are the signs by which one who transcends the
guṇas may be known? How does he behave? And how does he
overcome these three *guṇas*?
The Lord said:
That man does not abhor illumination, activism, and delusion[3]
when they are at work in himself, nor aspires to them when they are
not at work. A man is declared to have transcended the *guṇas* when
he sits aside as a disinterested party, is not moved by the *guṇas* and
does not react to them, knowing that it is just the *guṇas* at work;
who is equable in happiness and unhappiness, self-contained, equal-
minded toward a lump of clay, a rock of gold, the same toward the
pleasing and the displeasing, imperturbable, facing blame and praise
25 with equanimity, equable in honor and dishonor, and toward friend
and foe, and who relinquishes all undertakings. He who attends on me
unstrayingly with the discipline of the yoga of devotion and thus
transcends the *guṇas* is fit to become *brahman*. For I am the foundation
of *brahman*, of the immortal and intransient, of the sempiternal Law,
and of perfect bliss.

The Lord said:
37[15].1 They speak of the eternal Aśvattha[1] tree whose roots are above,
whose branches below, and whose leaves are the hymns: he who
understands it understands the Veda.

Its branches are stretching downward and up;
They thrive on the *guṇas* with buds that are objects;
The roots reach gradually down to the ground
In the world of men, connecting with *karman*.

na rūpam asyeha tathopalabhyate
nānto na cādir na ca saṃpratiṣṭhā /
Aśvattham enaṃ suvirūḍhamūlam
asaṅgaśastreṇa dṛḍhena chittvā //
tataḥ padaṃ tat parimārgitavyaṃ
yasmin gatā na nivartanti bhūyaḥ /
tam eva cādyaṃ puruṣaṃ prapadye
yataḥ pravṛttiḥ prasṛtā purāṇī //
5 *nirmānamohā jitasaṅgadoṣā*
adhyātmanityā vinivṛttakāmāḥ /
dvaṃdvair vimuktāḥ sukhaduḥkhasaṃjñair
gacchanty amūḍhāḥ padam avyayaṃ tat //
na tad bhāsayate sūryo na śaśāṅko na pāvakaḥ /
yad gatvā na nivartante tad dhāma paramaṃ mama //
mamaivāṃśo jīvaloke jīvabhūtaḥ sanātanaḥ /
manaḥṣaṣṭhānīndriyāṇi prakṛtisthāni karṣati //
śarīraṃ yad avāpnoti yac cāpy utkrāmatīśvaraḥ /
gṛhītvaitāni saṃyāti vāyur gandhān ivāśayāt //
śrotraṃ cakṣuḥ sparśanaṃ ca rasanaṃ ghrāṇam eva ca /
adhiṣṭhāya manaś cāyaṃ viṣayān upasevate //
10 *utkrāmantaṃ sthitaṃ vāpi bhuñjānaṃ vā guṇānvitam /*
vimūḍhā nānupaśyanti paśyanti jñānacakṣuṣaḥ //
yatanto yoginaś cainaṃ paśyanty ātmany avasthitam /
yatanto 'py akṛtātmāno nainaṃ paśyanty acetasaḥ //
yad ādityagataṃ tejo jagad bhāsayate 'khilam /
yac candramasi yac cāgnau tat tejo viddhi māmakam //
gām āviśya ca bhūtāni dhārayāmy aham ojasā /
puṣṇāmi cauṣadhīḥ sarvāḥ somo bhūtvā rasātmakaḥ //
ahaṃ vaiśvānaro bhūtvā prāṇināṃ deham āśritaḥ /
prāṇāpānasamāyuktaḥ pacāmy annaṃ caturvidham //
15 *sarvasya cāhaṃ hṛdi saṃniviṣṭo*
mattaḥ smṛtir jñānam apohanaṃ ca /
vedaiś ca sarvair aham eva vedyo
vedāntakṛd vedavid eva cāham //
dvāv imau puruṣau loke kṣaraś cākṣara eva ca /
kṣaraḥ sarvāṇi bhūtāni kūṭastho 'kṣara ucyate //
uttamaḥ puruṣas tv anyaḥ paramātmety udāhṛtaḥ /
yo lokatrayam āviśya bibharty avyaya īśvaraḥ //
yasmāt kṣaram atīto 'ham akṣarād api cottamaḥ /
ato 'smi loke vede ca prathitaḥ puruṣottamaḥ //

No form can here be perceived of it,
Neither end nor beginning nor final foundation—
Cut down this Aśvattha so thoroughly rooted
With the hardened axe of disinterest.

Then try to seek out that singular spot
Whence one does not return once he has found it:
"I draw near to that primordial Person
From whom has derived this ancient impulse."

5 Without pride or delusion or flaws of attachment,
Immersed in the self, all cravings abated,
From dualities freed, from joy and grief,
They attain, undeluded, that permanent spot.

Neither sun nor moon nor fire illumine it, that supreme domain of
mine, on reaching which they do not return. A particle of myself, as
the eternal individual soul in the order of souls,[2] pulls on the senses
and mind that are part of Prakṛti, the master[3] who takes on a body
and again escapes it, transmigrating out of it with these senses as the
wind moves on with the scents it has taken from their sources. He is
the one who oversees[4] the workings of hearing, sight, touch, taste,
10 smell, and thought and thus savors the objects. Whether he departs
from or remains in the body, or experiences things according to the
guṇas—the deluded do not perceive him: only those with the eyesight
of knowledge do. The yogins who exert themselves see him reside
within themselves, but those who have not mastered themselves and
lack insight do not see him, however hard they try.

Know that it is my light that in the sun illumines the entire universe, the light that is in moon and sun. Permeating the earth I support the creatures with my power; I nurture all the herbs as the Soma endowed with all tastes. As the digestive fire lying within the bodies of living beings, I consume with the aid of *prāṇa* and *apāna* the four kinds of food.

15 I dwell in the heart of everyone,
From me spring memory, knowledge, and reason;
I am known through the knowledge of all the Vedas,
I make the Vedānta,[5] I know the Veda.

In this world there are two Persons, the transient and the intransient.[6] The transient comprises all creatures, the intransient is called the One-on-the-Peak.[7] There is yet a third Person, whom they call the Supreme Soul, the everlasting lord who permeates and sustains the three worlds. Inasmuch as I have passed beyond the transient and transcend the intransient, therefore I am, in world and in Veda, renowned as the Supreme Person.

yo mām evam asaṃmūḍho jānāti puruṣottamam /
sa sarvavid bhajati māṃ sarvabhāvena Bhārata //
20 *iti guhyatamaṃ śāstram idam uktaṃ mayānagha /*
etad buddhvā buddhimān syāt kṛtakṛtyaś ca Bhārata //

Śrībhagavān uvāca /
38[16].1 *abhayaṃ sattvasaṃśuddhir jñānayogavyavasthitiḥ /*
dānaṃ damaś ca yajñaś ca svādhyāyas tapa ārjavam //
ahiṃsā satyam akrodhas tyāgaḥ śāntir apaiśunam /
dayā bhūteṣv aloluptvaṃ mārdavaṃ hrīr acāpalam //
tejaḥ kṣamā dhṛtiḥ śaucam adroho nātimānitā /
bhavanti saṃpadaṃ daivīm abhijātasya Bhārata //
dambho darpo 'timānaś ca krodhaḥ pāruṣyam eva ca /
ajñānaṃ cābhijātasya Pārtha saṃpadam āsurīm //
5 *daivī saṃpad vimokṣāya nibandhāyāsurī matā /*
mā śucaḥ saṃpadaṃ daivīm abhijāto 'si Pāṇḍava //
dvau bhūtasargau loke 'smin daiva āsura eva ca /
daivo vistaraśaḥ prokta āsuraṃ Pārtha me śṛṇu //
pravṛttiṃ ca nivṛttiṃ ca janā na vidur āsurāḥ /
na śaucaṃ nāpi cācāro na satyaṃ teṣu vidyate //
asatyam apratiṣṭhaṃ te jagad āhur anīśvaram /
aparasparasaṃbhūtaṃ kim anyat kāmahaitukam //
etāṃ dṛṣṭim avaṣṭabhya naṣṭātmāno 'lpabuddhayaḥ /
prabhavanty ugrakarmāṇaḥ kṣayāya jagato 'hitāḥ //
10 *kāmam āśritya duṣpūraṃ dambhamānamadānvitāḥ /*
mohād gṛhītvāsadgrāhān pravartante 'śucivratāḥ //
cintām aparimeyāṃ ca pralayāntām upāśritāḥ /
kāmopabhogaparamā etāvad iti niścitāḥ //
āśāpāśaśatair baddhāḥ kāmakrodhaparāyaṇāḥ /
īhante kāmabhogārtham anyāyenārthasaṃcayān //
idam adya mayā labdham idaṃ prāpsye manoratham /
idam astīdam api me bhaviṣyati punar dhanam //
asau mayā hataḥ śatrur haniṣye cāparān api /
īśvaro 'ham ahaṃ bhogī siddho 'haṃ balavān sukhī //
15 *āḍhyo 'bhijanavān asmi ko 'nyo 'sti sadṛśo mayā /*
yakṣye dāsyāmi modiṣya ity ajñānavimohitāḥ //
anekacittavibhrāntā mohajālasamāvṛtāḥ /
prasaktāḥ kāmabhogeṣu patanti narake 'śucau //
ātmasaṃbhāvitāḥ stabdhā dhanamānamadānvitāḥ /
yajante nāmayajñais te dambhenāvidhipūrvakam //
ahaṃkāraṃ balaṃ darpaṃ kāmaṃ krodhaṃ ca saṃśritāḥ /

He who is rid of his delusions and knows me thus as the Supreme
Person knows all there is to know; and he partakes of me with all his
20 being, Bhārata. Thus have I declared to you, prince sans blame, this
most mysterious doctrine: by understanding it one becomes an
awakened man who has completed his task, Bhārata.

The Lord said:

38[16].1 Fearlessness, inner purity, fortitude in the yoking of knowledge,
liberality, self-control, sacrifice, Vedic study, austerity, uprightness,
noninjuriousness, truthfulness, peaceableness, relinquishment,
serenity, loyalty, compassion for creatures, lack of greed, gentleness,
modesty, reliability, vigor, patience, fortitude, purity, friendliness, and
lack of too much pride comprise the divine complement of virtues of
him who is born to it, Bhārata. Deceit, pride, too much self-esteem,
irascibility, harshness, and ignorance are of him who is born to the
5 demonic complement, Pārtha. The divine complement leads to release,
the demonic to bondage. Have no qualms, Pāṇḍava, you have been
born to the divine. There are two kinds of creation in this world, the
divine and the demonic. I have spoken of the divine in detail, now
hear from me about the demonic, Pārtha.

Demonic people do not know when to initiate action and when to
desist from it; theirs is neither purity, nor deportment, nor truthfulness.
They maintain that this world has no true reality, or foundation, or
God, and is not produced by the interdependence of causes. By what
then? By mere desire. Embracing this view, these lost souls of small
enlightenment are with their dreadful actions capable of destroying
10 this world they seek to hurt. Embracing this "desire," which is
insatiable, they go about, filled with the intoxication of vanity and
self-pride, accepting false doctrines in their folly and following
polluting life rules. Subject to worries without measure that end only
with their death, they are totally immersed in the indulgence of
desires, convinced that that is all there is. Strangled with hundreds of
nooses of expectation, giving in to desire and anger, they seek to
accumulate wealth by wrongful means in order to indulge their
desire. "This I got today, that craving I still have to satisfy. This much
I have as of now, but I'll get more riches. I have already killed that
enemy, others I still have to kill. I am a master, I enjoy, I am
15 successful, strong and happy. I am a rich man of high family; who
can equal me? I shall sacrifice, I shall make donations, I shall enjoy
myself," so they think in the folly of their ignorance. Confused by too
many concerns, covered by a net of delusions, addicted to the
pleasures of desire, they fall into foul hell. Puffed up by their egos,
arrogant, drunk with wealth and pride, they offer up sacrifices in
name only, without proper injunction, out of sheer vanity.

Embracing egotism, overbearing strength, pride, desire, and anger,

mām ātmaparadeheṣu pradviṣanto 'bhyasūyakāḥ //
tān ahaṃ dviṣataḥ krūrān saṃsāreṣu narādhamān /
kṣipāmy ajasram aśubhān āsurīṣv eva yoniṣu //
20 *āsurīṃ yonim āpannā mūḍhā janmani janmani /*
mām aprāpyaiva Kaunteya tato yānty adhamāṃ gatim //
trividhaṃ narakasyedaṃ dvāraṃ nāśanam ātmanaḥ /
kāmaḥ krodhas tathā lobhas tasmād etat trayaṃ tyajet //
etair vimuktaḥ Kaunteya tamodvārais tribhir naraḥ /
ācaraty ātmanaḥ śreyas tato yāti parāṃ gatim //
yaḥ śāstravidhim utsṛjya vartate kāmakārataḥ /
na sa siddhim avāpnoti na sukhaṃ na parāṃ gatim //
tasmāc chāstraṃ pramāṇaṃ te kāryākāryavyavasthitau /
jñātvā śāstravidhānoktaṃ karma kartum ihārhasi //

Arjuna uvāca /
39[17].1 *ye śāstravidhim utsṛjya yajante śraddhayānvitāḥ /*
teṣāṃ niṣṭhā tu kā Kṛṣṇa sattvam āho rajas tamaḥ //
Śrībhagavān uvāca /
trividhā bhavati śraddhā dehināṃ sā svabhāvajā /
sāttvikī rājasī caiva tāmasī ceti tāṃ śṛṇu //
sattvānurūpā sarvasya śraddhā bhavati Bhārata /
śraddhāmayo 'yaṃ puruṣo yo yacchraddhaḥ sa eva saḥ //
yajante sāttvikā devān Yakṣa-Rakṣāṃsi rājasāḥ /
pretān bhūtagaṇāṃś cānye yajante tāmasā janāḥ //
5 *aśāstravihitaṃ ghoraṃ tapyante ye tapo janāḥ /*
dambhāhaṃkārasaṃyuktāḥ kāmarāgabalānvitāḥ //
karśayantaḥ śarīrasthaṃ bhūtagrāmam acetasaḥ /
māṃ caivāntaḥśarīrasthaṃ tān viddhy āsuraniścayān //
āhāras tv api sarvasya trividho bhavati priyaḥ /
yajñas tapas tathā dānaṃ teṣāṃ bhedam imaṃ śṛṇu //
āyuḥsattvabalārogyasukhaprītivivardhanāḥ /
rasyāḥ snigdhāḥ sthirā hṛdyā āhārāḥ sāttvikapriyāḥ //
kaṭvamlalavaṇātyuṣṇatīkṣṇarūkṣavidāhinaḥ /
āhārā rājasasyeṣṭā duḥkhaśokāmayapradāḥ //
10 *yātayāmaṃ gatarasaṃ pūti paryuṣitaṃ ca yat /*
ucchiṣṭam api cāmedhyaṃ bhojanaṃ tāmasapriyam //
aphalākāṅkṣibhir yajño vidhidṛṣṭo ya ijyate /
yaṣṭavyam eveti manaḥ samādhāya sa sāttvikaḥ //
abhisaṃdhāya tu phalaṃ dambhārtham api caiva yat /
ijyate Bharataśreṣṭha taṃ yajñaṃ viddhi rājasam //
vidhihīnam asṛṣṭānnaṃ mantrahīnam adakṣiṇam /
śraddhāvirahitaṃ yajñaṃ tāmasaṃ paricakṣate //

they hate and berate me in their own bodies and in those of others.
Those hateful, cruel, vile, and polluted men I hurl ceaselessly into
20 demonic wombs. Reduced to demonic wombs birth after birth, and
deluded, they fail to reach me, Kaunteya, and go the lowest road. The gateway to hell that dooms the soul is threefold: desire, anger, greed—so rid yourself of these three. The man who is freed from these three gates to darkness, Kaunteya, and practices what is best for himself, goes the highest road. He who throws away the precepts of teachings and lives to indulge his desires does not attain to success, nor to happiness or the ultimate goal. Let therefore the teaching be your yardstick in establishing what is your task and what is not, and, with the knowledge of what the dictates of the teaching prescribe, pray do your acts in this world.

Arjuna said:

39[17].1 People who sacrifice outside the injunctions of the teaching, yet are full of faith, what foundation do they have, Kṛṣṇa, that of *sattva*, of *rajas*, or of *tamas*?

The Lord said:

In embodied souls Faith is of three kinds: according to a person's nature it is typed as *sattva*, *rajas*, or *tamas*. Listen. Everyone's faith conforms to this nature, Bhārata: a person is as good as his faith. He is what his faith makes him. Creatures of *sattva* sacrifice to Gods;
creatures of *rajas* to Yakṣas and Rākṣasas; creatures of *tamas* to
5 ghosts and ghouls. Men who practice awful austerities not provided
for by the texts, and practice them out of exhibitionism and egotism, as they are filled with desires and passions, mindlessly wracking the composite of elements in their bodies, and me to boot within their bodies,[1] know that their own persuasion is demonic.

The preferred food of everyone is also of three kinds, as are their sacrifices, austerities, and donations; hear the specifics. Those kinds of food which increase lifespan, mettle, vigor, health, comfort, and pleasure, and are tasty, bland, fortifying, and agreeable are preferred by *sattva* creatures. *Rajas* creatures like foods that are bitter, sour,
salty, very hot, sharp, rough, and burning, and that cause discomfort,
10 misery, and sickness. The *tamas* person prefers food that is stale, has
lost all taste, smells badly, is kept overnight, even polluted leftovers.

Sattva rules a person who offers up sacrifices found in the injunctions which are performed by those who do not covet their fruits, and observes them in the pure conviction that the sacrifice must go on. Of the *rajas* type, best of Bharatas, is the sacrifice that is offered up both to obtain the fruit and to display oneself. They call a sacrifice ruled by *tamas* when it is not enjoined, lacks nourishing ingredients, is unaccompanied by Vedic *mantras*, carries no priestly stipend,[2] and requires no faith.

devadvijaguruprājñapūjanaṃ śaucam ārjavam /
brahmacaryam ahiṃsā ca śārīraṃ tapa ucyate //
15 *anudvegakaraṃ vākyaṃ satyaṃ priyahitaṃ ca yat /*
svādhyāyābhyasanaṃ caiva vāṅmayaṃ tapa ucyate //
manaḥprasādaḥ saumyatvaṃ maunam ātmavinigrahaḥ /
bhāvasaṃśuddhir ity etat tapo mānasam ucyate //
śraddhayā parayā taptaṃ tapas tat trividhaṃ naraiḥ /
aphalākāṅkṣibhir yuktaiḥ sāttvikaṃ paricakṣate //
satkāramānapūjārthaṃ tapo dambhena caiva yat /
kriyate tad iha proktaṃ rājasaṃ calam adhruvam //
mūḍhagrāheṇātmano yat pīḍayā kriyate tapaḥ /
parasyotsādanārthaṃ vā tat tāmasam udāhṛtam //
20 *dātavyam iti yad dānaṃ dīyate 'nupakāriṇe /*
deśe kāle ca pātre ca tad dānaṃ sāttvikaṃ smṛtam //
yat tu pratyupakārārthaṃ phalam uddiśya vā punaḥ /
dīyate ca parikliṣṭaṃ tad dānaṃ rājasaṃ smṛtam //
adeśakāle yad dānam apātrebhyaś ca dīyate /
asatkṛtam avajñātaṃ tat tāmasam udāhṛtam //
OṂ tat sad iti nirdeśo brahmaṇas trividhaḥ smṛtaḥ /
brāhmaṇās tena vedāś ca yajñāś ca vihitāḥ purā //
tasmād OM ity udāhṛtya yajñadānatapaḥkriyāḥ /
pravartante vidhānoktāḥ satataṃ brahmavādinām //
25 *tad ity anabhisaṃdhāya phalaṃ yajñatapaḥkriyāḥ /*
dānakriyāś ca vividhāḥ kriyante mokṣakāṅkṣibhiḥ //
sadbhāve sādhubhāve ca sad ity etat prayujyate /
praśaste karmaṇi tathā sacchabdaḥ Pārtha yujyate //
yajñe tapasi dāne ca sthitiḥ sad iti cocyate /
karma caiva tadarthīyaṃ sad ity evābhidhīyate //
aśraddhayā hutaṃ dattaṃ tapas taptaṃ kṛtaṃ ca yat /
asad ity ucyate Pārtha na ca tat pretya no iha //

Arjuna uvāca /
40[18].1 *saṃnyāsasya mahābāho tattvam icchāmi veditum /*
tyāgasya ca Hṛṣīkeśa pṛthak Keśiniṣūdana //
Śrībhagavān uvāca /
kāmyānāṃ karmaṇāṃ nyāsaṃ saṃnyāsaṃ kavayo viduḥ /
sarvakarmaphalatyāgaṃ prāhus tyāgaṃ vicakṣaṇāḥ //
tyājyaṃ doṣavad ity eke karma prāhur manīṣiṇaḥ /
yajñadānatapaḥkarma na tyājyam iti cāpare //
niścayaṃ śṛṇu me tatra tyāge Bharatasattama /
tyāgo hi puruṣavyāghra trividhaḥ saṃprakīrtitaḥ //

Askesis of the body comprises homage to Gods, brahmins, gurus,
15 and sages; purity; uprightness; continence; and nonviolence. Askesis
of speech comprises speech that does not hurt, is veracious, pleasant,
and beneficial, as well as the recitation of the daily lesson. Askesis of
the mind comprises serenity of mind, gentleness, taciturnity, self-
control, and inner purity. This triple askesis practiced with the highest
faith by committed men who expect no rewards is of the nature of
sattva. Askesis that is practiced with ostentation and in order to gain
the reputation and homage attendant on pious deeds is said to be of
the *rajas* type, and is ephemeral and unstable. Askesis undertaken
under foolish misconceptions, by means of self-molestation, or to
effect another's downfall is of the *tamas* type.
20 That donation is known to be of the nature of *sattva* which is
bestowed upon one who has not been a benefactor, in the simple
conviction that gifts must be given, at the right time, in the right
place, to the right recipients. A donation is of the *rajas* type when it is
made defectively, with the purpose of repaying another or with a
view to a later reward. A donation is characterized by *tamas* when it
is made at the wrong place and time and to unworthy recipients,
without proper hospitality and in a contemptuous manner.
OṂ tat sat is the traditional triple designation of *brahman*;[3] with it
were of yore ordained the brahmins, the Vedas, and the sacrifices.
Therefore among those who profess *brahman*, the acts of sacrifice,
donation, and askesis as prescribed by the injunctions always proceed
25 after invoking *OṂ*. The acts of sacrifice, and askesis, and those of
donation in all their variety, are performed by those who wish for
release and covet no mundane reward, while pronouncing *tad*.[4] *Sat* is
used for that which is and that which is good. Thus the word *sat* is
used for any laudable act, Pārtha. *Sat* is also used for sacrifice,
donation, and askesis; any act involving these is styled *sat*. But the
sacrifice offered up, the donation bestowed, and the askesis practiced
without faith is called *asat*, Pārtha; and it has no existence, either here
or hereafter.

Arjuna said:
40[18].1 Strong-armed Hṛṣīkeśa, I wish to hear the nature of relinquishment and renunciation, and what sets them apart, Slayer of Keśin.

The Lord said:

The wise call it "relinquishment" when one gives up acts that are motivated only by desires,[1] while they call "renunciation" the renouncing of all fruits of acts.[2] Some teachers propound that all acting should be renounced, as it is all tainted; while others hold that such acts as sacrifice, donation, and askesis are not to be renounced.

So hear from me, best of the Bharatas, tiger among men, the decision about what is renunciation. Of renunciation there are

5 *yajñadānatapaḥkarma na tyājyaṃ kāryaṃ eva tat /*
yajño dānaṃ tapaś caiva pāvanāni manīṣiṇām //
etāny api tu karmāṇi saṅgaṃ tyaktvā phalāni ca /
kartavyānīti me Pārtha niścitaṃ matam uttamam //
niyatasya tu saṃnyāsaḥ karmaṇo nopapadyate /
mohāt tasya parityāgas tāmasaḥ parikīrtitaḥ //
duḥkham ity eva yat karma kāyakleśabhayāt tyajet /
sa kṛtvā rājasaṃ tyāgaṃ naiva tyāgaphalaṃ labhet //
kāryam ity eva yat karma niyataṃ kriyate 'rjuna /
saṅgaṃ tyaktvā phalaṃ caiva sa tyāgaḥ sāttviko mataḥ //
10 *na dveṣṭy akuśalaṃ karma kuśale nānuṣajjate /*
tyāgī sattvasamāviṣṭo medhāvī chinnasaṃśayaḥ //
na hi dehabhṛtā śakyaṃ tyaktuṃ karmāṇy aśeṣataḥ /
yas tu karmaphalatyāgī sa tyāgīty abhidhīyate //
aniṣṭam iṣṭaṃ miśraṃ ca trividhaṃ karmaṇaḥ phalam /
bhavaty atyāgināṃ pretya na tu saṃnyāsināṃ kvacit //
pañcaitāni mahābāho kāraṇāni nibodha me /
sāṃkhye kṛtānte proktāni siddhaye sarvakarmaṇām //
adhiṣṭhānaṃ tathā kartā karaṇaṃ ca pṛthagvidham /
vividhāś ca pṛthakceṣṭā daivaṃ caivātra pañcamam //
15 *śarīravāṅmanobhir yat karma prārabhate naraḥ /*
nyāyyaṃ vā viparītaṃ vā pañcaite tasya hetavaḥ //
tatraivaṃ sati kartāram ātmānaṃ kevalaṃ tu yaḥ /
paśyaty akṛtabuddhitvān na sa paśyati durmatiḥ //
yasya nāhaṃkṛto bhāvo buddhir yasya na lipyate /
hatvāpi sa imāṃl lokān na hanti na nibadhyate //
jñānaṃ jñeyaṃ parijñātā trividhā karmacodanā /
karaṇaṃ karma karteti trividhaḥ karmasaṃgrahaḥ //
jñānaṃ karma ca kartā ca tridhaiva guṇabhedataḥ /
procyate guṇasaṃkhyāne yathāvac chṛṇu tāny api //
20 *sarvabhūteṣu yenaikaṃ bhāvam avyayam īkṣate /*
avibhaktaṃ vibhakteṣu taj jñānaṃ viddhi sāttvikam //
pṛthaktvena tu yaj jñānaṃ nānābhāvān pṛthagvidhān /
vetti sarveṣu bhūteṣu taj jñānaṃ viddhi rājasam //
yat tu kṛtsnavad ekasmin kārye saktam ahaitukam /
atattvārthavad alpaṃ ca tat tāmasam udāhṛtam //
niyataṃ saṅgarahitam arāgadveṣataḥ kṛtam /
aphalaprepsunā karma yat tat sāttvikam ucyate //
yat tu kāmepsunā karma sāhaṃkāreṇa vā punaḥ /
kriyate bahulāyāsaṃ tad rājasam udāhṛtam //
25 *anubandhaṃ kṣayaṃ hiṃsām anapekṣya ca pauruṣam /*
mohād ārabhyate karma yat tat tāmasam ucyate //

declared to be three kinds.[3] Acts of sacrifice, donation, and askesis are *not* to be renounced: They are one's task—sacrifice, donation, and askesis sanctify the wise. It is my final judgment, Pārtha, that these acts are to be performed, but with the performer renouncing all self-interest in them and all their rewards. It does not do to give up an act that is prescribed; giving acts up out of folly is the inspiration of *tamas*. If one renounces an act out of fear of physical hardship, because it is "too difficult," his renunciation is inspired by *rajas*. But renunciation is regarded as inspired by *sattva* if one performs a prescribed act because it is one's task, while renouncing all self-interest in it and all reward from it. The wise renouncer inspired by *sattva*, who has resolved his doubts, does not hate an act because it is unpleasant, or like one because it is pleasant. After all, no one who has a body can renounce all acts completely: he is the true renouncer who renounces the fruits of his acts.

Now, there are three kinds of fruits to an act: disagreeable, agreeable, and mixed; but such is the *karman* of the nonrenouncers hereafter,[4] but never of the renouncers. Hear from me, strong-armed prince, the five factors which in Sāṃkhyan doctrine are stated to lead to the successful performance of all acts: the realm of the object; the agent; the different means; the various sorts of action; and finally divine fate.[5] These five factors are present whatever act a man undertakes, whether with body, speech, or mind, and whether right or wrong. This being the case, when a man because of insufficient understanding looks upon himself as the sole agent, he is in error and does not see. He whose disposition is not dominated by his ego and whose understanding is not obscured, does not kill and is not bound by his act were he to kill off these three worlds.

There is a triple impulse to action: knowledge, its object, and its subject; while the act itself comprises these three: means, object, and agent. Knowledge, action, and agent are of three kinds, according to the prevailing *guṇa*. Hear then how this division has been set forth in the enumeration of *guṇas*. Know that that knowledge is of a *sattva* nature through which one perceives a single eternal being in all creatures, a being which, though parceled out, is indivisible. The knowledge that divisively perceives just various forms as being distributed over all the creatures is of the nature of *rajas*. To *tamas* is assigned that knowledge which, though limited and devoid of substance, groundlessly fixes on one object as though it were all.

Action is of the nature of *sattva* when it is done as prescribed, without self-interest, without love or hate, by one who does not wish to reap the reward. Action is assigned to *rajas* when it is painfully done by one who wants to gain something or who is motivated by egotism. Of *tamas* is declared to be that action which is mindlessly undertaken without considering consequences, possible death or

muktasaṅgo 'nahaṃvādī dhṛtyutsāhasamanvitaḥ /
siddhyasiddhyor nirvikāraḥ kartā sāttvika ucyate //
rāgī karmaphalaprepsur lubdho hiṃsātmako 'śuciḥ /
harṣaśokānvitaḥ kartā rājasaḥ parikīrtitaḥ //
ayuktaḥ prākṛtaḥ stabdhaḥ śaṭho naikṛtiko 'lasaḥ /
viṣādī dīrghasūtrī ca kartā tāmasa ucyate //
buddher bhedaṃ dhṛteś caiva guṇatas trividhaṃ śṛṇu /
procyamānam aśeṣeṇa pṛthaktvena Dhanaṃjaya //
30 *pravṛttiṃ ca nivṛttiṃ ca kāryākārye bhayābhaye /*
bandhaṃ mokṣaṃ ca yā vetti buddhiḥ sā Pārtha sāttvikī //
yayā dharmam adharmaṃ ca kāryaṃ cākāryam eva ca /
ayathāvat prajānāti buddhiḥ sā Pārtha rājasī //
adharmaṃ dharmam iti yā manyate tamasāvṛtā /
sarvārthān viparītāṃś ca buddhiḥ sā Pārtha tāmasī //
dhṛtyā yayā dhārayate manaḥprāṇendriyakriyāḥ /
yogenāvyabhicāriṇyā dhṛtiḥ sā Pārtha sāttvikī //
yayā tu dharmakāmārthān dhṛtyā dhārayate 'rjuna /
prasaṅgena phalākāṅkṣī dhṛtiḥ sā Pārtha rājasī //
35 *yayā svapnaṃ bhayaṃ śokaṃ viṣādaṃ madam eva ca /*
na vimuñcati durmedhā dhṛtiḥ sā Pārtha tāmasī //
sukhaṃ tv idānīṃ trividhaṃ śṛṇu me Bharatarṣabha /
abhyāsād ramate yatra duḥkhāntaṃ ca nigacchati //
yat tad agre viṣam iva pariṇāme 'mṛtopamam /
tat sukhaṃ sāttvikaṃ proktam ātmabuddhiprasādajam //
viṣayendriyasaṃyogād yat tad agre 'mṛtopamam /
pariṇāme viṣam iva tat sukhaṃ rājasaṃ smṛtam //
yad agre cānubandhe ca sukhaṃ mohanam ātmanaḥ /
nidrālasyapramādotthaṃ tat tāmasam udāhṛtam //
40 *na tad asti pṛthivyāṃ vā divi deveṣu vā punaḥ /*
sattvaṃ prakṛtijair muktaṃ yad ebhiḥ syāt tribhir guṇaiḥ //
brāhmaṇakṣatriyaviśāṃ śūdrāṇāṃ ca paraṃtapa /
karmāṇi pravibhaktāni svabhāvaprabhavair guṇaiḥ //
śamo damas tapaḥ śaucaṃ kṣāntir ārjavam eva ca /
jñānaṃ vijñānam āstikyaṃ brahmakarma svabhāvajam //
śauryaṃ tejo dhṛtir dākṣyaṃ yuddhe cāpy apalāyanam /
dānam īśvarabhāvaś ca kṣatrakarma svabhāvajam //
kṛṣigorakṣyavāṇijyaṃ vaiśyakarma svabhāvajam /
paricaryātmakaṃ karma śūdrasyāpi svabhāvajam //

injury, and one's own capacity for it.
An agent is of the nature of *sattva* when he is free from self-
interest, self-effacing, filled with fortitude and enterprise, and
undisturbed by success and failure. He is of *rajas* when he is
passionate, covetous of the fruits of his actions, greedy, injurious,
impure, and filled with joy and grief. He is assigned to *tamas* when he
is undisciplined, instinctive, insolent, crooked, deceitful, lazy, defeatist,
and procrastinating.
Likewise hear the triple divisions, determined by *guṇa*, of intelligence
and fortitude, as they are described severally and in sum, Dhanaṃjaya.
30 That intelligence proceeds from *sattva*, Pārtha, which understands
when to act and when not, what is a task and what not, what is a
cause of fear and what not, what is bondage and what deliverance.
To *rajas* goes the intelligence with which one incorrectly perceives
Law and lawlessness, task and non-task. An intelligence is inspired by
tamas, Pārtha, when, obscured by darkness, it mistakes lawlessness for
Law and perceives all matters topsy-turvy.
That fortitude with which one sustains the operations of mind,
prāṇas and senses in unswerving yoga is of the nature of *sattva*,
Pārtha. The fortitude with which one sustains Law, Profit, and
Pleasure out of self-interest, because one desires the rewards, Arjuna
35 Pārtha, is of the nature of *rajas*. While the fortitude with which a
mindless person does not rid himself of sleep, fear, grief, despair, and
inebriation is of the nature of *tamas*, Pārtha.
Hear from me now, bull of the Bharatas, about the three kinds of
happiness in which a person delights by practicing it assiduously and
finds the end of his sorrows. That is propounded to be happiness in
sattva which at first seems like poison but as it matures is like Elixir,
the happiness which springs from the serenity of one's own[6] spirit.
That happiness which springs from the contact of senses with objects,
and at first seems like Elixir but as it matures is like poison, is known
as a product of *rajas*. The happiness which, at first and ever after, is
the befuddlement of self which arises from sleep, sloth, and distraction
is declared a product of *tamas*.
40 There is not a creature on earth, nor in heaven among the Gods,
which is free from these three *guṇas* that spring from Prakṛti. The acts
of brahmins, barons, commoners, and serfs, enemy-burner, divide
themselves according to the *guṇas* that spring from nature.
Tranquillity, self-control, austerity, purity, patience, honesty, insight,
knowledge, and true faith are the brahmin's task, which derives from
his nature. Gallantry, energy, fortitude, capability, unretreating
steadfastness in war, liberality, and the exercise of power are the
baron's task, which spring from his nature. Husbandry, cattle herding,
and trade are the commoner's task, which derives from his nature;
while the natural task of the serf is to serve.

45 *sve sve karmaṇy abhirataḥ saṃsiddhiṃ labhate naraḥ /*
svakarmanirataḥ siddhiṃ yathā vindati tac chṛṇu //
yataḥ pravṛttir bhūtānāṃ yena sarvam idaṃ tatam /
svakarmaṇā tam abhyarcya siddhiṃ vindati mānavaḥ //
śreyān svadharmo viguṇaḥ paradharmāt svanuṣṭhitāt /
svabhāvaniyataṃ karma kurvan nāpnoti kilbiṣam //
sahajaṃ karma Kaunteya sadoṣam api na tyajet /
sarvārambhā hi doṣeṇa dhūmenāgnir ivāvṛtāḥ //
asaktabuddhiḥ sarvatra jitātmā vigataspṛhaḥ /
naiṣkarmyasiddhiṃ paramāṃ saṃnyāsenādhigacchati //
50 *siddhiṃ prāpto yathā brahma tathāpnoti nibodha me /*
samāsenaiva Kaunteya niṣṭhā jñānasya yā parā //
buddhyā viśuddhayā yukto dhṛtyātmānaṃ niyamya ca /
śabdādīn viṣayāṃs tyaktvā rāgadveṣau vyudasya ca //
viviktasevī laghvāśī yatavākkāyamānasaḥ /
dhyānayogaparo nityaṃ vairāgyaṃ samupāśritaḥ //
ahaṃkāraṃ balaṃ darpaṃ kāmaṃ krodhaṃ parigraham /
vimucya nirmamaḥ śānto brahmabhūyāya kalpate //
brahmabhūtaḥ prasannātmā na śocati na kāṅkṣati /
samaḥ sarveṣu bhūteṣu madbhaktiṃ labhate parām //
55 *bhaktyā mām abhijānāti yāvān yaś cāsmi tattvataḥ /*
tato māṃ tattvato jñātvā viśate tadanantaram //
sarvakarmāṇy api sadā kurvāṇo madvyapāśrayaḥ /
matprasādād avāpnoti śāśvataṃ padam avyayam //
cetasā sarvakarmāṇi mayi saṃnyasya matparaḥ /
buddhiyogam upāśritya maccittaḥ satataṃ bhava //
maccittaḥ sarvadurgāṇi matprasādāt tariṣyasi /
atha cet tvam ahaṃkārān na śroṣyasi vinaṅkṣyasi //
yad ahaṃkāram āśritya na yotsya iti manyase /
mithyaiṣa vyavasāyas te prakṛtis tvāṃ niyokṣyati //
60 *svabhāvajena Kaunteya nibaddhaḥ svena karmaṇā /*
kartuṃ necchasi yan mohāt kariṣyasy avaśo 'pi tat //
īśvaraḥ sarvabhūtānāṃ hṛddeśe 'rjuna tiṣṭhati /
bhrāmayan sarvabhūtāni yantrārūḍhāni māyayā //
tam eva śaraṇaṃ gaccha sarvabhāvena Bhārata /
tatprasādāt parāṃ śāntiṃ sthānaṃ prāpsyasi śāśvatam //
iti te jñānam ākhyātaṃ guhyād guhyataraṃ mayā /
vimṛśyaitad aśeṣeṇa yathecchasi tathā kuru //
sarvaguhyatamaṃ bhūyaḥ śṛṇu me paramaṃ vacaḥ /
iṣṭo 'si me dṛḍham iti tato vakṣyāmi te hitam //
65 *manmanā bhava madbhakto madyājī māṃ namaskuru /*
mām evaiṣyasi satyaṃ te pratijāne priyo 'si me //
sarvadharmān parityajya mām ekaṃ śaraṇaṃ vraja /
ahaṃ tvā sarvapāpebhyo mokṣayiṣyāmi mā śucaḥ //

45 Each man attains perfection by devoting himself to his own task:
listen how the man who shoulders his task finds this perfection. He
finds it by honoring, through the fulfillment of his own task, him who
motivates the creatures to act, on whom all this is strung. One's own
Law imperfectly observed is better than another's Law carried out
with perfection. As long as one does the work set by nature, he does
not incur blame. One should not abandon his natural task even if it is
flawed, Kaunteya, for all undertakings are beset by flaws as fire is by
smoke. He whose spirit is free from any personal interest in anything,
who has conquered himself, who is rid of cravings, attains by his
renunciation the ultimate perfection of freedom from *karman.*
50 Hear from me in brief, Kaunteya, how by reaching perfection one
attains to *brahman,* which is the pinnacle of knowledge. Yoked with a
pure spirit and subduing himself with fortitude, renouncing the sense
objects of sound, etc., and discarding love and hatred, seeking
solitude, eating lightly, restraining speech, body, and mind, intent
upon the yoga of contemplation, cultivating dispassion, ridding
himself of egotism, displays of strength, pride, lust, wrath, and
possessions, and being no longer acquisitive but serene, he is able to
become *brahman.* Having become *brahman,* serene of spirit, he does not
grieve, he does not crave: equable to all creatures, he achieves the
55 ultimate *bhakti* of me. Through this *bhakti* he recognizes me for who
I am and understands how great I really am, and by virtue of his true
knowledge he enters me at once. Even though performing all the acts,
he has his shelter in me and by my grace attains that supreme abode
that is everlasting.
Relinquish all your acts to me with your mind, be absorbed in me,
embrace the yoga of the spirit, and always have your mind on me.
With your mind on me you will by my grace overcome all hazards;
but when you are too self-centered to listen, you will perish. If you
self-centeredly decide that you will not fight, your decision is
60 meaningless anyhow: your nature will command you. Fettered by
your own task, which springs from your nature, Kaunteya, you will
inevitably do what you in your folly do not want to do, Arjuna. The
lord of all creatures is inside their hearts and with his wizardry he
revolves all the creatures mounted on his water wheel. Go to him for
shelter with all your being, Bhārata, and by his grace you shall reach
the eternal abode which is ultimate peace.
Reflect upon this knowledge I have propounded to you, this mystery
of mysteries, in its entirety, and then do as you are pleased to do.
Listen to one more final word of mine that embodies the greatest
mystery of all. I shall tell it for your own good, for you are profoundly
65 dear to me. Keep your mind on me, honor me with your devotion and
sacrifice, and you shall come to me. Abandon all the Laws and
instead seek shelter with me alone. Be unconcerned, I shall set you

idaṃ te nātapaskāya nābhaktāya kadācana /
na cāśuśrūṣave vācyaṃ na ca māṃ yo 'bhyasūyati //
ya idaṃ paramaṃ guhyaṃ madbhakteṣv abhidhāsyati /
bhaktiṃ mayi parāṃ kṛtvā mām evaiṣyaty asaṃśayaḥ //
na ca tasmān manuṣyeṣu kaścin me priyakṛttamaḥ /
bhavitā na ca me tasmād anyaḥ priyataro bhuvi //
70 *adhyeṣyate ca ya imaṃ dharmyaṃ saṃvādam āvayoḥ /*
jñānayajñena tenāham iṣṭaḥ syām iti me matiḥ //
śraddhāvān anasūyaś ca śṛṇuyād api yo naraḥ /
so 'pi muktaḥ śubhāṃl lokān prāpnuyāt puṇyakarmaṇām //
kaccid etac chrutaṃ Pārtha tvayaikāgreṇa cetasā /
kaccid ajñānasaṃmohaḥ pranaṣṭas te Dhanaṃjaya //
Arjuna uvāca /
naṣṭo mohaḥ smṛtir labdhā tvatprasādān mayā-Acyuta /
sthito 'smi gatasaṃdehaḥ kariṣye vacanaṃ tava //
Saṃjaya uvāca /
ity ahaṃ Vāsudevasya Pārthasya ca mahātmanaḥ /
saṃvādam imam aśrauṣam adbhutaṃ romaharṣaṇam //
75 *Vyāsaprasādāc chrutavān etad guhyam ahaṃ param /*
yogaṃ yogeśvarāt Kṛṣṇāt sākṣāt kathayataḥ svayam //
rājan saṃsmṛtya saṃsmṛtya saṃvādam imam adbhutam /
Keśava-Arjunayoḥ puṇyaṃ hṛṣyāmi ca muhur muhuḥ //
tac ca saṃsmṛtya saṃsmṛtya rūpam atyadbhutaṃ Hareḥ /
vismayo me mahān rājan hṛṣyāmi ca punaḥ punaḥ //
yatra yogeśvaraḥ Kṛṣṇo yatra Pārtho dhanurdharaḥ /
tatra śrīr vijayo bhūtir dhruvā nītir matir mama //

Saṃjaya uvāca /
41.1 *tato Dhanaṃjayaṃ dṛṣṭvā bāṇa-Gāṇḍīvadhāriṇam /*
punar eva mahānādaṃ vyasṛjanta mahārathāḥ //
Pāṇḍavāḥ Somakāś caiva ye caiṣām anuyāyinaḥ /
dadhmuś ca muditāḥ śaṅkhān vīrāḥ sāgarasaṃbhavān //
tato bheryaś ca peśyaś ca krakacā goviṣāṇikāḥ /
sahasaivābhyahanyanta tataḥ śabdo mahān abhūt //
atha devāḥ sa-Gandharvāḥ Pitaraś ca janeśvara /
Siddha-Cāraṇasaṃghāś ca samīyus te didṛkṣayā //
5 *ṛṣayaś ca mahābhāgāḥ puraskṛtya Śatakratum /*
samīyus tatra sahitā draṣṭuṃ tad vaiśasaṃ mahat //
tato Yudhiṣṭhiro dṛṣṭvā yuddhāya susamudyate /
te sene sāgaraprakhye muhuḥ pracalite nṛpa //
vimucya kavacaṃ vīro nikṣipya ca varāyudham /
avaruhya rathāt tūrṇaṃ padbhyām eva kṛtāñjaliḥ //
pitāmaham abhiprekṣya Dharmarājo Yudhiṣṭhiraḥ /
vāgyataḥ prayayau yena prāṅmukho ripuvāhinīm //
taṃ prayāntam abhiprekṣya Kuntīputro Dhanaṃjayaḥ /

free from all evils.[7]

This is not to be revealed, ever, to one without austerities or
devotion to me, nor to one who does not wish to listen or who
disbelieves in me. But he who propounds to my devotees this ultimate
mystery and thus shows me his perfect devotion shall beyond a doubt
come to me. No one among humankind does me greater favor than
he, nor shall anyone on earth be more dear to me than he.
70 He who commits to memory this our colloquy informed by Law, he
will offer up to me a sacrifice of knowledge, so I hold. And he who,
filled with belief and trust, listens to it, will be released and attain to
the blessed worlds of those who have acted right.

Pārtha, have you listened to this with concentrated attention?
Dhanaṃjaya, is your ignorant delusion now gone?

Arjuna said:

The delusion is gone, Acyuta, and by your grace I have recovered
my wits. Here I stand with no more doubts. I shall do as you say.

Saṃjaya said:

Thus have I heard this Colloquy[8] of Vāsudeva and the great-spirited
75 Pārtha, marvelous and enrapturing. By Vyāsa's grace I have heard
this supreme mystery, this yoga, from that Master of Yoga Kṛṣṇa
himself, who told it in person. Sire, whenever I reflect on this
wondrous, holy Colloquy of Keśava and Arjuna, I rejoice anew.
Whenever I recall that miraculous form of Hari, I am stunned to the
core, sire, and rejoice anew. Wherever Kṛṣṇa the Master of Yoga and
Pārtha the archer are, there, I hold, are fortune, victory, prosperity,
and a steady course.

Saṃjaya said:

41.1 Then, seeing that Dhanaṃjaya again held his Gāṇḍīva bow and
arrows, the great warriors again roared their approval. The Pāṇḍavas,
the Somakas[1] and their followers cheerfully and gallantly blew their
sea-born conch shells. Kettledrums, hand drums, cymbals, and cow
horns were sounded in unison; and the noise was tremendous. Gods,
Gandharvas, Ancestors, hosts of Siddhas and Cāraṇas assembled to
5 watch, O lord of the people. The lordly seers, placing the God of the
Hundred Sacrifices[2] at their head, gathered there to watch the great
holocaust.

When Yudhiṣṭhira saw the two oceanlike armies once more on the
move ready for battle, sire, the hero unfastened his armor and put
down his fine weapon. He quickly dismounted from his chariot and
proceeded on foot with folded hands. Yudhiṣṭhira the King Dharma
espied Grandfather and strode in silence eastward to the enemy army.
Kuntī's son Dhanaṃjaya also dismounted at once, when he saw the
10 other stride forward, and followed him with his brothers. The blessed

avatīrya rathāt tūrṇaṃ bhrātṛbhiḥ sahito 'nvayāt //
10 *Vāsudevaś ca bhagavān pṛṣṭhato 'nujagāma ha /*
yathāmukhyāś ca rājānas tam anvājagmur utsukāḥ //
Arjuna uvāca /
kiṃ te vyavasitaṃ rājan yad asmān apahāya vai /
padbhyām eva prayāto 'si prāṅmukho ripuvāhinīm //
Bhīmasena uvāca /
kva gamiṣyasi rājendra nikṣiptakavacāyudhaḥ /
daṃśiteṣv arisainyeṣu bhrātṝn utsṛjya pārthiva //
Nakula uvāca /
evaṃgate tvayi jyeṣṭhe mama bhrātari Bhārata /
bhīr me dunoti hṛdayaṃ brūhi gantā bhavān kva nu //
Sahadeva uvāca /
asmin raṇasamūhe vai vartamāne mahābhaye /
yoddhavye kva nu gantāsi śatrūn abhimukho nṛpa //
Saṃjaya uvāca /
15 *evam ābhāṣyamāṇo 'pi bhrātṛbhiḥ Kurunandana /*
novāca vāgyataḥ kiṃcid gacchaty eva Yudhiṣṭhiraḥ //
tān uvāca mahāprājño Vāsudevo mahāmanāḥ /
abhiprāyo 'sya vijñāto mayeti prahasann iva //
eṣa Bhīṣmaṃ tathā Droṇaṃ Gautamaṃ Śalyam eva ca /
anumānya gurūn sarvān yotsyate pārthivo 'ribhiḥ //
śrūyate hi purākalpe gurūn ananumānya yaḥ /
yudhyate sa bhaved vyaktam apadhyāto mahattaraiḥ //
anumānya yathāśāstraṃ yas tu yudhyen mahattaraiḥ /
dhruvas tasya jayo yuddhe bhaved iti matir mama //
20 *evaṃ bruvati Kṛṣṇe tu Dhārtarāṣṭracamūṃ prati /*
hāhākāro mahān āsīn niḥśabdās tv apare 'bhavan //
dṛṣṭvā Yudhiṣṭhiraṃ dūrād Dhārtarāṣṭrasya sainikāḥ /
mithaḥ saṃkathayāṃ cakrur neśo 'sti kulapāṃsanaḥ //
vyaktaṃ bhīta ivābhyeti rājāsau Bhīṣmam antikāt /
Yudhiṣṭhiraḥ sasodaryaḥ śaraṇārthaṃ prayācakaḥ //
Dhanaṃjaye kathaṃ nāthe Pāṇḍave ca Vṛkodare /
Nakule Sahadeve ca bhīto 'bhyeti ca Pāṇḍavaḥ //
na nūnaṃ kṣatriyakule jātaḥ saṃprathite bhuvi /
yathāsya hṛdayaṃ bhītam alpasattvasya saṃyuge //
25 *tatas te kṣatriyāḥ sarve praśaṃsanti sma Kauravān /*
hṛṣṭāḥ sumanaso bhūtvā cailāni dudhuvuḥ pṛthak //
vyanindanta tataḥ sarve yodhās tatra viśāṃ pate /
Yudhiṣṭhiraṃ sasodaryaṃ sahitaṃ Keśavena ha //
tatas tat Kauravaṃ sainyaṃ dhikkṛtvā tu Yudhiṣṭhiram /
niḥśabdam abhavat tūrṇaṃ punar eva viśāṃ pate //
kiṃ nu vakṣyati rājāsau kiṃ Bhīṣmaḥ prativakṣyati /
kiṃ Bhīmaḥ samaraślāghī kiṃ nu Kṛṣṇa-Arjunāv iti //
vivakṣitaṃ kim asyeti saṃśayaḥ sumahān abhūt /

Lord Vāsudeva followed behind, and after him came eagerly the other kings according to their rank.

Arjuna said:

King, what do you have in mind, leaving us behind and going on foot eastward to the enemy army?

Bhīmasena said:

Where are you going, Indra of kings, doffing armor and weapons while the enemy troops are armed to the teeth, leaving your brothers behind?

Nakula said:

Terror is striking my heart, when I see you, my eldest brother, in this state, Bhārata! Tell me, where are you going?

Sahadeva said:

While there are a score of terrible battles to be fought, where are you going, facing the enemies?

Saṃjaya said:

15 Ignoring his brothers' questions, O scion of Kuru, Yudhiṣṭhira went
silently onward without making a reply. Then, with a hint of laughter,
the wise and great-minded Vāsudeva said to them, "I know what he
intends to do. This king will fight his enemies only with the consent
of Bhīṣma, Droṇa, Gautama, Śalya, and all his other gurus. It is said[3]
that in a former age, when a man openly did battle without first
seeking the consent of his gurus, he was despised by his betters. But if
he did seek their consent and then fought his betters, his victory in
battle was assured. That is my opinion."

20 While Kṛṣṇa was speaking there rose a loud wail of anguish among
the troops of the Dhārtarāṣṭra, but the others remained silent. Seeing
Yudhiṣṭhira in the distance, the soldiers of the Dhārtarāṣṭra exclaimed
to one another, "He has lost control of himself, he defiles his family!
Surely that king is going to Bhīṣma because he is afraid! Yudhiṣṭhira
and his brothers are begging for mercy! How is it possible that the
Pāṇḍava approaches in fear, when he has protectors in Dhanaṃjaya,
the Pāṇḍava Wolf-Belly, Nakula, and Sahadeva? He certainly cannot
be a son of a baronial lineage famous on earth, if his coward's heart
25 panics at battle!" Thereupon all those barons sang the praises of the
Kauravas and full of joy and cheer waved their robes about. All the
warriors there cried shame on Yudhiṣṭhira and his brothers as well as
Keśava, O lord of your people. The Kaurava troops reviled
Yudhiṣṭhira, but soon they fell silent, lord of your people. A grave
doubt grew in both armies about Yudhiṣṭhira, sire. "What will the
king say?" they wondered; "how will Bhīṣma respond? What will
battle-famed Bhīma say, and Kṛṣṇa and Arjuna? What does he have
in mind to say?"

ubhayoḥ senayo rājan Yudhiṣṭhirakṛte tadā //
30 *sa vigāhya camūṃ śatroḥ śaraśaktisamākulām /*
Bhīṣmam evābhyayāt tūrṇaṃ bhrātṛbhiḥ parivāritaḥ //
tam uvāca tataḥ pādau karābhyāṃ pīḍya Pāṇḍavaḥ /
Bhīṣmaṃ Śāṃtanavaṃ rājā yuddhāya samupasthitaṃ //
Yudhiṣṭhira uvāca /
āmantraye tvāṃ durdharṣa yotsye tāta tvayā saha /
anujānīhi māṃ tāta āśiṣaś ca prayojaya //
Bhīṣma uvāca /
yady evaṃ nābhigacchethā yudhi māṃ pṛthivīpate /
śapeyaṃ tvāṃ mahārāja parābhāvāya Bhārata //
prīto 'smi putra yudhyasva jayam āpnuhi Pāṇḍava /
yat te 'bhilaṣitaṃ cānyat tad avāpnuhi saṃyuge //
35 *vriyatāṃ ca varaḥ Pārtha kim asmatto 'bhikāṅkṣasi /*
evaṃ gate mahārāja na tavāsti parājayaḥ //
arthasya puruṣo dāso dāsas tv artho na kasyacit /
iti satyaṃ mahārāja baddho 'smy arthena Kauravaiḥ //
atas tvāṃ klībavad vākyaṃ bravīmi Kurunandana /
hṛto 'smy arthena Kauravya yuddhād anyat kim icchasi //
Yudhiṣṭhira uvāca /
mantrayasva mahāprājña hitaiṣī mama nityaśaḥ /
yudhyasva Kauravasyārthe mamaiṣa satataṃ varaḥ //
Bhīṣma uvāca /
rājan kim atra sāhyaṃ te karomi Kurunandana /
kāmaṃ yotsye parasyārthe brūhi yat te vivakṣitam //
Yudhiṣṭhira uvāca /
40 *kathaṃ jayeyaṃ saṃgrāme bhavantam aparājitam /*
etan me mantraya hitaṃ yadi śreyaḥ prapaśyasi //
Bhīṣma uvāca /
na taṃ paśyāmi Kaunteya yo māṃ yudhyantam āhave /
vijayeta pumān kaścid api sākṣāc Chatakratuḥ //
Yudhiṣṭhira uvāca /
hanta pṛcchāmi tasmāt tvāṃ pitāmaha namo 'stu te /
jayopāyaṃ bravīhi tvam ātmanaḥ samare paraiḥ //
Bhīṣma uvāca /
na śatruṃ tāta paśyāmi samare yo jayeta mām /
na tāvan mṛtyukālo me punar āgamanaṃ kuru //
Saṃjaya uvāca /
tato Yudhiṣṭhiro vākyaṃ Bhīṣmasya Kurunandana /
śirasā pratijagrāha bhūyas tam abhivādya ca //
45 *prāyāt punar mahābāhur ācāryasya rathaṃ prati /*
paśyatāṃ sarvasainyānāṃ madhyena bhrātṛbhiḥ saha //
sa Droṇam abhivādyātha kṛtvā caiva pradakṣiṇam /
uvāca vācā durdharṣam ātmaniḥśreyasaṃ vacaḥ //
āmantraye tvāṃ bhagavan yotsye vigatakalmaṣaḥ /

30 Surrounded by his brothers, Yudhiṣṭhira plunged into the enemy's
ranks, which were bristling with arrows and spears, and silently
stepped forward toward Bhīṣma himself. King Pāṇḍava pressed with
his hands the feet of Bhīṣma Śāṃtanava, who had come to wage war,
and he spoke to him—

Yudhiṣṭhira said:

I seek permission from you who are inviolate[4] to me, so that I may fight you, father. Give your consent and wish me well.

Bhīṣma said:

If you had not come to me like this on the field of battle, I would
have sworn an oath to your total defeat, great King Bhārata, lord of
the earth! I am pleased, son. Fight and win victory, Pāṇḍava. Obtain
35 whatever it is you seek to obtain in this battle. Choose a boon, son of
Pṛthā: what do you desire of us? Thus, great king, you will not meet
defeat. It is the truth that man is the slave of wealth and that wealth
is no man's slave: I have been held captive by the Kauravas with
their wealth.[5] Hence I can only speak to you like a eunuch, scion of
Kuru: I have been the slave of wealth, Kauravya. What do you wish
except battle?

Yudhiṣṭhira said:

Counsel me, wise one. You have always wished me well. Wage war for the Kauravas, for this has always been the boon of my choice.

Bhīṣma said:

King, what help can I give you, scion of Kuru? Surely I must fight on the side of your enemy. What is it you want to say? Tell me.

Yudhiṣṭhira said:

How can I defeat you in battle, you who are invincible? Counsel me for my good, if you see any good in it.

Bhīṣma said:

Son of Kuntī, I do not see a man who could fight me in battle and win, were he Indra himself!

Yudhiṣṭhira said:

Then let me ask you this, Grandfather, and my homage to you: tell me by what means enemies can overcome you in war.

Bhīṣma said:

Son, I do not see a foe who could defeat me. The hour of my death has not yet come. Now return.

Saṃjaya said:

Yudhiṣṭhira accepted Bhīṣma's reply with bowed head, O scion of
45 Kuru. And after saluting him again, the strong-armed king went on
to the chariot of the Teacher with his brothers while all the troops
looked on. He greeted Droṇa, circumambulated him, and spoke to the
inviolate man these words for his own benefit, "I seek your permission,
reverend lord, so that I may fight you without guilt. With your

jayeyaṃ ca ripūn sarvān anujñātas tvayā dvija //
Droṇa uvāca /
yadi māṃ nābhigacchethā yuddhāya kṛtaniścayaḥ /
śapeyaṃ tvāṃ mahārāja parābhāvāya sarvaśaḥ //
tad Yudhiṣṭhira tuṣṭo 'smi pūjitaś ca tvayānagha /
anujānāmi yudhyasva vijayaṃ samavāpnuhi //
50 *karavāṇi ca te kāmaṃ brūhi yat te 'bhikāṅkṣitam /*
evaṃ gate mahārāja yuddhād anyat kim icchasi //
arthasya puruṣo dāso dāsas tv artho na kasyacit /
iti satyaṃ mahārāja baddho 'smy arthena Kauravaiḥ //
atas tvāṃ klībavad brūmo yuddhād anyat kim icchasi /
yotsyāmi Kauravasyārthe tavāśāsyo jayo mayā //
Yudhiṣṭhira uvāca /
jayam āśāssva me brahman mantrayasva ca maddhitam /
yudhyasva Kauravasyārthe vara eṣa vṛto mayā //
Droṇa uvāca /
dhruvas te vijayo rājan yasya mantrī Haris tava /
ahaṃ ca tvābhijānāmi raṇe śatrūn vijeṣyasi //
55 *yato dharmas tataḥ Kṛṣṇo yataḥ Kṛṣṇas tato jayaḥ /*
yudhyasva gaccha Kaunteya pṛccha māṃ kiṃ bravīmi te //
Yudhiṣṭhira uvāca /
pṛcchāmi tvāṃ dvijaśreṣṭha śṛṇu me yad vivakṣitam /
kathaṃ jayeyaṃ saṃgrāme bhavantam aparājitam //
Droṇa uvāca /
na te 'sti vijayas tāvad yāvad yudhyāmy ahaṃ raṇe /
mamāśu nidhane rājan yatasva saha sodaraiḥ //
Yudhiṣṭhira uvāca /
hanta tasmān mahābāho vadhopāyaṃ vadātmanaḥ /
ācārya praṇipatyaiṣa pṛcchāmi tvāṃ namo 'stu te //
Droṇa uvāca /
na śatruṃ tāta paśyāmi yo māṃ hanyād raṇe sthitam /
yudhyamānaṃ susaṃrabdhaṃ śaravarṣaughavarṣiṇam //
60 *ṛte prāyagataṃ rājan nyastaśastram acetanam /*
hanyān māṃ yudhi yodhānāṃ satyam etad bravīmi te //
śastraṃ cāhaṃ raṇe jahyāṃ śrutvā sumahad apriyam /
śraddheyavākyāt puruṣād etat satyaṃ bravīmi te //
Saṃjaya uvāca /
etac chrutvā mahārāja Bhāradvājasya dhīmataḥ /
anumānya tam ācāryaṃ prāyāc Chāradvataṃ prati //
so 'bhivādya Kṛpaṃ rājā kṛtvā cāpi pradakṣiṇam /
uvāca durdharṣatamaṃ vākyaṃ vākyaviśāradaḥ //
anumānaye tvāṃ yotsyāmi guro vigatakalmaṣaḥ /
jayeyaṃ ca ripūn sarvān anujñātas tvayānagha //

consent I shall defeat my enemies, brahmin."

Droṇa said:

If you had not come to me, although your mind is set on war, I
would have sworn an oath to your total defeat, great king. Therefore,
Yudhiṣṭhira, prince sans blame, I am pleased with your homage.
50 I give my consent: fight and win victory. I shall do your desire, tell
me what you want. In these circumstances, what do you wish except
war, great king? Man is the slave of wealth, but wealth is nobody's
slave, that is the truth, great king. I have been kept captive by the
Kauravas with their wealth. Therefore we speak to you like a eunuch
—what do you want except war? I shall fight for the Kauravas, but I
must hope that you win.

Yudhiṣṭhira said:

Wish me victory, brahmin, and counsel me for my good. Fight for the Kauravas, that is the boon I ask.

Droṇa said:

Your victory is assured, king, for you have Hari as your counselor.
55 I recognize you: you shall defeat your foes in battle. Where the Law
is there is Kṛṣṇa, and where Kṛṣṇa is lies victory. Go and fight,
Kaunteya. What can I tell you? Ask me.

Yudhiṣṭhira said:

Then I shall ask you, best of brahmins, and listen to what I have to say. How can I defeat you in battle, you who are invincible?

Droṇa said:

You shall not have your victory as long as I am still fighting. You and your brothers will have to try your utmost if you are to kill me soon.

Yudhiṣṭhira said:

Then, strong-armed one, tell me by what means we may kill you. Teacher, I am asking you while I lie at your feet. Tell me! Homage to you!

Droṇa said:

Son, I do not see an enemy who could kill me while I am on the
battlefield, fighting furiously and causing vast showers of arrows to
60 rain down. Not a one of your warriors will be able to kill me until I
am ready to die, king, and, bereft of my wits, lay down my arms—
this I swear to you. And I swear to you, I shall put down my weapons
only when I have heard most grievous tidings from a man whose
word I trust.[6]

Saṃjaya said:

Having heard this from the wise Bhāradvāja, sire, Yudhiṣṭhira took leave from his teacher and went on to Śāradvata.[7] The king saluted Kṛpa and circumambulated him. Then he eloquently spoke to that most inviolate man, "I seek your consent, guru, so that I may fight you, guru, without guilt and, permitted by you, defeat all my enemies, lord sans blame.

Kṛpa uvāca /
65 *yadi māṃ nābhigacchethā yuddhāya kṛtaniścayaḥ /*
śapeyaṃ tvāṃ mahārāja parābhāvāya sarvaśaḥ //
arthasya puruṣo dāso dāsas tv artho na kasyacit /
iti satyaṃ mahārāja baddho 'smy arthena Kauravaiḥ //
teṣām arthe mahārāja yoddhavyam iti me matiḥ /
atas tvāṃ klībavad brūmi yuddhād anyat kim icchasi //
Yudhiṣṭhira uvāca /
hanta pṛcchāmi te tasmād ācārya śṛṇu me vacaḥ //
Saṃjaya uvāca /
ity uktvā vyathito rājā novāca gatacetanaḥ /
taṃ Gautamaḥ pratyuvāca vijñāyāsya vivakṣitam /
avadhyo 'haṃ mahīpāla yudhyasva jayam āpnuhi //
70 *prītas tv abhigamenāhaṃ jayaṃ tava narādhipa /*
āśāsiṣye sadotthāya satyam etad bravīmi te //
etac chrutvā mahārāja Gautamasya vacas tadā /
anumānya Kṛpaṃ rājā prayayau yena Madrarāṭ //
sa Śalyam abhivādyātha kṛtvā cābhipradakṣiṇam /
uvāca rājā durdharṣam ātmaniḥśreyasaṃ vacaḥ //
anumānaye tvāṃ yotsyāmi guro vigatakalmaṣaḥ /
jayeyaṃ ca mahārāja anujñātas tvayā ripūn //
Śalya uvāca /
yadi māṃ nābhigacchethā yuddhāya kṛtaniścayaḥ /
śapeyaṃ tvāṃ mahārāja parābhāvāya vai raṇe //
75 *tuṣṭo 'smi pūjitaś cāsmi yat kāṅkṣasi tad astu te /*
anujānāmi caiva tvāṃ yudhyasva jayam āpnuhi //
brūhi caiva paraṃ vīra kenārthaḥ kiṃ dadāmi te /
evaṃ gate mahārāja yuddhād anyat kim icchasi //
arthasya puruṣo dāso dāsas tv artho na kasyacit /
iti satyaṃ mahārāja baddho 'smy arthena Kauravaiḥ //
kariṣyāmi hi te kāmaṃ bhāgineya yathepsitam /
bravīmy ataḥ klībavat tvāṃ yuddhād anyat kim icchasi //
Yudhiṣṭhira uvāca /
mantrayasva mahārāja nityaṃ maddhitam uttamam /
kāmaṃ yudhya parasyārthe varam etad vṛṇomy aham //
Śalya uvāca /
80 *brūhi kim atra sāhyaṃ te karomi nṛpasattama /*
kāmaṃ yotsye parasyārthe vṛto 'smy arthena Kauravaiḥ //
Yudhiṣṭhira uvāca /
sa eva me varaḥ satya udyoge yas tvayā kṛtaḥ /
sūtaputrasya saṃgrāme kāryas tejovadhas tvayā //
Śalya uvāca /
saṃpatsyaty eṣa te kāmaḥ Kuntīputra yathepsitaḥ /

Kṛpa said:

65 If you had not come to me, although your mind is set on war, I would have sworn an oath to your total defeat, great king. Man is the slave of wealth, but wealth is nobody's slave, that is the truth, great king. I have been held captive by the Kauravas with their wealth, and I know that I shall have to fight for them. Therefore I speak only as a eunuch. What do you wish except war?

Yudhiṣṭhira said:

Then let me ask you, teacher, listen to my words . . .

Saṃjaya said:

Having said this much the king fell silent, out of his mind with grief. But Gautama, surmising his meaning, replied, "I cannot be
70 killed, king of the earth. Fight and gain victory. Your coming has pleased me. Upon every awakening I shall wish you victory. This I swear to you."

When he had heard this reply of Kṛpa Gautama, sire, Yudhiṣṭhira took his leave from him and went on to the king of the Madras. He saluted Śalya and circumambulated him. Then the king spoke to his inviolate uncle these words that served his own interest, "I seek your permission so that I may fight you, guru, without guilt and, with your consent, defeat my enemies, great king."

Śalya said:

If you had not come to me, although your mind is set on on war,
75 I would have sworn an oath to your total defeat, great king. Now I am both pleased and honored. May what you wish come true. I give you my permission: fight and gain victory. And say further, hero, what do you need, what can I give you? In these circumstances, great king, what do you wish except war? Man is the slave of wealth, but wealth is nobody's slave, that is the truth, great king. The Kauravas have held me captive with their wealth.[8] But indeed, I shall carry out your desire, son of my sister, whatever it is you want. But I speak as a eunuch—what do you wish except war?

Yudhiṣṭhira said:

Counsel me, great king, about what shall forever be of great profit to me. By all means, fight for the enemy—that is the boon I choose.

Śalya said:

80 Tell me how I can be of help to you, best of kings. Surely I must fight at your enemy's side, for the Kauravas have laid claim to me with their wealth.

Yudhiṣṭhira said:

Let that boon be true which you pledged to me at the time of the *Effort*: you are to obscure the splendor in battle of the *sūta's* son![9]

Śalya said:

Your desire shall be fulfilled the way you want it, son of Kuntī. Go

gaccha yudhyasva visrabdhaṃ pratijāne jayaṃ tava //
Saṃjaya uvāca /
anumānyātha Kaunteyo mātulaṃ Madrakeśvaram /
nirjagāma mahāsainyād bhrātṛbhiḥ parivāritaḥ //
Vāsudevas tu Rādheyam āhave 'bhijagāma vai /
tata enam uvācedaṃ Pāṇḍavārthe Gadāgrajaḥ //
85 *śrutaṃ me Karṇa Bhīṣmasya dveṣāt kila na yotsyasi /*
asmān varaya Rādheya yāvad Bhīṣmo na hanyate //
hate tu Bhīṣme Rādheya punar eṣyasi saṃyuge /
Dhārtarāṣṭrasya sāhāyyaṃ yadi paśyasi cet samam //
Karṇa uvāca /
na vipriyaṃ kariṣyāmi Dhārtarāṣṭrasya Keśava /
tyaktaprāṇaṃ hi māṃ viddhi Duryodhanahitaiṣiṇam //
Saṃjaya uvāca /
tac chrutvā vacanaṃ Kṛṣṇaḥ saṃnyavartata Bhārata /
Yudhiṣṭhirapurogaiś ca Pāṇḍavaiḥ saha saṃgataḥ //
atha sainyasya madhye tu prākrośat Pāṇḍavāgrajaḥ /
yo 'smān vṛṇoti tam ahaṃ varaye sāhyakāraṇāt //
90 *atha tān samabhiprekṣya Yuyutsur idam abravīt /*
prītātmā Dharmarājānaṃ Kuntīputraṃ Yudhiṣṭhiram //
ahaṃ yotsyāmi miṣataḥ saṃyuge Dhārtarāṣṭrajān /
yuṣmadarthe mahārāja yadi māṃ vṛṇuṣe 'nagha //
Yudhiṣṭhira uvāca /
ehy ehi sarve yotsyāmas tava bhrātṝn apaṇḍitān /
Yuyutso Vāsudevaś ca vayaṃ ca brūma sarvaśaḥ //
vṛṇomi tvāṃ mahābāho yudhyasva mama kāraṇāt /
tvayi piṇḍaś ca tantuś ca Dhṛtarāṣṭrasya dṛśyate //
bhajasvāsmān rājaputra bhajamānān mahādyute /
na bhaviṣyati durbuddhir Dhārtarāṣṭro 'tyamarṣaṇaḥ //
Saṃjaya uvāca /
95 *tato Yuyutsuḥ Kauravyaḥ parityajya sutāṃs tava /*
jagāma Pāṇḍuputrāṇāṃ senāṃ viśrāvya dundubhim //
tato Yudhiṣṭhiro rājā saṃprahṛṣṭaḥ sahānujaiḥ /
jagrāha kavacaṃ bhūyo dīptimat kanakojjvalam //
pratyapadyanta te sarve rathān svān puruṣarṣabhāḥ /
tato vyūhaṃ yathāpūrvaṃ pratyavyūhanta te punaḥ //
avādayan dundubhīṃś ca śataśaś caiva puṣkarān /
siṃhanādāṃś ca vividhān vineduḥ puruṣarṣabhāḥ //
rathasthān puruṣavyāghrān Pāṇḍavān prekṣya pārthivāḥ /
Dhṛṣṭadyumnādayaḥ sarve punar jahṛṣire mudā //
100 *gauravaṃ Pāṇḍuputrāṇāṃ mānyān mānayatāṃ ca tān /*
dṛṣṭvā mahīkṣitas tatra pūjayāṃ cakrire bhṛśam //
sauhṛdaṃ ca kṛpāṃ caiva prāptakālaṃ mahātmanām /
dayāṃ ca jñātiṣu parāṃ kathayāṃ cakrire nṛpāḥ //

and fight with confidence, I promise you victory.

Saṃjaya said:

After seeking the consent of his maternal uncle, the lord of the
Madrakas, the son of Kuntī withdrew amidst his brothers from that
huge army.

But Vāsudeva betook himself on the battlefield to Rādheya, and
85 Gada's elder brother said to him in the Pāṇḍava's cause, "I have
heard it rumored that you have declined to fight out of hatred for
Bhīṣma. Choose our side, Rādheya, for as long as Bhīṣma survives.
When Bhīṣma has been slain, you can return to the battle, Rādheya,
and help the Dhārtarāṣṭra, if you look equably on both sides.[10]

Karṇa said:

I shall do nothing to displease the Dhārtarāṣṭra, Keśava, for you
should know that I am Duryodhana's friend unto death.

Saṃjaya said:

And upon hearing Karṇa's reply, Bhārata, Kṛṣṇa too withdrew in
the company of the Pāṇḍavas, who were led by Yudhiṣṭhira.

Thereupon the eldest Pāṇḍava cried in the middle of that army,
90 "I choose him for an ally who chooses us!" Then Yuyutsu[11] gazed
upon them and, filled with affection, he spoke to Kuntī's son
Yudhiṣṭhira the King Dharma, "If you are willing to choose me, prince
sans blame, then I shall fight for you on this battlefield against the
sons of Dhṛtarāṣṭra, before their very eyes, great king!"

Yudhiṣṭhira said:

Come then, come! We shall all fight your benighted brothers!
Yuyutsu, Vāsudeva and all of us say to you, "I choose you, strong-
armed man, fight on my side, for on you there are seen to depend
now both the funeral offering for Dhṛtarāṣṭra and his future line.[12]
Side thou, son of a king, with us who shall side with thee, illustrious
Yuyutsu, and the truculent, evil-spirited Dhārtarāṣṭra shall be no
more!"

Saṃjaya said:

95 So Yuyutsu Kauravya abandoned your sons and, accompanied by
a peal of drums, went over to the army of the sons of Pāṇḍu. Then
King Yudhiṣṭhira and his younger brothers joyously took up again
their glistening armor which sparkled with gold. All the bull-like men
mounted their chariots and arrayed their ranks as before. They
sounded their drums and cymbals by the hundreds, those bulls among
men, and roared forth with their various battle cries. When
Dhṛṣṭadyumna and the other kings saw the tigerlike Pāṇḍavas on
100 their chariots, they were beside themselves with joy. Now that they
had witnessed the filial respect of the Pāṇḍavas, who paid honor to
those who deserved honor, the kings held them in even greater
esteem. The princes recounted the brotherly spirit and
compassionateness of the great-spirited men with tales that fitted the

sādhu sādhv iti sarvatra niśceruḥ stutisaṃhitāḥ /
vācaḥ puṇyāḥ kīrtimatāṃ manohṛdayaharṣiṇīḥ //
Mlecchāś cāryāś ca ye tatra dadṛśuḥ śuśruvus tadā /
vṛttaṃ tat Pāṇḍuputrāṇāṃ rurudus te sagadgadāḥ //
tato jaghnur mahābherīḥ śataśaś caiva puṣkarān /
śaṅkhāṃś ca gokṣīranibhān dadhmur hṛṣṭā manasvinaḥ //

occasion, and their surpassing sympathy for their kinsmen; and applauding shouts went up everywhere, and songs of praise, and prayers of blessing, which gladdened the hearts and the minds of those famous men. Barbarian and Aryan alike, everyone who heard of that feat of the sons of Pāṇḍu choked and wept; and the spirited warriors beat their kettledrums and cymbals by the hundreds and joyfully blew their milk-white conches.

Notes

Preface

1. S. K. Belvalkar, ed., *Bhīṣmaparvan* (1) (fascicule 15) (Poona: Bhandarkar Oriental Research Institute, 1947), pp. 74–203.

2. Rāmānuja, *Vedāntācārya-Śrī-Veṅkaṭanātha-kṛtatātparyacandrikā-khyaṭīkāsaṃvalita-Śrīmad-Rāmānujācārya-viracitabhāṣyasahitā Śrīmad-Bhagavadgītā*, ed. by V. G. Apte, Ānandāśrama Sanskrit Series 92 (Bombay, 1923); Etienne Lamotte, *Notes sur la Bhagavadgītā* (Paris, 1929); Emile Senart, *La Bhagavad-Gîtâ* (Paris, 1944[2]); Franklin Edgerton, *The Bhagavad Gītā*, Part 1, Harvard Oriental Series 38 (Cambridge, Mass., 1946).

Introduction

1. *MBh.* 1.94; I, 224 ff.

2. *MBh.* 1.95; I, 227. This seems a likely explanation of the account that Citrāṅgada fought a losing battle with a Gandharva for three years. For another historic case of possession by a Gandharva, see *Bṛhadāraṇyaka Upaniṣad* 3.3.1.

3. *MBh.* 1.96; I, 227 ff.

4. The story in *MBh.* 1.99 f.; I, 233 ff. That Pāṇḍu's "pallor" indicates a disease as an effect of his mother's fright at his conception is made very probable by the effect of blindness that *his* frightened mother had on Dhṛtarāṣṭra. This catalog of physical defects in the offspring of Śaṃtanu ("healthy of body," hence curing by touch; his own brother Devāpi had a skin disease) indicates the general disorder in the royal succession.

5. *MBh.* 1.102, at the end; II, 239; cf. also 5.147; III, 459.

6. *MBh.* 1.129 ff.; I, 283 ff.

7. *MBh.* 1.174 ff.; I, 346 ff.

8. *MBh.* 1.199; I, 387 ff.

9. *MBh.* 2.43 ff.; II, 109 ff.

10. *MBh.* 5.57; III, 324 ff.

11. Cf. *MBh.* 6.41.36 ff.

12. *MBh.* 5.153; III, 470 f.

13. Franklin Edgerton, *The Bhagavadgītā*, Part 2, Harvard Oriental Series 38 (Cambridge, Mass., 1946), pp. 3 f.

14. *MBh.* 5.151.20 ff.; III, 467 f.

15. E.g., *MBh.* 12, 269; 270 f.; 279 ff.

16. *MBh.* 14.16 ff.

17. *MBh.* 5.197.17 ff.; III, 532.
18. *MBh.* 5.7; III, 197.
19. *MBh.* 1.183; I, 358 f.
20. *MBh.* 1.191; I, 377 f.; more gifts at Arjuna's and Subhadrā's wedding: *MBh.* 1.213; II, 409 ff.
21. *MBh.* 1.214 f.; I, 413 ff.
22. *MBh.* 1.212; I, 407 f.
23. *MBh.* 2.12 ff.; II, 55 ff.
24. *MBh.* 2.22 ff.; II, 67 ff.
25. *MBh.* 2.37 ff.; II, 97 ff.
26. *MBh.* 5.70 ff.; III, 343 ff.
27. *MBh.* 3.19 f.; II, 258 ff.
28. *MBh.* 4.36; III, 82 ff.
29. *MBh.* 3.13.38 f.; II, 248; also 3.41; II, 302; and 5.109.4 f.; III, 402.
30. Notably 5.129; III, 428.
31. *MBh.* 2.13; II, 59; 2.38 f. and 41 f.; II, 98 ff.; 3.21 ff.; II, 261 ff.
32. For instance, in their *Vedāntasūtra* commentaries Śaṅkara quotes the *Gītā* 42 times, the *MBh.* once, and *Manu* 8 times (the only *smṛti* quotations of the text); and Rāmānuja the *Gītā* 104 times, the *MBh.* never, *Manu* 9 times, and *Yājñavalkya* once (with the *Viṣṇu Purāṇa* the only *smṛtis* quoted).
33. The best general introduction to Mīmāṃsā is found in Ganganatha Jha, *Pūrva-Mīmāṃsā in Its Sources* (Madras, 1942 and 1946).
34. *Sūtras* 3.1.
35. Śaṅkara, *Bhagavadgītābhāṣya* (Ānandāśrama Sanskrit Series 34; Bombay, 1936[3]), *Upodghāṭa* 3–5.
36. Bhāskara, *Bhagavadāśayānusaraṇa* (MS.5828, Sarasvati Bhavana Library, Benares), Introduction.
37. Rāmānuja, *Bhagavadgītābhāṣya* (AAS Series 92; Bombay, 1923), Introduction.
38. In the next chapter, pp. 18 ff.
39. *Chāndogya Upaniṣad*, ch. 5.
40. Chandragupta Maurya favored the Jainas, Aśoka the Buddhists.
41. 18.76 f. and 73 respectively.
42. For the role of the *yajamāna*, cf., e.g., *Śatapatha Brāhmaṇa* 7.4.1.15; he is called *ātman*, e.g., *Taittirīya Āraṇyaka* 10.64.1. See also my discussion in *The Maitrāyaṇīya Upaniṣad* (The Hague, 1962), ch. 3.
43. *Suttanipāta* 2.7.15–21; 26; 32.
44. E.g., *MBh.* 5.149.47; III, 464.
45. Cf. Jha, *op. cit.*, pp. 258 ff.
46. *Śrautakośa* (Poona: Vaidika Saṃśodhana Maṇḍala, 1958), vol. I, pt. i, pp. 199 ff.
47. *MBh.* 5.42.6 ff.; III, 268; see my comments III, 182 ff.
48. Etienne Lamotte, *Notes sur la Bhagavadgītā* (Paris, 1929), p. 20.
49. Cf. my remarks in "Studies in Sāṃkhya: II. Ahaṃkāra," *Journal of the American Oriental Society* 77, no. 1 (1957): 22 ff., and "Studies in Sāṃkhya: III. Sattva" ibid. 77, no. 2 (1957): 101 ff., where there are further references.
50. That school recognizes the existence of an archetypal soul that has never been involved in transmigration and functions as a model for aspiring but bound souls.

Text

15.47b. The confusion of *śastra* with *śāstra* in manuscripts is so constant that I have no hesitation in adopting the former.

16.4a. We should read the *avagraha 'nikṛti°* where the cr. ed. omits it.

21.2b. I take *kalpitam* as similar in meaning to *°kalpa* ifc., "like."

22.10b. Note this rare spelling of *Gāṇḍīva*, *metri causa*.

23[1]. Bhāskara's commentary on the *Gītā*, the *Bhagavadāśayānusaraṇa*, has a number of variants that have not been noticed by the editor of the cr. ed., and some of which are distinctly preferable to the Vulgate readings. I have listed and discussed the variants in "A Contribution to the Critical Edition of the Bhagavadgītā," (*J.A.O.S.* 85.1, 1965). I have accepted into the text only those readings that make any difference to the translation.
10. *Bhīṣma*° and *bhīma*° should be transposed; so Bh.
19d. I read *vyanunādayat* with Bh. as an augmentless imperfect for Vulgate *vyanunādayan*.
33cd. I read with Bh. *ta eva naḥ sthitā yoddhuṃ prāṇāṃs tyaktvā sudustyajān* for Vulgate *ta ime 'vasthitā yuddhe prāṇāṃs tyaktvā dhanāni ca.*

25[3.]35d. So Bh. for Vulgate *paradharmo bhayāvahaḥ.*
39d. For *ca* Bh. reads *vā* in the sense of *iva.*

33[11]8a. I would prefer to read *śakṣyase* for the anomalous *śakyase* of the Vulgate.

Translation

14.

1. Saṃjaya, the old King Dhṛtarāṣṭra's personal bard, acts as his reporter on the progress of the war between the Pāṇḍavas, his nephews, and the Kauravas, his sons. After ten days Saṃjaya returns from the field with his first report.

2. Saṃjaya identifies himself because Dhṛtarāṣṭra is blind.

3. Reference to the dicing match between Duryodhana and Yudhiṣṭhira; see *MBh.* 2.43 ff.; II, 109 ff. No special mention is made there of Bhīṣma's active encouragement rather than his distressed resignation.

4. Bhīṣma had appeared at the Bridegroom Choice of the three daughters of the king of the Kāśis, defeated all other suitors, and carried off the three sisters for his younger brother. The eldest, Ambā, pled a previous commitment of her love to King Śālva, and was let go, but was rejected by Śālva. She called on Rāma Jāmadagnya (= Paraśu-Rāma) for revenge on Bhīṣma, but their battle was a standoff. She was later reborn as the Pāñcāla hero Śikhaṇḍin in order to kill Bhīṣma. See *MBh.* 5.170 ff., the *Story of Ambā*; III, 493 ff.

5. According to one account Bhīṣma was Dyaus reborn, one of the Vasu gods; cf. *MBh.* 1.93; I, 220 ff.

15.

1. Arjuna, who used Śikhaṇḍin as a human shield.

2. Droṇa was Bhīṣma's friend and the teacher of the younger generation.

3. Kṛpa, the first teacher of the Pāṇḍavas.

4. A race of demons defeated by Indra.

5. Duryodhana.

16.

1. The Pāṇḍavas had to go into a twelve-year forest exile as penalty for losing the dicing match.

2. I.e., Dhṛtarāṣṭra's natural father, Kṛṣṇa Dvaipāyana Vyāsa (*MBh.* 1.99 f.; I, 233 ff.), who also bestowed on Saṃjaya the vision of a universal narrator.

3. Warriors slapped their left forearms with the flat of their right palms as a sign of challenge.

4. I.e., ready to die.

17.

1. *Maghā*: the Sickle constellation in the sign of Leo.

2. Droṇa.

3. Insulted by Bhīṣma, Duryodhana's friend and ally Karṇa swore not to fight until Bhīṣma lay dead.

4. Aśvatthāman.

5. Aśvatthāman.

19.

1. *Saubhadra*: metronymic of Arjuna's son Abhimanyu; *Draupadeyas*: the five sons of Draupadī by the five Pāṇḍavas.

2. Arjuna, whose bow was named Gāṇḍīva.

21.

1. *Dhārtarāṣṭra*: patronymic of Dhṛtarāṣṭra's eldest son Duryodhana; in the plural his brothers and troops.

22.

1. Arjuna, who bore the ape Hanumān on his banner, and Kṛṣṇa.

23[1].

1. I.e., Dhṛṣṭadyumna, commander-in-chief of the Pāṇḍava forces.

2. Kṛṣṇa.

24[2].

1. I.e., between being and nonbeing.

2. *Spirit*: *buddhi*, the psychophysical faculty of alertness and decisiveness.

3. *Theory*: *sāṃkhya*, which here has the meaning of "reflection."

4. *Practice*: *yoga*, in the general *BhG*, sense of "consistent endeavor aimed at a specific goal," esp. unselfishly performed acts.

5. In contradistinction to an act (*karman*) as defined by the Mīmāṃsakas, which can be voided by interruption or disruption, an act inspired by the single *buddhi* remains valid.

6. *Law*: term borrowed from Mīmāṃsā, where *dharma* is tantamount to the (ritual) act.

7. This against the ritualists who recognize a separate "intention" (*abhiprāya*, *saṃkalpa*) for every act, while the act itself can vary according to different schools (*śākhā*) of the Veda.

8. I.e., the injunction of ritual acts in *Brāhmaṇas* and *Sūtras*, all prescribed for specific and limited purposes.

9. *Vedavāda*: frequent indeed are arguments about how certain acts should be performed.

10. A play on the words *samādhi* and *vidhīyate. Samādhi* is the emptying-out from consciousness of all distracting perceptions and notions in order to concentrate on the ultimate object, an achievement impossible to the ritualists as long as there is enjoined (*vidhīyate*) the need to perform a variety of acts, many of which are *kāmya*, "inspired by a specific desire," often enough a desire for pleasure (heaven, son, rain, etc.) and dominion (overlordship, etc.).

11. I.e., the phenomenal, polarized domain of the material creation (*prakṛti*), which is dominated by the three *guṇas* (cf. below).

12. A metaphor for the plenitude of spiritual experience transcending the ephemeral consequences of a strict Vedic ritualism.

13. *Entitlement: adhikāra*: a technical Mīmāṃsā term for the sum of properties in a prospective performer of a ritual act which qualify him to perform that act. If the injunction declares that "he who has a desire for heaven (*svargakāma*) should sacrifice with the *jyotiṣṭoma*," it is specifically one's desire to obtain heaven that entitles him to perform the rite. The Mīmāṃsaka therefore would take issue with Kṛṣṇa here, and maintain that it is his desire for the fruit that is the person's entitlement. But Kṛṣṇa expressedly condemns such *kāmya* (desire-motivated) acts as conducive to rebirth, and he upholds as ultimately beneficial only those acts that are naturally incumbent on one (e.g., as fighting a just war is on a *kṣatriya*), so that no desire for a fruit need arise.

14. *To avoid acting: akarmaṇi*: Kṛṣṇa attempts to steer a middle course between the inflated ritualism of the orthodox and the complete rejection of all Vedic ritual (including the *varṇāśrama* acts at issue) of the heterodox. Traditional acts, he claims, are necessary, and are beneficial if performed selflessly.

15. *Application*: *yoga* in the above sense of "the application of the spirit (*buddhiyoga*) to acting": success and failure in acts performed selflessly are indifferent to the performer.

16. Karman: here, as so often, in the sense of the consequences (*phala*) of the act.

17. *Capacity: kauśala*: one is not deterred by possible failure. *Kauśala* may also translate as "good fortune," sc., through avoiding the binding consequences of acting.

18. *Rebirth*: as the result of those acts that have not fructified in this life.

19. *Śrotavyasya śrutasya ca*: i.e., in the rejected narrow sense of having to act for a self-seeking purpose.

20. *Withdraws*: though he may see, he will not look; he may hear but not listen, etc.

21. Figuratively: he who does not feed on, thrive on, external objects.

22. Nirvāṇa: surely a reply to the Buddhists, declaring that even while taking a brahmanistic stance in a life of social activity, a person can attain the serenity which the Buddhists have arrogated to themselves while not socially active.

25[3].

1. *By not performing acts*: in certain circles orthodox and heterodox, the abjuration of acts (*saṃnyāsa*, etc.) was considered a precondition to the higher insight. Kṛṣṇa implies that the "discipline of knowledge" does not require such a renunciation at all.

2. *Three forces*: viz., the three *guṇas*.

3. In the sense of karmic consequences.

4. *Sacrifice: yajña*: here understood ideally as selflessly acting. In the sequel Kṛṣṇa endeavors to show that orthodox Vedic opinion supports his views on acting.

5. Brahman *of the Veda*: i.e., its sacred contents.

6. *Syllable* OṂ: the *Akṣara*, to which the entire Veda can be meaningfully reduced.

7. *Ubiquitous* brahman: *brahman* as the substantial cause of creation.

8. *By acting alone*: i.e., without ulterior, selfish purpose, since they had no incentive. Janaka is the ideal Vedic king, imbued with the true spirit of Veda and sacrifice.

9. *What holds together the world: lokasaṃgraha*. Edgerton renders "the mere control of the world," which is inappropriate because it implies a transcending self-interest.

10. This paragraph introduces a Sāṃkhyan concept which is really inconsistent with the above, viz., that the "self" (*puruṣa, ātman*) is not an agent at all, but that the categorically different *prakṛti* through its *guṇas* acts within the domain of *prakṛti* only, leaving the self as spectator (*sākṣin*) and experient (*bhoktṛ*) of the fruits of those acts.

11. This seems to modify the previous paragraph by identifying *prakṛti* with God, who is its substantial cause; Sāṃkhya itself considers *prakṛti* to be uncaused.

26[4].

1. *Nature which is mine*: God on occasion takes flesh ("descends") in the nature of which he is the substantial cause.

2. *Karmaṇy akarma yaḥ paśyet*: here *karman* is used in the sense of "act" (*karmaṇi*: "in the acting"), while in *akarma* it has the connotation of "[the persistence of the act in] its binding consequences." The catchy phrase can be rendered more prosily: "He who sees that in acting [there need be] no [binding consequences normally resulting from] acting, and that [there may be binding consequences of] acting in the abstention from acting . . . ."

3. *Spirit*: *buddhi*, as set forth above.

4. *Intention*: *saṃkalpa*, once more the technical ritual term for the solemn declaration of one's intention in performing one's act, which precedes its performance. Thus the sage relinquishes any selfish purpose in his act.

5. Karman: again, the consequences of the act.

6. Viz., the *buddhiyoga* applied to acting.

7. Viz., without *saṃkalpa*, "intention."

8. In this context *brahman* signifies at once the complex of the (sacrificial) act and the supreme being.

9. *Yogins*: i.e., performers of acts with *karmayoga*.

10. *Deities*: Indra, etc., to whom Vedic sacrifices are ordinarily directed.

11. *Offer the senses*: i.e., practice withdrawal of sensory activity.

12. *Sacrifice the objects*: i.e., with the realization that the objects have no functional existence outside sensory perception.

13. Here *prāṇa* and *apāna* clearly have the sense of inhalation and exhalation.

14. *Offer* prāṇas *into* prāṇas: i.e., reduce the functioning of their vital faculties (*prāṇas*) to the mere maintenance of life (*prāṇas*).

15. *The mouth of* brahman: i.e., the sacrificial fire, both figurative and literal.

16. *Sacrifice of knowledge*: i.e., the interiorized sacrifice.

27[5].

1. *Relinquishment of acts*: this indicates that Arjuna has not yet understood Kṛṣṇa's distinction between *karman*, "act," and *karman*, "its binding consequences." Kṛṣṇa now proceeds on the basis of Arjuna's imperfect understanding, showing that the outcome remains the same.

2. *A perpetual renouncer*: Kṛṣṇa lifts the notion of renunciation out of the nonaction vs. action controversy.

3. I.e., *karmayoga.*

4. *Does in fact do nothing*: i.e., he incurs no *karman.*

5. I.e., the consequences.

6. *Nine-gated fortress*: i.e., the body, its "gates" being the orifices.

7. *Svabhāva* should here be taken in its technical sense of *prakṛti.* The doctrine that agency, acts, and their fructification all belong to the domain of *prakṛti* and do not ultimately affect the *puruṣa* is Sāṃkhyan and contradicts the doctrine generally espoused by Kṛṣṇa that the self as such is in fact the agent.

8. *Vibhu* is to be taken here as the "lord of the body," the soul/self (*ātman, puruṣa*). I supply to *kasyacit*, sc., *karmaṇaḥ*, which the context requires.

9. *Ignorance*: viz., of the absolute separateness of *puruṣa* and *prakṛti*; the confusion is that people mistake the active self in the body for the real self.

10. *Indifferent*: *samam*, i.e., indifferent to phenomenal distinctions of genus and species and therefore the same in every individual; *brahman* here equals *ātman/puruṣa.*

11. Yoga here in the sense of the unifying knowledge of the *brahman/ātman.*

28[6].

1. E.g., the Buddhists and other unorthodox who reject Vedic ritual.

2. *Yoga*: viz., the *karmayoga* of above.

3. *Intention*: *saṃkalpa* in the ritualist sense.

4. The text works here with two meanings of the word *ātman*: the reflexive "oneself," i.e., the phenomenal self that needs to be conquered; and the transcendent self.

5. *Yogin*: the *karmayogin* now shades into the solitary yogin of the technical Yoga.

6. *Beyond* nirvāṇa: *nirvāṇaparamām*: because it is not pure extinction but a positive union of the persisting *ātman* with the personal God.

7. *Candle flame outside a draft*: *dīpo nivātasthaḥ*: a correction of the Buddhist *nirvāṇa* in the sense of "extinction." Kṛṣṇa appears to maintain that this is the right interpretation of the traditional metaphor (*sopamā smṛtā*), which accepts an ultimately persisting *ātman*, but in that case overlooks the force of the preverb *niḥ.*

8. *Ubhayavibhraṣṭaḥ*: failing both in gainful acting and in reaching *brahman*—lost like a torn-off cloud.

9. *Shares in me*: *bhajate*; or: has *bhakti*; but it is important to retain here also the central meaning of the root *bhaj.*

29[7].

1. *Nature*: *prakṛti*: this eightfold differentiation of the *prakṛti* is an old Sāṃkhyan-type doctrine attested to in passages of the *Mokṣadharma* of the *Mahābhārata.*

2. *Another, higher nature*: *anyāṃ prakṛtiṃ parām*: a notion which is definitely not Sāṃkhyan, for Sāṃkhya denies the existence of a God transcendent to the *puruṣas.* But the idea is in line with occasional views in the *Upaniṣads* that perceive of creation as the creator's body, views adopted and adumbrated especially by Rāmānuja.

3. *Ether*: *ākāśa*: which is held to be the medium of sound.

4. On the *guṇas*, see *in extenso* below, chs. 13 ff. Here the *guṇas* are still viewed as cosmic constituents producing modes of being in creation.

5. *Seek my love*: *bhajante*; or: have *bhakti.*

6. Kṛṣṇa thus distinguishes four sorts of *bhakti*: of those who implore him to alleviate

their sufferings; of those who seek but have not yet found knowledge of him; of those who pray to him for material benefits; and of the "knowers," which I here translate as "adepts." All of them are "persons of stature," inasmuch as they recognize the paramountcy of Kṛṣṇa.

7. *Ekabhakti*: "whose loving loyalty is directed to one person only."

8. *Any loyal person*: *bhakta*, who faithfully worships a god without necessarily knowing that that god is an embodiment of Kṛṣṇa.

30[8].

1. *Nature: svabhāva* in the sense of *prakṛti*: that is, the second, higher *prakṛti* of God.

2. *Kṣara*, the world of the elements, as opposed to *akṣara*.

3. *Spirit: puruṣa = akṣara*.

4. *Sacrificial*: the one to whom all sacrifices are directed.

5. I.e., in a new life one derives new being from that of which one thinks at the hour of death.

6. *Worlds*: i.e., domain and circumstances of existence; the World of Brahmā is the highest such, but still phenomenal.

7. *Beyond the unmanifest: avyaktāt*: *avyakta* is the description of *prakṛti* in germinal state; the order of God is beyond that.

8. *Supreme Person: purusaḥ paraḥ*: i.e. supreme, transcendent to the order of *puruṣas*.

9. Notions derived from *Upaniṣadic* sources, cf. *Chāndogya Up*. 5.3 ff., *Bṛhadāraṇyaka Up*. 6.2 ff.

31[9].

1. Kṛṣṇa works here with two meanings of *avyakta* he has just described: as the *avyakta = prakṛti*, he is the domain of phenomenal life, in which all creatures have their being, so that "they exist in me," *matsthāni*. But even as the lower *avyakta* he is not summed up by these creatures.

2. *They do not exist in me*: as the *Avyakta* beyond the lower *avyakta* God represents an order of being completely transcendent to the creatures.

3. Here yoga has practically the sense of "divine wizardry, unpredictable power," close to *māyā*, but not identical with it, since *māyā* can be overcome (cf. 7.14), whereas this *aiśvara yoga* is an expression of real power.

4. *By the force of nature: prakṛter vaśāt*: this inherent creative and destructive pulsation of God is automatic.

5. The herb (*auṣadha*) is undoubtedly the soma.

6. *Be it without proper rite* (vidhi): i.e., not by a rite devoted to Kṛṣṇa himself. Or: *avidhipūrvakam* can also be rendered: "though no such provision is made in the injunction (*vidhi*)."

7. *Ghouls: bhūtāni*: rites for gods and ancestors are orthodox, those for *bhūtas* are heterodox. *Bhūtas* are the ghosts of those deceased whose remains have not properly been disposed of by ceremonial cremation. One might in this context think of relic worship by the Buddhists.

8. Such offerings are both plain and personal; they remind us of *pūjā*.

32[10].

1. *Seven seers*: group of brahmin ancestors also celebrated as a constellation; *four*

Manus: a Manu is the progenitor of creation in a circumscribed period (*manvantara*) which he rules. *Manusmṛti* 1.63 gives their number as fourteen, which has remained canonical ever since. The number four here, it has been reasonably argued, may derive from the four *yugas*, *Kṛta*, etc.

2. *Ubiquity*: I find this rendering of *vibhūti* more helpful than "power manifestation," etc. The root *bhū-* with preverb *vi* indicates a pervasive, ubiquitous display of appearances, cf. below, vs. 19, where Kṛṣṇa exemplifies this display among all manner of groups. *Yoga*: as above, in the sense of divine power.

3. *Nārada*: a seer and frequent visitor from the gods.

4. *Asita Devala*: a vague but possibly historic sage in the *MBh.*, who also appears in the Buddhist scriptures; *Vyāsa*: the "author" of the *MBh.*

5. *Vibhūti*; see above, n. 2.

6. The 27/28 *nakṣatras*, "lunar mansions," are the constellations in which the moon rises in the course of a lunation; hence it is the moon that makes them significant and rules them.

7. *Skanda*: the army commander of the gods.

8. I.e., at the churning of the ocean for the Elixir of immortality; see *MBh.* 1.15 ff.; I, 72 ff.

9. The god of love.

10. *Who tame: saṃyamatām*: play on *yama/yam-*.

11. *Things that count: kalayatām*: from root ²*kal-*; or: "things that impel," from root ³*kal-*. Since Time is so often represented as being counted off in its component periods, and as counting down all existence, I prefer the first derivation.

12. *The* a: the first sound of the alphabet and/or in OṂ.

13. Dvaṃdva: name of the copulative compound in Sanskrit, here elevated as the foremost compound because it refers to many things at a time.

14. *Mārgaśīrṣa*: the first month of the year (November/December).

15. *Kavi Uśanas*: priest of the Asuras.

16. *Mysteries: guhya*; *mauna* is munihood which is especially characterized by a refusal to speak.

33[11].

1. *Yoga*: divine unpredictable power.

2. Groups of Vedic gods.

3. Descriptions like this prompt the question whether the author had certain icons in mind.

4. *Muṇḍaka Up.* 2.1.4, cf. below, 37[15], n. 6.

5. Karṇa.

6. This predicts the imminent death of these heroes in battle.

7. Rare use of Viṣṇu who does not at all figure in the *Gītā* as the author of the Kṛṣṇa *avatāra*.

8. Note the double *saṃdhi sakheti* for *sakha iti*.

9. In which matters of precedence are meticulously observed.

10. *Bhaktyā . . . ananyayā*: with *bhakti* directed at none other.

34[12].

1. I.e., those who pursue knowledge and attainment of the *ātman* alone.

2. *Kūṭastha*, a qualification of the pure *ātman* which is insufficiently explained. In a technical sense it seems to appear first in the *Gītā* (here; 6.8; 15.16). The commentators explain it as "immovably fixed" (somewhat unexpected on a high, windy peak), but this may be based on context: here it is followed by *acalaṃ sthiram*, "immovable and fixed"; in 15.16 it seems glossed with *akṣara*, "intransient." Two possible explanations come to mind: (1) "Standing at the top of the crown of the head," the place to which the soul proceeds through one of the channels (*nāḍī*) emanating from the heart, before it leaves the body for good. Compare *Chāndogya Up.* 8.6, particularly vs. 6: "The heart has 101 channels; one of them goes out to the crown (*mūrdhan*); going upward by way of it he goes to immortality; the others, in every direction, are for the purpose of leaving the body (in the ordinary way: *utkramaṇe*)." (2) "Standing on the top of a mountain," and thus taking a disinterested view of things, cf. the context in 6.8.

3. I.e., *bhaktiyoga*.

4. The ascending order is *abhyāsa* (which I take in the sense of *Vedābhyāsa*) → knowledge → contemplation (sc., on the contents of this knowledge) → *karmayoga* → serenity (= release); this is perhaps the most unequivocal statement of the superiority of *karmayoga* to *jñānayoga*.

5. *Undertakings*: *ārambhāḥ*, esp. of actions; here: "the fruits of such actions."

35[13].

1. *Kṣetrajña*: the sense of "guide" (cf. *Śatapatha Br.* 13.2.3.2) brings out more clearly the active role of the individual soul than the literal "knower of the field."

2. While the meaning of this verse is not entirely clear, I prefer *chandas* in the sense of "metrical utterance" rather than "Vedic hymns" (though these meters are no doubt those of the *saṃhitās*), parallel and contrastive to *pada*, metrically unbound words.

3. *Arguments in the* Brahmasūtras: lit., "the reasoning words in the *Brahmasūtras*." *Brahmasūtras*, technically a corpus of *sūtras* about Vedānta and *brahman* ascribed to Bādarāyaṇa, is here best taken more broadly as "*sūtras* about *brahman*." But I see no reason either to seek here a reference to the *Upaniṣads* (which I doubt would be called *hetumat*, *sūtras*, or for that matter *padas*), or to deny that there existed corpora of *sūtras* prior to Bādarāyaṇa, who himself quotes predecessors.

4. This describes the Sāṃkhyan view of the psychophysical entity of the body: (1) the *prakṛti*, unevolved, *avyakta*; (2) the evolutes (a) *buddhi*, (b) *ahaṃkāra*, (c) objects, *ākāśa*, etc.; (3) the ten faculties reacting to the objects, i.e., the five sensory ones, hearing, etc., and the five motoric ones, with the five realms (*gocara*) of the senses (sound, etc.); (4) the positive and negative emotional reactions to sense contacts; (5) the bodily organisms (*saṃghāta*) comprising them all; (6) the correlated body consciousness (*cetana*, perhaps = mind); and (7) the continuity (*dhṛti*) of the field. I see no reason to construe another meaning for *saṃghāta* (so Edgerton); if one insists on reading in it a quality, "cohesion" will do, without change of meaning.

5. I.e., *bhaktiyoga*.

6. I see no compelling reason to prefer (with Edgerton) Rāmānuja's division of *anādimatparam* into *anādi matparam*. I think Rāmānuja is too zealous here.

7. *Ābhāsa* in the sense of "false appearance."

8. Edgerton's interpretation is fetching: "Among the lights it is the light that is beyond darkness," and would have gained in credibility if he had noted that *jyotiḥ* means particularly "celestial luminary," which of course is subject to periodic darkening. But compare also *Bṛhadāraṇyaka Up.* 4.4.16: "Below which the year revolves with its days, that the gods contemplate as the light of lights, the full lifespan," i.e., the sum total of all

the lights of every year of one's life. Here *jyotiṣām* is more a possessive genitive. Also *Chāndogya Up.* 3.17.7: "High beyond darkness discerning light all around, we have gone to the highest light," where the implication is clearly superlative, e.g., Song of Songs.

9. *Kāryakāraṇakartṛtve hetuḥ prakṛtir ucyate*: I take the compound ending in *-tve* as an elliptic absolute locative, sc., *sati*: "in that it is . . . ," which seems to me the obvious way of reading it since it is true to Sāṃkhya doctrine. *Prakṛti* is the uncaused cause, it is *not kārya* and *kāraṇa*, which are evolutes. *Pace* Edgerton, I find his own interpretation very forced and artificial: he takes *-tva* as a collectivizing suffix (other exx. in *Gītā*?) of three items, as he must in order to avoid a plural (*kāryatvakāraṇatvakartṛtveṣu*, or *kāryakāraṇakartṛtveṣu*). His reference to 18.18 is no help since *prakṛti* does not equal *karman*.

10. I.e., spontaneously, without any propaedeusis. The text once more juxtaposes the reflexive and absolute uses of *ātman*: *ātmanā* and *ātmani* are reflexive; *ātmānam* is absolute.

11. *Acquired insight*: *sāṃkhyena*: in contrast to the spontaneous insight of the previous one.

12. *Hurts the self* (i.e., the lord): sc., in himself by mortification, etc., or by ignorance; cf. 17.17.

36[14].

1. *Worlds*: *lokān*: sc., domestic environment and social position.

2. I take *dehasamudbhavān* as a *tatpuruṣa* compound which fits the doctrine better than a *bahuvrīhi* (so Edgerton).

3. The qualities of *sattva*, *rajas*, and *tamas* respectively.

37[15].

1. *Aśvattha*: *ficus religiosus*, which however does not drop roots. Here (in vs. 1) the image is the positive one of the upside-down sacred tree rooted in heaven and stretching down. Vss. 2 and 3, in *triṣṭubh* metre, pervert the image.

2. This line is difficult and the interpretation hinges on the meaning of *jīvabhūtaḥ*, which is usually rendered "having become the *jīva*." But this rendering implies that God emanates the individual souls, an idea that runs counter to the view that they are eternal (*sanātana*). I take the line as follows: the individual souls, eternal and existing in the order of souls (*jīvaloke*, parallel to the *jīvabhūtā prakṛti* of 8.5), are altogether a particle (*aṃśa*) of God from whom they derive their properties as souls. What makes the line difficult is that a three-order universe (God, *jīvas*, *prakṛti*) is superimposed on a Sāṃkhyan two-order universe (*puruṣas*, *prakṛti*), with the implications not wholly thought through.

3. I.e., their individual souls.

4. *Adhiṣṭhāya*; *adhi-sthā-* is frequently used to describe the control of the soul over the workings of the body.

5. *Vedāntakṛt*; or: "give voice to the *Vedānta*," in this context certainly the *Upaniṣads*.

6. This notion resembles closely that of *Bṛhadāraṇyaka Up.* 2.3.1: "Brahman indeed has two forms, substantial (*mūrta*) and insubstantial, mortal and immortal, the existing (*sat*) and the yon (*tyad*)," and *Muṇḍaka Up.* 2.1.4 f.: "There are two knowledges to be had . . . a higher and a lower one. The lower is [the *Vedas* and *Vedāṅgas*], while the higher is the one by which the intransient (*akṣara*) is to be known." Again, on this bipartite universe a third order, God, is imposed.

7. See above, 34[12], n. 2.

39[17].

1. I.e., God as *jīva*, which is an *aṃśa* of him (see above, 37[15], n. 2).

2. *Adakṣiṇa*: the priestly stipend (*dakṣiṇā*) makes a rite complete as well as Vedic.

3. *OṂ* as the summation of the *Veda*, the word-*brahman*; *tad* as the "yon," frequent *Upaniṣadic* reference to *brahman*; *sat*, as, e.g., *Chāndogya Up.* 6.2 ff.

4. *Tad* here seems to carry the connotation: "that much only," without the fruits.

40[18].

1. I.e., the *kāmya* rites.

2. I.e., the fixed rites to which incidental rewards may accrue. The distinction here made between *saṃnyāsa* and *tyāga* is interesting and lexically correct: *saṃnyāsa*, "giving up entirely" (lit., "throwing it all down"), and *tyāga*, "giving up with generosity what one could properly have kept."

3. *Three kinds*: viz., (1) out of folly (*tamas*); (2) as too hard (*rajas*); and (3) by renouncing the rewards (*sattva*).

4. *Hereafter*: *pretya*: viz., after death in a new birth.

5. *Realm of the object*: *adhiṣṭhāna*: the senses and objects governed by the soul (*adhiṣṭhātṛ*). *Divine fate*: *daiva*: the unpredictable forces influencing actions, sc., the sudden death of the agent, etc.

6. *Ātmabuddhiprasādaja*, where I take *ātman* as reflexive. Or: "insight (*buddhi*) into the self."

7. The famous *caramaśloka*, "the final, summarizing verse" of the *Gītā*. *Abandon all the Laws* (= actions): sc., those actions undertaken for rewards or not dedicated to God.

8. *Colloquy*: *saṃvāda*: a term very frequently used of similar discourses in the *Mokṣadharma*. Since the term here occurs in the colophon, one may wonder whether it was the original title of (part of?) the *Gītā*, e.g., *Keśavārjunasaṃvāda*, that was soon replaced (cf. *Anugītā*) by the more honorific *Bhagavadgītā*.

41.

1. *Somakas*: often = the Pāñcālas: sometimes they are a division of them under Dhṛṣṭadyumna.

2. Indra, because many sacrifices include him.

3. Reference is here probably to a similar gesture of Bhīṣma to his guru Rāma Jāmadagnya, cf. *MBh.*, 5(60).180.10 ff.; III, *Ambā*, 509.

4. Since he is the "grandfather."

5. Both Bhīṣma and Droṇa, as well as Kṛpa, felt obligated to the court of Dhṛtarāṣṭra for giving them a livelihood.

6. These are the circumstances described in *MBh.* 7.164.

7. Kṛpa Śāradvata (patronymic) Gautama (clan name) was the teacher of the Pāṇḍavas before Droṇa Bhāradvāja.

8. In the case of Śalya, who is a guru insofar as he is the brother of the mother of Nakula and Sahadeva, it was because of the rich rest houses Duryodhana built for him on his journey to the Pāṇḍavas; cf. *MBh.* 5(49).8.25 ff.; III, 198 f.

9. Quoted from the *Book of the Effort*, *MBh.* 5(49).8.25 ff.; III, 199 f.

10. Cf. Kṛṣṇa's temptation of Karṇa, *MBh.* 5.138 ff.; III, 444 ff.

11. Yuyutsu was born to Dhṛtarāṣṭra by a *vaiśya* woman, besides his 100 sons by Gāndhārī.

12. The presumption is that Yuyutsu, now fighting on the Pāṇḍava side, stands a better chance to survive the war, as he does.

Index